LOVE TO GROW

LOVE TO GROW

Remove Your Financial Barriers, Grow Your Wealth and Succeed in Your Business

Trish Love

NEW YORK

LOVE TO GROW
Remove Your Financial Barriers, Grow Your Wealth and Succeed in Your Business

ISBN 978-1-61448-553-7 paperback
ISBN 978-1-61448-554-4 eBook
ISBN 978-1-61448-555-1 audio
Library of Congress Control Number: 2013932144

Morgan James Publishing
The Entrepreneurial Publisher
5 Penn Plaza, 23rd Floor,
New York City, New York 10001
(212) 655-5470 office • (516) 908-4496 fax
www.MorganJamesPublishing.com

Cover Design by:
Chris Treccani
www.3dogdesign.net

Stephen Reid
www.ramp.co.nz

Interior Design by:
Bonnie Bushman
bonnie@caboodlegraphics.com

To Craig, Jax, Jenn, Kaz, Mars, Bailey and Annie.
I love you more and more and more and more!

CONTENTS

Foreword   Keith Randell, Business Psychologist
and Brain Science Researcher   ix

Acknowledgments   xi

Note from the Author   xiii

Part I   Looking After You   1

Chapter 1   Your Independence Day   3

Chapter 2   How's Your Relationship With Wealth?
"Happily Married" or Heading For "Divorce?"   10

Chapter 3   How to Permanently Improve Your Finances
What Do You WANT, What Do You BELIEVE
and What Are You Going to DO About it?   20

Chapter 4   Identifying Your Money Style   34

Chapter 5   Communicating Effectively About Finances   54

Chapter 6   From Survival to Sorted—Shifting Your
Money Style "Actions"   65

Chapter 7   From Fear to Love—Climbing Your Way
Through the Financial Beliefs Ladder   89

Chapter 8   Traps for Young Players—How to Get Out
(and Stay Out) of Survival Mode   116

Chapter 9   Seven Steps to Wealth Creation—Where Are You
Now? And How to Get You Where You Want to Be   139

Part II   Looking After Your Business   **159**

Chapter 10   Start as We Mean to Go On—
             The Basics of Business Value   161

Chapter 11   The Journey to Financial Freedom and Leverage—
             Combining Business Competencies
             With Business Values   173

Chapter 12   From "Mission Impossible" to
             "Mission Accomplished"—Getting Better
             Leadership and Knowledge into your Business   188

Chapter 13   Stepping Up and Taking Charge—When to Get
             Advisors on Board and When to "Do it" Yourself   202

Chapter 14   Building a Great Team in Your Business—
             Important Things to Not Forget   210

Chapter 15   How to Delegate—Make Your Business Better
             Instead of Worse When You Release Control   229

Chapter 16   Managing that Oh So Lovely Symptom
             of Poor Cash Flow   244

Chapter 17   How to Get the Best Out of an Internal
             Chief Financial Officer (CFO)—Why Does the
             CFO Sit at Your Right Hand?   259

Chapter 18   We are Here to Learn, What We Are Here to Teach:
             The Love to Grow Story   274

FOREWORD

Keith Randell, Business Psychologist and Brain Science Researcher

Making a Difference Financially

Most people do not have the wider wealth, money and/or time they desire and yet many of them don't know why. In Love to Grow, Trish Love explains the underlying reasons that create a gap between what you have wanted until now, versus what you have actually achieved financially. Much of this information is sourced in three main areas being what you 1) want, 2) believe and 3) do with your financial situation. Trish shares this compelling information in Love to Grow so you can bridge the gaps in any or all of these areas.

Looking After YOU, Versus Looking After Your BUSINESS

The first part of this book explains why you are financially operating the way you are. And more importantly, it explains how to improve your financial situation in a very easy, practical and permanent way. It specifically helps you look after you. Much of the information in part one is based in how to improve your financial belief system.

As a business psychologist specializing in researching many leading brain scientists, I know that being able to create permanent change is more than a mere fantasy. Applying the stepped change principles outlined in Love to Grow is significant to creating permanent financial improvement. Much of this improvement occurs when we apply simple, practical habits, and as a by-product, we also improve our underlying belief systems housed in some of the oldest parts of our unconscious minds. Trish Love's information and easy exercises will allow you to directly access both your mind's left and right hemispheres. Both are critical for creating improvements and improving barriers that might have previously held you back.

The second part of this book explains how to 'look after your business'. It is important to note however that most of the principles in part two are relevant for business owners and individuals alike. Applying the same concepts to your personal world, job, or business, Love to Grow explains the principles needed to improve your leadership skills and business knowledge. Again the easy pathway suggested is critical for forming the habits needed to achieve sound business growth for the type of wealth and success you seek.

Keith Randell,
Bachelor of Psychology, Cambridge University, England.

Keith Randell is a Business Psychologist who brings together research and published works of many leading scientists in personality style assessments and cognitive research. He feels privileged to be included into information resulting from recent international studies to explain how the left and right brain works together to optimize people potential. As well as working with many companies and business owners, he is assisted by leading scientists from elite Universities and Schools of Medicine in America, England and Australia who are involved with brain research projects and modern resonance imaging which measure the brain's control functions.

ACKNOWLEDGMENTS

To Craig Love: You're such a special person for your unconditional love, undying belief, support, incredible non-judgment and patience. Love that you keep me grounded.

To Jacksen, Jennah, Kareina and Mariah Love: You are very cool kids, thanks for letting me have the time to also help others. I just can't stop loving you, more and more, all the time. No matter what.

To Mom and Dad: You showed how to love the good and forgive the rest. You taught integrity, honor, courage, compassion, unconditional love, patience and to stand up for what we believe in.

To Pete Foster, Jude Foster, Jill Stevens: You have been caring and supportive forever. I love that we don't need many words, we just understand each other. Aren't we lucky that we love the fun.

To Kirsten Rattray, Susan Carpenter, Dianne Davern, Charmaine Brown, Christine Moore, Grant Stephen, Leanne Brockelbank, Rupert Webb, Jo Thoms, Susan Little, Joyce Spellacy, Chrystal Rains: You have needed more patience than anyone, which I really appreciate, thank you. Thanks for being part of the L2G journey.

To Joy & Peter Love: Thanks for all your love and support over the past 25 years.

To Duncan & Karen Holland and Euan & Sue Robertson: Thanks for showing me how to blend integrity with all things business. My hat is off for your early day's patience and support. And thanks also Duncan for your more recent business assistance.

To Janice Roth: love your friendship and expertise. Thanks for "calling it" whenever needed. Don't stop.

To Ady Dale and Keith Randell: I appreciate you helping me learn that it's fun to grow into our skin and be 100% comfortable with ourselves, whatever that is, or becomes.

To Carla Sherriff: the children and us adore you. Thanks for being "Camp Mother."

To Todd Stevens and Chris Leatham: thanks for your friendship and expertise. I love feeling you enjoy being part of the journey.

To Sally Anderson: You helped me find the dream. Thanks for guidance in how to grab it.

To Warwick Walker, Helen Down, Haydn Virtue, Karl Baker, Michael Major, Sharn Rayner, Lauchie Griffin, Dave Morgan, Peter McMenamin, Stephen Reid: Love your involvement in our projects. Thank you for your friendship, support and expertise.

To Wutee Amohia, Ruth Horsley, Kate McSweeney, Vanessa Hendry, Julie Prout: Thanks for being there at times we could listen and share.

To Rhys Barlow, George Domett, Victor Wu, Robert Walker and Ian Evans: Thanks for together giving me such a well rounded, safe and balanced work foundation. And for allowing me to grow.

To Liam Fennell: Phew, we actually finished it! Thanks for your amazing tact, patience, editing expertise and guidance.

To all our Love to Grow clients: Thanks for working with us over the years. We wouldn't achieve anything without you.

NOTE FROM THE AUTHOR

Trish Love, Business Advisor, Chartered Accountant, Financial Intelligence Specialist.

My 'Why'

In 1988, I got my first full time job working in a medium sized international accounting firm. Over the years I have experienced many business owners and I very quickly became fascinated by the reasons some people "thrive" while others "survive" financially.

It took me a while to learn the formula for building and also keeping wealth in my own world. I am gifting that formula to you in this book. It explains 25 years of working out how to best deal with my own financial beliefs and actions, as well as those of many of my clients.

My fascination around the "why" of financial dynamics originated in my own personal learnings. Coming from a dysfunctional background, there was a lot for me to learn. The irony of training as an accountant is that the educational system seems to presume that we already know about *how* to deal with our own money. After all, we specialize in the field, so of course we must know. Think again. Well, they forgot to tell me at least; perhaps I was absent for that lecture. Admittedly accountants are probably better at some things (as a gross generalization) than other stereotypical occupations. But

I also believe that as a general group, another generalization is that at times we can have serious shortcomings around issues such as fear and control, allowing these to "run the show."

I can tell you that everything explained in this book has also been practiced by me personally. A few of my colleagues use the saying "we are here to learn what we are here to teach." Like many, I learn at an experiential level. I jokingly add that trust me, there was a fair bit to work with when I first started out. And like all of us, this will continue forever. I welcome my own learnings and invite you to do the same.

I am privileged to have experienced my own learnings and witnessed those of others. My "why" is to pass this knowledge on to you and those you love. So improvements in your financial domain can assist other areas of your life.

How to Read this Book

I suggest you apply your entire mind to the points I am suggesting. Try not to rush ahead. If you are unsure what I mean about a point, stop. Consider for yourself what I might be talking about. I am unlikely to give you all the answers on a plate, but I will give you the vast majority of them. Some answers however are relevant to only you and these ones will need your own personal understanding. Consider my comments from a number of different contexts and vantage points.

Highlight sentences you find relevant and come back to them later. There are some nuances that will continue to reveal themselves as you grow through your own financial belief system. You will begin to apply your own interpretation to my words, and this interpretation will likely change over time.

This is a good thing. Actively try to engage with my mind and mentally ask me questions as you go. The answers will most likely come to you intuitively. Allow yourself to listen from an empowered place. You will know if you are instead feeling negative about a topic or comment. Recognize that if you are feeling this way it is unlikely to be an empowered response. Listen for the answers that are inspired, and allow these ones to be the seeds of possibility.

The answers you receive will change and grow as you do. After a few months, study the book again and see if your perception has changed. My goal is for you to think that perhaps somebody has rewritten the book in the interim—I would love for your perception of my words to change that much over time. I imagine I will have the same process also occur for myself.

As these changes in your perception occur, your own relationship with wealth will also change. Be open for that to happen. If you continue to ask questions, you will innately find the answers.

Part I

LOOKING AFTER YOU

Chapter One

Your
Independence
Day

Allow me to draw you into our world and welcome you to it. Grab yourself a drink and make yourself comfy so you can wrap yourself around this book. Please seek a deeper meaning in my words while you read with an open mind and heart and you will learn how to create 'financial magic.' I will explain this phrase soon. For now, know that I am glad that you are here and that it is not by accident. It's time…for us to share what we know.

Your Future Story

Rolling time forward 5, 20, 100 years, I want to help you share the story you and your loved ones will be able to tell from the future looking back. Applying what you learn from this book, you will create a powerful family legacy. With this in mind, I will share parts of my own and also others' stories, so you can see how you and your business (if you have one) can create your desired future.

If you do not have a business, rest assured, this book is still for you. Regardless of your working situation, you will learn how to:

1. achieve what you want, so you can create your own Independence Day.
2. learn how to operate financially from a place where fear no longer exists.
3. grow in practical, easy steps.

Together we can create this future story for both you and your succeeding generations.

The Wonder of A Fairy Tale

Some years ago, one simple question changed the path of my own business significantly. Surprisingly it came from my then three-year-old son, Jacksen. Despite it not being "business like," it was to have a huge impact.

Flashback to 2000. I was reading the fairy tale "Jack and the Beanstalk" at story time (yet again!) Jacksen loved that story. However when reading it this time he became upset for Jack, asking me, "Mommy, how come Jack didn't ask people to help him to get rid of the giant?" He added "Then he could have played on the beanstalk as much as he wanted, without needing to chop it down."

I smiled to myself as my mind immediately sparked, "Wow! Imagine if people applied those thoughts to explain what is needed in a healthy business. If the business was the beanstalk, what would be needed for it to thrive and grow so it didn't need to be chopped down?"

"Hmmm...I wonder," I continued to think, "how could we work with that idea?" Applying the metaphor, I began thinking that if we could help people get rid of their "giants" (in their business or personal worlds), they would have a lot more fun playing on whatever type of beanstalk they wanted. And they could also go get their treasure without problems.

That bedtime story with Jacksen was a defining moment. But like all of us, there are many other experiences that have shaped my path. Understanding the lessons these experiences have taught me has been key to my personal success, and also created my apprenticeship for learning to grow both myself and my business. This apprenticeship as an entrepreneur started well before Jacksen's question...

My First Independence Day

It was the 4th of July 1997, my last day ever as an employee. I picked the date intentionally, Independence Day. It marked three years of working at Telecom NZ, principally as Financial Controller for Xtra, the Internet division in its start-up phase. Xtra had launched eighteen months prior, achieving massive growth rates.

In our planning meetings the GM had been known to literally stand on top of the board room table, exclaiming "I don't care what else is happening, we just need to get more fish in the boat!" Our main goal was getting customers signed up and interested in all things online. Like any business leader, he was rightly focused on ensuring we had enough customers engaged.

I now bemusingly recall conversations about us wondering whether this "Internet thing" would really take off. International statistics suggested the Internet would indeed be popular, but few were using it in New Zealand at the time. In only six weeks we achieved our twelve-month target. Clearly we got that part of our planning wrong! We had underestimated how people love technology.

In management meetings our American GM enthused us by saying we would tell our grandchildren we had played a part in bringing the Internet to NZ. Looking back now I see that this is true. We were pioneers, because this was necessary for the business to succeed. Thriving today needs a similar focus.

We learned lots about what to do, as well as what not to do. In particular, the deep financial pockets of the mother ship helped us be well capitalised. Very quick decision making, using intuition and sound business practice, meant we could adapt quickly. Importantly, the division had external eyes watching out for its safety too. All of these lessons, along with my professional accountancy background, contributed to the foundation of my own business, my advice to clients and what I share throughout this book.

My Second Independence Day

Roll forward to July 4th 2012. This marked 6 months since our Love to Grow team (Love to Grow is also the name of my business) had been running the vast majority of our accountancy division, fifteen years after my first Independence Day. You'd be forgiven for thinking this took a pathetically long time—take comfort in my slowness and know that you can do it too. I tell you the details below so you can think about how to celebrate your own Independence Day in the not-too-distant future.

We planned our celebration six months before July 4th 2012, after setting a business maturity date per Chuck Blakeman's book, *Making Money is Killing Your Business*. The ideas set out in his book were made more real for me because I met Chuck on his own business celebration, a holiday he chose to take in New Zealand.

When I set my Independence Day goal, I had no idea how we would fund it. Plan A didn't work. Plan B didn't work. Plan C worked, only four weeks before July 4th. As always, back up plans were crucial to make sure we achieved this goal.

July 4th 1997 was my last day as an employee. And on July 4th 2012, I took my wider team and family for a champagne breakfast to celebrate my business's Independence Day. One sister flew in to celebrate and my brother sent his well wishes.

Everyone was given rewards—cash, massage appointments and shopping vouchers to enjoy their day. Lunch with my Advisory Board was followed with my immediate family and I flying from Wellington to San Francisco. We crossed the dateline, meaning it was still July 4th when we arrived.

This meant we could continue to celebrate. My last Board member arrived from Michigan, and we watched the Independence Day fireworks together at Fisherman's Wharf. Another sister and her partner arrived from a 50th birthday trip through Europe, a celebration she had been saving up for over 15 years. It was very special that our celebrations collided. We managed to enjoy Independence Day celebrations in two countries with my family, staff and Board, all of whom I view as my wider family. I loved it.

My July 4th celebration was a small but important step in my business and personal progress. But it is only one step. Rest assured, there is a lot more to do yet. Importantly, I don't believe it would have happened unless I had been helped along the way by guidance from others.

Learning From Those Who Have Gone Before Us

Our lives and businesses are built on values we learn along the way; being mindful of these contributes to our success. One of my values was learnt from my dad. He believed we have a duty to become the best we can, not only for ourselves, but also for the betterment of society. I agree with him. Mom and Dad often spoke of integrity and honesty. They taught me that sometimes we even need to remove ourselves instead of doing something lacking in integrity. Even resign from a job if need be. Although I have yet to do that, I have at times had some intentional conversations to ensure I didn't have to. This is something we all need to be able to do: have difficult but necessary conversations when required with our loved ones, colleagues and clients.

Dad used to always espouse Hamlet's famous quote, "*This above all: to thine own self be true, and it must follow, as the night the day, thou canst not then be false to any man.*" Sometimes others' perspectives of our actions may differ to our own because of miscommunication. But as long as we know we are being true, it doesn't matter what others think. Just be the compass that always points north.

Outside of business, my parents and I have sometimes fallen short on the integrity barometer. I have compassion for our learning; we are all human after all. When we strive to learn from our mistakes, and preferably make them only once, we are growing. And that is what matters most.

My perspectives have changed significantly over time as I have matured and got closer to achieving something akin to wisdom. And encountering differing perspectives along the way has helped bring a richness to my world that I would hate to lose. There is the saying that dogs only bark when they don't know a person. People are similar.

Everyone we come into contact with teaches us, by who they be, how they guide, and how they share themselves with us. In particular, my parents taught me a great deal in the relatively short time I had with them. Mom said to me early on to "not judge a book, or its cover." She deliberately changed the standard saying to suggest people have an inner authentic self that is often packaged with a different facade. And she also reminded me regularly that regardless of where someone was operating "love the good and forgive the rest." I can still hear her saying those words many years after her death. Her ability to be unconditionally loving was remarkable.

Much of my parents teachings were intentional, some not. And some of it was via their actions and inaction. There were also challenges which enable me now to highly cherish the contrast in my world. I was taught unconditional love, loyalty, honor and compassion at a very experiential level. Some by what not to do. Reading and applying Love to Grow will help you understand how some of your challenges are relevant for your own financial domain.

Everything explained in this book are things we practice ourselves. Occasionally we need to remember our own advice! We have failed at much, and succeeded at most. But all of it has given us a deeper understanding of business and our clients. And I will use it to help you change your world to the one you want. We "Love it. Live it. Teach it." ("it" is whatever is relevant at hand.)

Our Future and the Journey to Get You There

Not enough small and medium business owners achieve the cash and time freedom they seek. We also know that many people operate from a place of fear with financial matters, so we want to help improve this. We know these things both from our own personal experiences, as well as from those shared with us by our clients and colleagues involved with my business. Dad taps me on my shoulder and reminds me that if we can help, we should. Writing this book, is one way of listening to his message and sharing knowledge to help others.

We want to inspire people like you to create financial magic. I hope this will occur much quicker than twenty or a hundred years from now. And I also hope the teachings will last at least that long. It's best when we grow honourably, as well as from a place of holistic wisdom and sound business knowledge. We want this is for the betterment of society and to help us all improve our place in it. Imagine a world where survival mode mentality is no longer tolerated and instead we all operate from beliefs that transcend fear and unhelpful elements of control.

So, buckle in, we are on a journey together. Whether you are in our world for a reason, a season, or a lifetime, I welcome you to it. I know you will teach us as much as we teach you. And thank you in advance for your contribution for as long as it lasts. I trust you will find this book helpful and I look forward to hearing about your own personal Independence Day.

Summary of chapter

- Think about your future from you and your loved ones looking back in 10, 20, 50, 100 years time.
- This book will help you:
    - ◊ Work out how to achieve your own Independence Day and create your own legacy
    - ◊ Gain the time, cash and wealth balance you seek
    - ◊ Learn to operate financially from a place which is no longer sourced in fear
    - ◊ Grow in practical, easy steps.

Chapter Two

How's Your Relationship With Wealth?

"Happily Married" or Heading For "Divorce?"

Creating Magic.

I opened chapter 1 by saying I want to help you create more financial magic. Another word I could use for magic is ease. So by financial magic I am referring to achieving your financial goals more easily. I am not necessarily here to convince you that financial magic exists, but I am here to teach you how to create more of it in your life. I will show you *how* to apply beliefs and actions that support you in this cause.

In the beginning, this may be in spite of you getting in the way. Often we don't know why things aren't working the way we think they should be financially. Once you have fully digested this book, you will understand why.

I often think to myself, wouldn't it be great if we could all live in "fun," allowing the big kids in each of us to play and enjoy our lives more. What would that look like for you? This is the type of magic I am referring to—where we create the life we truly want to live, a life where we are free to play, are happy, and have financial security.

If there is one thing I ask of you when reading this book, it would be this; do not be fooled by the simplicity of what I am teaching. It is in the simplicity that you will find the magic.

Results from Reading this Book

I will have done my job if you can put a tick next to the following five goals by the time you have finished reading:

- You think of wealth topics as *Fun* (this might be a shift for you, I acknowledge that).
- I have helped you create *Magic* in your world and for those close to you.
- You have *learned* relevant, compelling, practical strategies to apply to your life—and these have become permanent, positive changes.
- You totally understand *why* this information is *important.*
- You create *balance* in your world as part of creating your wealth.

The above results are very achievable. We will do this by raising the quality of your financial understanding and actions. I refer to this as improving your *financial intelligence.*

The Need For Us to Step Up,
to Improve Wider Financial Intelligence

Wouldn't it be fabulous if masses of us could improve our ability to have fun in our life? A key part of achieving this is improving our financial intelligence. Some of us need to improve financial intelligence for ourselves, whilst some of us can help raise it in others. If you are thinking that you don't *need* to continue learning around finances, or your life is just peachy right now, then I'm calling you out. We need self-interest for our own financial benefit. But I believe we also need to see interest in wanting to help others. Well done those of you that already have this. I feel our collective job is to continue to help with the evolution of everyone's financial awareness.

Imagine helping yourself, your siblings, your parents, your neighbors, friends, colleagues, workmates, and strangers improve their enjoyment of life. To transcend culture, religion, discrimination, demographics, education levels, and biases. Each person we reach in a positive way is one more person than if we never even tried.

Some people are very stuck in survival mode; they cannot see how they can help others because they need to look after themselves financially first. That is a reality for some, I agree. But we can still all help others to some extent, even if we need it ourselves. And we need to be able to see the self-interest in wanting to do so. Sometimes we can do this with our spare time— we don't necessarily need money to help others improve financial intelligence and results. We all benefit, when we all benefit.

People often resonate with the concept of helping others, but why should we apply this to finances? I believe it is because finances are so fundamentally important to our society that we need to re-examine the type of financial awareness we bring to money issues for ourselves and others. We will all be better off when everyone is financially stronger and enjoying themselves more, while still operating from a place of sound values.

There is some irony here. As part of helping others create the wealth and enjoyment they seek, we also need to help ourselves; we need to do both. This is because we are more effective at helping others when we have financial strength and stability, rather than struggling financially. So it doesn't matter whether it is us that needs improved financial intelligence or someone else needs our help to raise theirs—our world needs both. It is time more of us did our part in stepping up to help improve the overall wealth of the planet.

Your Version of Wealth

When I use the word wealth throughout this book, please remember that I mean so much more than just money. It can take on a lot of different meanings and include any part of your life that is especially important to you.

Arhh, now, one point. If any of you sense your reactions might be getting into something similar to "stinking thinking" (i.e. operating from a disempowered place), allow me to alleviate one thing for you. The word "wealth" is whatever you want it to be. It's your world, so your definition. What does the word *currently* mean for you? Okay, now, what *do you want it to mean*? And what can you do to steer your current worldview of wealth toward that? Ask yourself, how much more could you benefit others if your own financial situation was completely sorted?

Your Worldview about Money and Wealth

Rest assured, I'm not trying to change your worldview. But I am trying to extend you beyond it to see other possibilities. I want you to be open to a *really easy way* to achieving the honorable pursuits you want. Whatever they are.

Staying open to the possibility is all I ask. It will be your decision whether or not you go into shut down, judgment, or get stuck in *how* to apply this information. If you notice yourself doing any of these, know that we will address them all later.

I want to be very clear about one specific point. I am not professing that my opinions are 100% correct from every vantage point. We each have varying belief systems that drive the way we operate. To profess that mine are exactly "the right way" would be highly arrogant and definitely not my intent: I am instead inviting your perceptions and debate. Together we can widen all of our views, and become richer for them.

I also invite you to trust me a little bit more than you normally might. I get that for some of you this might be difficult. Your situation to date has kept you safe. I don't want to take away or discredit that; quite the contrary. I just want you to allow me to help *enhance* it, and to do so would be a privilege. So keep an open mind and read my words from a place of empowerment, not disempowerment.

The First Step—Taking a Stand for Your Version of Wealth

We need to work out your personal version of wealth and for you to take a stand for it. What does it currently include for you and all the extensions of who you are in your life? My personal version is partly based on Napoleon Hill's understanding of "life's riches." If you haven't already read his books, I suggest you do.

As a result of reading them myself and also my upbringing, my version of wealth centers on the concept of unconditional love. It also includes elements such as having a positive mental attitude, an absence of fear, a hope for achievement, an open mind on all subjects, great relationships, the capacity to understand people, a willingness to share my blessings, a capacity for faith, and yes, financial security. It also includes, somewhat reluctantly at first, self-discipline.

Like all of us, the realization of my wealth is a work in progress. I hope it always will be. And importantly, my version of wealth is irrelevant for you. I refer to it only to help you think about the *types of things* you might include in your own. It is probably very different to yours, and that is exactly how it is meant to be. Whatever your version is, choose to take a stand for obtaining it.

Your Why, Your What, Your How

Our minds are very powerful. I know you know that. But often we get so busy in our day-to-day lives *doing* things that we forget how to just *be*. It's important to wake up to this. We need to acknowledge for ourselves our life purpose, the gifts we already have, and learn how to use these to our best advantage.

There is a voice inside you that knows what you are already good at, and what causes you can assist with. It is the one you may have put to one side because it couldn't possibly be you who did something like that. Listen to it. Some of you already have been, and taking action, leading to results. Well done if that is you.

We all need to do this and become the person we were born to be. Consider for yourself your purpose for being on the planet. This may be as big or as small as you feel fits. It doesn't have to be overly deep and meaningful, if you don't want it to be. But just think about it for a bit. What is your "*why?*", your "*what?*" Once you know this I can help you with the "*how.*"

So, why is it important to know your purpose for being on the planet when discussing finances? Well, consider this: once you know your "why," is it easier to achieve this if you are financially secure or if you are in survival mode?

The accumulation of financial wealth in itself should never be viewed as a negative (or a positive for that matter). It is the *purpose* underlying your financial wealth that matters. You don't need to be the same as others whose actions you do not align with. The more we wish to assist others, our loved ones and the causes we wish to promote, the more having spare cash is handy. It helps us be agile and adaptive.

If you find thinking about your life purpose difficult, forget about it for now, finish reading this book, and then come back to it later. Your purpose will come to you over time as you digest more about your life. Meet yourself at a place that is comfortable right now. Stay open to possibilities and things will continue to reveal themselves.

Our "Financial Baggage" Mirrors Our Life – Finding the Keys to Understanding the Rest of Our World

Taking a stand is one thing and so too is learning what is holding us back. Since our unhelpful beliefs or "baggage" impact our results greatly, it is useful to know what these are so we can be more effective and achieve faster financial results. Whatever that baggage is, it will show up in our finances.

When we look closely at our financial domain, it becomes a mirror for our underlying behaviors to show what is also happening for us beyond our finances. *My role is to assist you to pass through this looking glass to see things from the other side.* Stop for a moment. Applying your whole mind and intuition to this last sentence, what might I mean by this?

There are a number of layers to explore about this sentence. Think about this sentence in terms of 1) how others might see you operate with money, 2) the relevance of your spiritual beliefs (if any), or 3) what you can see about the natural energy and flow with your money.

It can be helpful to use our imagination. Pretend you have ultimate power and can choose who deserves to enjoy financial freedom. Would you choose to allow money to flow towards someone just like you, knowing everything you know about yourself? Or would you instead stop, or reduce the money flow for some reason, until that person learned something first?

Put another way, if you held ultimate power would you send lots of money to someone if they had any of the following elements operating too often; disbelief, mistrust, resentment, ungratefulness, laziness, dishonorableness, fear, too much pride, frivolousness, disrespectfulness, or a lack of awareness about their financial situation?

Or might you instead resist, concerned they might be disrespectful about the money you were about to send them? Would you instead prefer to flow money towards others who operate from places of respect, belief, trust, love, compassion and an unselfish ability to give, financially or otherwise?

Whether we realize it or not, the natural energy of money chooses to flow this way. If we genuinely set the level of money we want for ourselves from an honorable position of power, there is a good chance that we will receive money to the extent we need it. We define for ourselves the level we need. Some people sadly manage to set their bar much lower than they want.

These type of questions are designed to help us think about our financial dynamics from the outside of our world looking in, so we can gain more self-awareness about what is holding us back.

But let's also consider why our financial dynamics can show us the keys to understanding the rest of our world. Our financial situation is an output, a result. It is a symptom of how we generally operate in our life in areas like career or business, relationships, health, and spirituality. For example, cash flow is only ever a symptom: if we look closely we will see the underlying cause of it found in what we have done, thought or felt earlier. We tend to do, think and feel the same way in other areas. So the same baggage plays out in most parts of our lives. It's just usually easier to see the effects of it in our finances.

Sometimes it's easier for us to see another person's issues than it is for them. So one of the easiest ways to see what might be true about ourselves is to imagine we are someone else looking at us. From their perspective they might see that we are *scared, untrusting, controlling, or financially reckless*. All of these can impact our financial situation and also our life generally.

There will be a few doors to pass through to understand yourself better and create your version of wealth. Each door will need a key. And each key is found by resolving the unhelpful beliefs underpinning your financial baggage.

Don't be Fooled by the Value Involved

Sometimes an unhelpful belief takes a while to reveal itself in our finances, but eventually it will. It could show up with something involving a small dollar value, or it could involve many more zeros. Whatever the monetary size, it's important to see the underlying issue. For example, a lack of trust in ourselves or others will likely have a flow on effect to our financial results.

If distrust is relevant, consider how this has contributed to your current financial situation. How might things have played out differently if you had allowed yourself to trust more? Under the circumstances, would this have been appropriate? The answer depends on whether your original perspective was valid and coming from an empowered space. A lack of trust is only one example of beliefs that may hold us back. Most others are also based in some form of fear. Understanding this can provide insight when we look for the connections between our beliefs and our results.

Whether we realize it or not, each day we receive lessons through our financial results that highlight our beliefs. Part of the magic is created when we see them. And if we learn from these lessons, we will improve our financial situation quickly.

Some people are provided a lesson only once, while others get them again and again until they actually learn and change. Do you have something bad that always happens financially? It could be as simple as constantly receiving parking tickets. This could indicate that you believe you cannot afford to pay for parking, or that you might be disrespectful of, or disassociated from, the financial rules of others. We need to wake up and pay attention to the lessons being shown to us in our financial realm. Lack of awareness around this will likely result in these unhelpful beliefs continuing to inhibit us financially.

Your Financial Relationship—Are Your Finances "Happily Married" or "Heading For Divorce?"

My discussion above is centered on the concept that we all have a relationship with our finances. You might not be aware of it, but you definitely have one. Self-awareness is key. My sister Jill jokes that "denial is a beautiful place, as long as we don't stay there too long."

Consider some questions below that will help provide insight to your relationship with money. Is it conscious, intentional, well-nurtured and well-managed, or are you completely disassociated from the concept of having a relationship with money? Perhaps you don't know? If you don't know, therein lies a clue.

What words would you use to describe your relationship with money?

Do you dislike talking about money, or are you okay discussing the topic? How freely do you "let people in financially" and who does it need to be?

On a scale of 1–10, how vulnerable do you feel about others knowing your real financial situation?

What needs to change financially to shake your certainty? What needs to change financially to make you feel more secure?

What emotions do you feel about money?

Remember the answers to these questions for later. Remember also the feelings that have arisen in you.

Wanting to Change versus Feelings Getting in the Way

There is little point you reading about financial intelligence unless you want to achieve a better situation *in some way*, for either yourself or someone you love. If everything is absolutely fabulous, great, I salute you. And if you want to move away from financial conversations, that's okay, truly. But I do believe you might be doing yourself a disservice.

If deep down you know that one reason you want to move away from financial conversations is because they make you feel less than ten feet tall and bullet proof, this is a strong clue that you should hang around instead. I want you to understand that you are not broken and haven't failed. If your intent is decent, whatever is holding you back is unlikely to be your fault. Your financial belief system may just be playing out in a way that might be unhelpful and inconsistent with your desires.

Often we simply need to better understand our relationship with wealth and money. Note the distinction between the two, as I really want you to see this. And if one or the other of these words leaves you feeling charged, simply notice this and we will explore further when looking at your financial beliefs.

Make a Decision. Make a Commitment. To Grow

If you have not yet decided you want to change your financial domain, know that not much happens unless we first decide we want it, then make a commitment. Whatever you define as your wider version of wealth, dare to consider that you are worth it. (You are by the way.)

In the next chapter are some exercises on exactly how to define your personal version of wealth. In the meantime, entertain the idea that a shift in your perception of wealth and what that means can be positive for you.

Summary of the Chapter

- Help me help you create some *magic, fun, learning, balance and understanding* about *why* all of this is *important* for you
- Define your version of wealth in a wide context. What do you want it to be?
- Find our your "why" for wanting to change your finances and your "why" for reaching your life's fullest potential
- We all bring our own "stuff" into our financial dynamics—this book is designed to help you become aware and change them. Consider how you would rate your relationship with money. What do you want it to be?
- Make a decision. Make a commitment. To Grow.

Chapter Three

How to Permanently Improve Your Finances.

What Do You WANT, What Do You BELIEVE and What Are You Going to DO About it?

So you have made a decision and commitment to improve your finances right? Great. Before we go on, I want to explain one of the most fundamental basics about wealth creation. Our wealth dynamics and results achieved are directly impacted by:

1. our wants
2. our beliefs
3. our actions

Anything else, while possibly relevant, is still fluff by comparison. Most people only address one or two of these and therefore don't get the results they want.

1. What Do You WANT

Imagine organizing a trip from destination A to *somewhere, i.e. anywhere.* Once you left your house, which way would you turn, if you didn't know where you were headed?

Learning about wealth is as much about the journey as the destination, but it is still fundamental to know *where* we want to head. Remind yourself about the factors you have so far considered to be important in your own definition of wealth. At the end of this chapter there is an exercise to help you with defining this. For now know that it is really important to be specific.

Imagine this. You get onto a plane of a major airline and when the flight crew, (including the pilot), discuss the flight, they tell you they aren't sure where they are headed, but they are really excited about it and think you will have a lovely trip. They will let us know once they have found a good airport to land in. They are not sure how long it will take, which country we will arrive in, or whether we will run out of fuel before getting there. But that's okay. Isn't it?

They are also not certain if all your luggage is aboard and suspect they might have forgotten the food and life rafts. They are not really sure about that either though; they forgot to check. They also failed to check whether the plane itself was in good working order prior to embarking. But rest assured, in case of emergency, they have a high belief they will be able to work things out at the time and although they do not know why or how, things will probably be okay. They are very confident everything will be fine, no matter what. All aboard!

Who's willingly going with them? Nobody, right? Well a few of us adventure seekers might (including most of my family actually, come to think of it) but most people wouldn't trust this situation enough to place their lives in the hands of the crew.

We all reasonably want the pilot and crew to have all of the above issues covered. It is a given. And yet many of us are effectively taking a similar approach when generating our own version of wealth. Why is that?

Whenever we operate without being clear about the financial world we want, we are potentially heading for disaster. Not all of us like disasters. We need to plan and consider our aspirations if we are to ever safely reach our version of wealth.

Wants versus Beliefs and Getting Specific

This list of wants is not a replacement for having a high level of belief: it is important to have both. I still strongly advocate having faith in everything working out okay, through consistent and strong beliefs about finances.

When I use the word faith, I simply mean belief in things yet unseen coming to fruition, belief in things working out without knowing *how* that might occur. It doesn't have to have a religious or spiritual connotation if you don't view the world that way—simply think belief. This belief is a critical element of financial success.

Right now though let's stay focused on what you want rather than what you believe. As in the plane story, it is normally when you know specifics of what you want that things work out better. Otherwise the plane may fly around forever, eventually running out of fuel. And you may do the same. There is always a chance that your plane will find exactly the right airport for your needs/wants, even if you haven't really worked out what they are yet. But given the variables involved, how many people would rely on the pilot getting that right? The irony is we do this with our financial lives daily.

When you specifically know what you want, things just become easier. You plan better, have more efficient use of fuel to get you there, manage risks better, and have a much higher level of confidence in all those around you to get the plane to the correct destination, safely and on time.

So find out what you want by imagining your ideal world. Expand on your version of wealth to an extent that you know what you would achieve if you had all the time and money at your fingertips.

Take a "fresh sheet" approach. And please hear this: do not worry about *how* to achieve what you decide. If you want to know what to focus on, firstly pick *why*. Then pick *when*. We will sort out the how together in later chapters.

Consider each of these questions below. Get your partner to do the same if you have one. Build a combined list using the exercise at the end of this chapter and ensure that everyone's views are fairly represented. Dare to be bold. Take a "dance as if nobody is watching" approach to these questions.

- What types of relationships are most important for you to have in your world?

- What personal values are most important for you to operate under?
- What do you *not* want in your world? What is the opposite of that?
- What beliefs do you dislike or think might be holding you back? What beliefs are the opposite of these?
- What type of person do you want to be?
- What things need to change in order for you to be that person— one example might be you would need to learn to operate *without* coming from a place of fear or control.
- How much time do you want to spend in creating income per week or per month?
- At what stage would you want your income to be self-supporting and not require your personal input in time?
- What type of support do you want to be able to provide to your family and friends?
- How much money do you think would be good to have in your world each year?
- Now multiply that value by 10. What would you do with the difference?
- How about if you multiply the value by 100? Or a 1000? What could you do differently in terms of helping others?
- Who would you help? Why?
- What would you actually DO?
- What would you do differently to now? When would you do it by?
- Who would you get to help you?
- Which of your skills can you readily use to fulfill your purpose (that you have been hiding away for whatever reason)?
- What would you like to do more of when you are not working?
- What activities would you like to do more of with your friends or family?
- How often and where would you like to travel?
- What is your burning desire? Does this take time, money, or both?

The above is designed to evoke a conversation with yourself. Note if your thinking went anywhere disempowered. If so, acknowledge this and choose to remove any drama about it.

2. What do you BELIEVE

If we are to transform our finances, it is critical to understand our belief system around money. Here are a few key points before we cover this in detail later.

You need to understand and apply a sound financial belief system to transform your finances. To a very large extent, your belief system runs the show. Not everyone is aware of what these beliefs are, or where they come from.

Consider whether your financial beliefs are sourced in empowerment, from a sound basis of trust, high self-worth, respect towards yourself and others, and an ability to give unconditionally.

Often they are actually sourced in disempowerment: based in fear, anger, guilt, pride, a need for control, low self-worth, greed, mistrust and/or disrespect towards yourself and others. Where we sit on the 0–10 beliefs scale is connected to our overall, long-term financial results. More on this in chapter 7.

3. What are you going to DO financially

This step is so obvious yet people often forget it. Most people know what they are supposed to do in order to have better finances, yet they just don't do it. Why is that? It is totally and completely illogical not to do so, yet we all sometimes realize we don't take the action we need to.

Failing to do the basics is part of human nature. Often it isn't until we feel enough pain or fear that we choose to act. Isn't that a sad indictment on our psyche!

Knowing what specific actions to take, and actually taking them, will impact our results greatly. The following five action steps are critical:

1. Always live within our means.
2. Have a consistent habit of savings.
3. Have a consistent habit of philanthropy (time and money).
4. Know your financial situation.
5. Have and operate a budget.

These five actions form the first significant step to wealth creation. Most importantly is living within our means. Making more cash than you spend. And not spending it until you actually have it.

We will address points 2) and 3) more fully in chapter 6, but with these it is the habit that matters most, not the actual amounts.

Your relationship with wealth can shift significantly in a reasonably short space of time by simply taking a higher level of responsibility around your finances. It still surprises me how quickly this can happen. It occurs because of the laws of nature or the universe that relate to finances. We will explain these a bit later too.

Finding the Balance between Beliefs and Actions

Your financial belief system accounts for 90 percent of your success, whilst your financial actions are the other half. I get that this doesn't add up to 100 percent. That's actually the point; it's not supposed to. The concepts of beliefs and actions live in different paradigms to each other.

What do you think I mean by this comment? It might mess with your head a little; on some levels I hope that it does. Consider this for a moment and consider it again once you have finished the book.

Applying the inter-relationships between your financial beliefs and financial actions is an art more than a science. This is because there is a balance to be found between the two that is sometimes intuitive, and sometimes logical. Sometimes we need to recognize it is our financial beliefs that need more focus, while other times improving our financial actions is key. We figure out which of the two we need to favor by applying both intuition and logic. Combining beliefs and actions with appropriate balance is what creates financial magic.

We tend to use our right brain for intuitive beliefs and our left brain for logical actions. We each naturally favor one side of our brains, so like many aspects of natural order, balance between the two can sometimes be elusive. In essence, equilibrium is constantly being sought as we adjust our financial beliefs and actions to ever-changing circumstances. If we tip the scales too far one way, we need to recognize this and bring ourselves back to a place of balance by adjusting either our beliefs or our actions.

Balance will come in time if you allow your intuition to guide you as to which of the two factors is most important at any given stage. Be patient, and remember to not discount the finger mentally tapping on your shoulder when you are making decisions. Our minds often try to remind us of information we have learned but easily forgotten, especially where there is information that does not naturally sit in our top of mind awareness.

Connection With Our Own Attitudes and Financial Situation

Everyone has moments (some longer than others) when we are disconnected from our financial situation. Sometimes we don't hear, or choose not to act on, that finger tapping in our head. This can result in us running around pretending everything is fine, when in fact the exact opposite is true. Sometimes we might actually be aware of it, but approach the situation from a place of fear or control instead of faith, empowerment, and an ability to give.

To enable a financial shift, it is critical for each of us to be aware of what we believe about money. When we can see what is present in our beliefs, we then have the ability to change instead of going to our "automatic default" settings.

JACK AND THE BEANSTALK

In Chapter One I wrote about the well-known fairy tale Jack and the Beanstalk, and how my son Jacksen loved hearing it at bedtime.

The tale has many parallels with the teachings in this book. So we are going to use Jack and his story throughout, to illustrate key points that you are learning. Most of these comments are sourced in real life events either for myself or my clients and colleagues. I have wrapped them up into Jack's story to use as an example throughout.

So imagine if you were Jack (or Jacqui) and you have grown up. You might be a thriving accomplished adult, or someone who would like to have a very different world to what you have currently. Jack represents you, either as an individual or as a business owner.

As a child, Jack wanted to help out his mother and create a better life for both of them. He did this the best way he knew how. He had a sense of responsibility as well as adventure, and a lot of courage and honor. He also had a cow.

But some things Jack did were not well thought out. Jack managed to get into trouble a few times, even coming across a giant who, understandably on some level, did his best to prevent him achieving the financial wellbeing he sought. Jack's mother's perspective of his actions differed greatly to her son's.

Because the giant was a risk to his safety, Jack chopped down the beanstalk to save himself and his mother. But this meant he couldn't use the beanstalk any more as a pathway to the treasure, or play on the beanstalk for pure enjoyment.

It's true that Jack enjoyed success via procuring the golden egg laying goose. But imagine that if after the story ended, the goose died or was stolen before Jack had managed to build a healthy financial nest egg. Or the goose simply ran out of golden eggs when Jack and his family were relying on them to live within their means.

What might have happened if Jack had all his financial eggs in one basket (i.e. the goose itself) and it was no longer available to him? And what else might he have been able to achieve if he had gotten rid of the risk of the giant, without chopping the beanstalk down?

Just for now, let's forget that the treasure didn't actually belong to Jack, but assume it was treasure that anyone could claim freely, similar to any income generated honorably.

What would the treasure you want in your world look and feel like? How would you want Jack's story to end if you were him? What picture would you hold in your mind about what is important to you? To what extent do you already have this picture? Your next step is to define any gaps and to help you become the person you want to be. And throughout this book we will check in with Jack's progress too.

EXERCISE : Defining Your Wider Version of Wealth

For many of us, our imagination is one part of ourselves we waved goodbye to in kindergarten, seldom to be seen again. But harnessed well, imagination can be one of our biggest strengths. Albert Einstein said "imagination is everything. It is a preview of life's coming attractions." In order to achieve something, we must first think of it, preferably involving both our beliefs and actions.

Now is when our imagination needs to come out from behind the shadows of our auto response habits. We want to dust off any sense of negativity, disinterest, or low self-confidence which helped it slink away in the first place.

For this exercise to work, we need our imagination to be center stage, using child-like wonder to contemplate any possibility. We need to think about our "why," our "what" and our "when," and only after considering these, work out "how" to achieve what we want.

Dare to be bold when completing this exercise. Dare to allow yourself to express your hidden most desired accomplishments. Own for a few moments that part of you that has always wanted to achieve something, but has previously allowed itself to get stuck in a sense of inertia or confusion about how to do it.

The worksheet below walks you through how to define your wider version of wealth. This is for both you and your business. These questions focus on how you want to live, and what you are here to achieve for yourself and for others.

Once you have defined your desired wealth, the next action is to prioritize the importance of achieving each component, then figure out the steps needed to achieve each one. Trust for now that one of the most important steps is simply to clarify what you are aiming for.

Something special starts to happen when we crystallize our intent from a place of burning desire and drive for high achievement. Things almost magically start to create the results we seek. Sometimes the path is totally different to what we originally envisaged, but the results start occuring anyway.

If you are unsure how to answer any of the questions, request assistance from those you love or trust to help facilitate your ideas. Add to your answers over time as more ideas surface.

Questions to Define Your Own Wealthy World

1. What aspects of your life are most important to you?

   You might include your life relationship, family, friends, career, health, recreation, travel, personal development/spirituality, physical environment/material possessions, specific causes you want to support like charities or particular sections of society, financial security, savings for your future, an inheritance to leave for your family, or enduring donations to causes.

2. What emotional/wellbeing aspects would you like to always operate from?

   You might include things like highly constructive thoughts, ability to be self- aware, always feel and show respect, receiving and giving unconditional love, having freedom from fear, high self-confidence, high self-worth, high self-esteem, always having an open mind, being able to freely disagree with others, high emotional intelligence, high spiritual intelligence, low rigid thought, high ability to trust, to give unconditionally, high belief in things yet unseen, low prejudice, low judgement, high ability to adapt perspective, high ability to understand other's views, low negative thoughts, or low internal impact from other's actions.

Include anything you think is genuinely relevant for you and how you would want to live.

3. What activities/aspects are important for you to be able to do now? Next to each point, note the amount of time and money needed for these.

4. What activities/aspects are important for you to be able to do in your future? Next to each point, consider what date, either month or year, you want to do these by. Also note the time and money needed for these.

5. What people or causes are important for you to be able to assist?

6. What is relevant about your past or the skills you have developed that you can draw on to help yourself or others?

7. What do you want to be able to do in the future that you believe is impossible (or very difficult) to achieve for you?

Review all of your answers. Remember to not get stuck about how to achieve these things. Rank every point listed on a scale of 0–10 as to its importance for you, with 10 being the most important.

Now list them all below, consider how you want the issue to be different to how it is now, and express the issue in terms of what you want—e.g. an improved relationship with your son could be one specific point to put below.

List the issues in order of priority, starting with the highest rankings out of ten. If you have a number of them with the same ranking, put the ones you perceive as most important first as well. This may not be possible but that's okay—they may genuinely rank equally. There may be a real mix between tangible things like an ability to travel overseas every second year, as well as highly intangible things such as having freedom from fear in all your interactions. Consider if there is anything obvious missing.

8. Consider the extent to which the above is impacted by the activities of your business or job, and vice versa (how would the activities of your business or job be impacted by achieving your wider definition of wealth).

9. How does your own involvement in your business or job need to differ in order to achieve the above definition of wealth?

10. Which of your business or job activities have a direct impact on achieving the above list?

11. How much profit does your business need (or income from your job) in order to achieve the above wealthy life? (you can complete this later if need be.)

12. How much time would you spend in your business or job if you were living your wealthy life?

13. How much time would you spend on your chosen causes if you were living your wealthy life?

14. What is specifically needed for you to transition from your current world to your desired world?

Now print out a summary of your desired wealth factors. Next to each attribute/factor, list your perspective of what is needed in order to change this so it becomes a reality. Some of the attributes might be very intangible, some might require money, some might require time. I suggest you discuss the above with your partner if you have one and/or your closest advisors. Now that we know what we are aiming for, we can start to achieve it.

Summary of the Chapter

- As obvious as this may be, your financial situation is made up of three main elements: what you WANT, what you BELIEVE and what you DO
- The reason most people do not have the financial success they seek is because although they know what is needed, they are blocked because they simply do not DO the five simple actions, or improve their underlying financial beliefs.
- Determining what you WANT is an obvious step—and yet seldom done at a conscious level
- Diagnosing and increasing your self-awareness about what you BELIEVE impacts your finances and helps you understand why you might be stopping yourself from doing the five financial actions.
- When we do start to DO the five suggested financial actions, our financial flow or energy shifts and we often see a significant improvement in our results. We need to understand our beliefs and actions to diagnose our money style and use this information to shift our results.
- Complete the wealth definition exercise above. Now that we know what you are aiming for, we can start to achieve it.

Chapter Four

IDENTIFYING YOUR MONEY STYLE

When we recognize our financial situation is made up of what we WANT, what we BELIEVE and what we DO, we are able choose whether we want our results to change.

Sometimes we love the struggle. I know this because sometimes we insist on the struggle continuing. It is what we are used to, and some of us wouldn't operate well if things were too easy. It's just not in our psyche. Why on earth would we feel more comfortable with struggle instead of it being easy? The answer is in our subconscious minds.

Before exploring this further, I first want to explain a key concept: money style. Money style refers to how we be around money. Our attitudes, our actions, and the results we either "allow" or "prevent" for ourselves.

Our money style is strongly connected with our financial results. And our results are directly impacted by the combination of our underlying financial beliefs and actions.

Our Beliefs + Our Actions = Our Money Style

Within the construct that Our Beliefs + Our Actions = Our Money Style, there are four main money style quadrants.

1. Stable.
2. Survival.
3. Sold out.
4. Sorted.

At some point I have personally lived in every one of these. And it was sometimes a struggle to stay in the quadrant my logical mind desired. This is because my subconscious had different ideas and influences. I needed to work out how to move beyond my current reality, so I was no longer bound by self-imposed constraints.

The Money Style Quadrants and Why Knowing Your Money Style is Important

Once we understand our money style, we can more easily see what beliefs and actions have been holding us back. When we diagnose which money style we naturally operate under, we can use this information to help us learn how to shift into a more financially sorted place.

The first step is understanding where we naturally operate. This gives us insight around what might be improved to effect change. We need a stake in the ground for our current reality; use the explanations below to help you get the first clues as to your natural style.

Within each main money style quadrant, there are a few different variations. Firstly find the quadrant that you feel best describes you, then find the specific style you identify with most. Don't worry if this is not immediately obvious to you. That may come later.

1. Stable Quadrant— Low Financial Beliefs / High Financial Actions

When we operate financially from a place of fear or control, (such as from low self-worth), I refer to this as operating from a "low belief system."

Fear can be what generates a need for feeling in control. In this situation, actions taken around finances are well-disciplined, but sourced in a need to know, rather than a desire for best practice.

It is not wrong to have this combination of low beliefs and high actions. It is just not as empowered as if our belief system had more depth and trust, and coming from a place of genuine ability to give financially with no fear or control present.

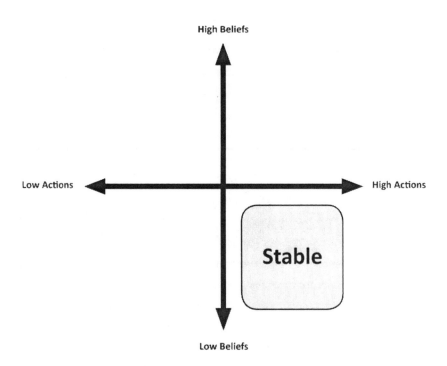

This quadrant is the second most useful quadrant to naturally operate under, in terms of long-term growth and financial stability. So if you are naturally a stable money style, know that you could do a lot worse. The main issue for us in this quadrant is when our financial actions are based in fear or too much control (to an unhelpful extent).

If we were an animal, we would be an elephant—powerful, strong and dependable. Yet under certain circumstances scared by something as small as a mouse! (In cartoons anyway.)

The specific money styles that live in this quadrant are:

- Saver.
- Severed/saver.
- Saver/severed.

Savers tend to need control, normally based in some type of fear or low self-worth. The flow of money is therefore assisted via a slight release on the grip of fear—sometimes these people strangle their financial lives with the need for certainty.

To improve your money situation, try "living" a little more. Don't be reckless with that (I know you won't be). Just for fun, practice taking a small risk occasionally. One suggestion is to sometimes not pay for parking, risking a parking ticket—or only pay a few cents, so if you get a ticket it would be lower in value. Take small, calculated risks often and your need for financial control may lessen.

Allowing a higher level of trust in things outside your own control means money can flow to you from places that aren't totally constrained by your own abilities. Release the grip on fear or control just a little, and see what happens to your cash and enjoyment. Do this a little bit at a time, until you can trust all is well with the changes you experience.

Savers are at risk of being too safe in their investment choices. Learn to understand the need to have your eggs in more than one basket. And learn to be at peace with the chance that over time, at least one investment may go bad.

Understand though that if done correctly, your investments overall are still more valuable than if you just have them in the safest place you could find. A good financial planner can assist with how to achieve this for you. Be discerning in your choice of advisor.

You are an easy style to work with because you have most things sorted, just a few things to improve around the edges. Deal to your control and fear issues and your results will start to change. Fear and unhelpful levels of control stop the flow of money more than anything else. Most of the other styles also have fear and control elements underpinning them, so you are not alone. You know that some control is wise and best practice. Do not lose all of this in your quest. Lose the parts that are based in fear, but keep the parts that are based in best practice.

A **Severed /saver** money style is someone who is predominantly naturally "severed" or emotionally disconnected from their finances, but also has high saver qualities. Their disconnection is strong and out ranks their fear or control based preferences. They are unconscious to these two factors of fear or control so they perpetuate them until they can see the relevance of how they are holding them back.

Both fear and control tend to be sourced in low self-worth. These people are characterized by not realizing they are operating from a place of fear and/ or control; they are disconnected from this.

While fear and control continue to operate at unhelpful levels, results will remain bound and constrained. Conversely, reducing fear and control will improve your results.

A **Saver/severed** style is someone very similar to the severed/savers. The subtle difference is how often the saver qualities of fear and control are present, relative to the level of emotional disconnection.

Sometimes people are more present to their fear, so they intuitively know it is their nemesis. Yet they feel unable to change the fear and control that binds them. This style can see their fear, but feel ill equipped to change it.

If this is you, Chapter 7 on climbing the beliefs ladder will help you improve these financial dynamics.

2. Survival Quadrant—
High Financial Beliefs / Low Financial Actions

Those of us naturally aligned with the survival quadrant tend to be diametrically opposed to stable quadrant people. We thrive on crisis. Stability bores us. In fact we repel it. This is my natural quadrant. This means my self-discipline needs to be more vigilant so I do not drift back there. You may be the same.

Survival quadrant people have a high level of belief. High beliefs can be the reason for our biggest strengths and also the cause of our biggest weaknesses. The irony is that it's our high beliefs that keep us bound. The trick lies in working out which part of our belief system is doing this.

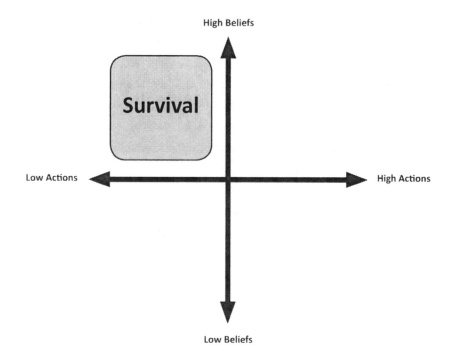

On some level, it is a bit like having an addiction. For example, if I was an alcoholic I would need to decide today whether or not to have a drink. This is the same decision anybody who enjoys alcohol might need to make. But the difference is that if I were an alcoholic, I would need to employ a much higher level of self-discipline in order to achieve the same result of not having a drink. It is fairly simple to achieve this if I do not have addictive tendencies running. Once I know refraining from drinking is the main issue, self-discipline makes the difference.

With survival quadrant people, the first thing to consider is what might be the equivalent of alcohol for yourself in relation to your finances. In other words, what is the equivalent of an unhealthy addiction in your financial belief system? Consider this question for a moment. There may be many examples, or you may think of only one or two. For example, do you have unhealthy levels of compulsion with spending in particular areas such as food, beverages, clothes, shoes, gambling, travelling, giving to others at a level beyond your means, or putting too much investment into your business compared to how much it is returning?

We may recognize we need to change something to live within our means, but our high belief system keeps us feeling everything will be okay "if only"...and when we do ABC or have XYZ, then everything will be okay.

We fail to recognize we need to act today to live within our means. Not next month once things are better, but now. Wake up! If you are not living within your means this month, change it right now. There is always a better way; always a way to improve if you want to badly enough. Find the way.

But hear this caution: protect your important relationships in the process. Do not compromise your important relationships through unilateral decisions to change your finances. Instead compromise in your finances via joint decisions to change. Be committed together to honoring your decisions. This could be with your partner, your children, your roommates or your business partners, depending on the situation.

If you don't want to find a way, acknowledge this to yourself. Get associated with your beliefs and the results being achieved from them. Decide if that is okay or not. If so, great. If not, change some actions or beliefs. Make a decision whether you want to stay in survival mode. It is a choice, day-by-day. If you love it, stay there. Personally I think there is a better way, but it is your call.

If we were an animal we would be a lemming, occasionally throwing ourselves off a cliff into the water for no apparent reason. Our belief system is so strong we cannot see these actions may be highly risky. We congregate with others of a similar belief system hence our actions seem perfectly reasonable to ourselves, even if others of a very different belief system view us another way.

But we do have the ability to swim in the waters below and we can often find our way back to the top of the cliff. Unless our belief system changes though, we are at risk of jumping off again.

Sometimes lacking self-discipline, we work very hard, but not in all the right areas. Our beliefs keep us bound and yet at the same time assist us in having a better chance of "surviving the fall." There is a big irony present. We have massive skills and yet our beliefs, as positive as they are most of the time, keep us bound until we change our ways.

We need to adapt a little so our efforts are focused in slightly different places. We employ small changes around focus and self-discipline. More on this in chapter 6 where we learn how to shift from the survival to sorted quadrants. Master this and your financial results will improve.

The money styles in this survival quadrant are:

- **Self-saboteurs** in the low–medium range
- **Spenders** who only just live within their means

Self-saboteurs are those amongst us with many gifts, yet for some undefined reason kick ourselves in the guts. Others can see it, but we cannot. I find that self-saboteurs tend to be the most fun to work with. We can achieve phenomenal results. Well for a while at least, before we "do it again." The trick with self-saboteurs is to allow them to do so!

Don't resist your own self-sabotage tendencies. Budget it in! Give yourself a play account to allow yourself some self-sabotage. After a while you may get sick of this. But if it doesn't hurt that much, you may not.

Every now and then, give yourself the freedom you so desperately need (but please, do so within your budget). It doesn't take long to decide a different game when you have an increased awareness of what you are actually doing to yourself financially. Have a mentor. This is critical. The time to listen most is the day you want to fire them.

Remind yourself what it is costing you to not live within your means. What are you missing out on? What costs are there in terms of things like your relationships, stress, self-worth, harmony, and opportunity costs of what else you could do?

Our biggest threat in this quadrant is we do not live within our means. There are many tricks to help you achieve this. One example is to put a credit card in a plastic cup of water and keep it in the freezer. You then need to defrost it before using, buying yourself time for decision making. A cooling off period, excuse the pun. It's a bit different if you do online shopping and like every good retail therapist, remember your credit card number. Put a post-it note on your computer to remind yourself not to shop online unless it's absolutely necessary, and why the note is there. Add a reference to remind you what else you want instead.

Do the same activities you want, but decide to do them in a cheaper way. See your friends via a potluck dinner and not an expensive restaurant—be honest about why and they are likely to thank you for it. It's about them, not the venue. Buy an OJ or get water instead of a wine; it will halve the cost and be better for you. Still have fun, but spend less money while enjoying similar activities a little differently or slightly less often.

You are the style voted most likely to buy something because you have a sense of self-entitlement, instead of whether you can afford it. You deserve the thing, so you go out and get it. It doesn't work that way. You need to be able to afford it first.

If you respect money it will respect you back. If you don't, it won't. Financial things will continue to go wrong until you learn this. The law of compensation, (which is similar to the concept of Karma), although slow, is very thorough. And it applies itself with a high level of accuracy. Honor it. Your choices will repay you in kind.

Spender money styles are similar to self-saboteurs, but they consider themselves to be slightly more sophisticated, which they are. This level of sophistication can be their downfall. They sabotage in a much more subtle way. They are the Kings/Queens of justification, making their every decision seem valid.

Self-saboteurs have the decency to admit their failings. Spenders always find a way to make it the "right thing to do." They even plan for it as well. None of this is a problem unless it is a problem. However, please carefully digest the specific definition of 'living within your means" outlined in chapter 6. Many spenders fool themselves. If you are a spender who does actually live within your means, then well done. We can't take it with us.

I would suggest however adding a long-term view to your perspective. Check in on whether your retirement is going to be as much fun as your current life—if not hang out with a saver to learn their views on financial topics. Allow them to rub off on you and vice versa. You create a good balance for each other.

If you are a spender that does not live within your means, you are a self-saboteur. So see above and admit to yourself your true money style. You may have been hiding this from yourself very well. Start living within your means so your long-term position is both protected and optimized.

If you want to be more like a different style (they each have fabulous positive attributes as well as challenging aspects) hang out with one of them.

Ask them their views. You may be really surprised. Allow your worldview to change a little via people you respect.

3. Sold Out Quadrant—
Low Financial Beliefs / Low Financial Actions

I lived in this quadrant for a period of my younger life. It wasn't fun. No fun at all. Those who have low beliefs/low actions characterize this quadrant, as well as those disconnected from a relationship with finances.

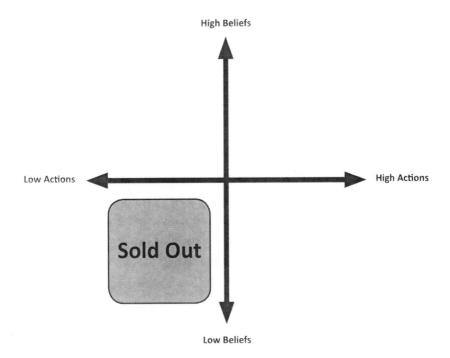

We tend to either not recognize we are spending more than we make, or else we simply don't believe it is important to *change something* to start living within our means. It's just not a priority.

Like the survival quadrant, we have a "she'll be alright" attitude that abdicates responsibility, or else we operate out of fear to an extent that it paralyses us. Either way, it is abdication. Either way we need a very special blend of self-compassion and an ability to grow so we can choose to shift.

If we were an animal, we would be an ostrich, head well buried in the sand. We lack self-awareness that effectively results in us not being all that bright. That's nothing to do with our IQ—just our awareness of what we are doing to ourselves and our continued ability or insistence to tolerate it.

Wake up and we will understand more. We need to see what we are doing and what it is costing us. Ostriches are able to pull their heads out of the sand. Sometimes they just need a reason, like wanting to breathe. What is stopping you from wanting to breathe more? You deserve to be allowed to breathe better. Do you agree with me? You will need to be in a place where you inherently agree if you want the information in this book to work.

You could also be a dodo, roaming around your finances in a clumsy and sluggish manner. If you are not careful, you may be destined for financial extinction. You need to wake up and start to pay attention, increasing both actions and beliefs so you begin showing up as slightly less dim. This is also a choice and not a judgment by the way; it just is what it is.

The money styles in this sold out quadrant are:

- **Severed**
- **Self-saboteurs** in the high range

Severed money styles tend to be disconnected and don't really know, or care, where money things are at. You tend to be easy to work with if you change to a point where you 1) have a goal and 2) live within your means.

Set up a savings automatic payment for the specific purpose of living within your means. I don't care how little the savings value is; any level of habit is the important part for now. Get savings account statements delivered in paper form so you get reminded of how your savings are going. Decide to take an active interest in this information.

Once a month look at your bank account transactions and notice for yourself where you are spending and how much. Change it if it's not working for you. It IS a choice.

It is also important to work out what in your life created a sense of disassociation and consider working on improving that. Money, like anything, tends to lose interest if the relationship you have with it is nondescript or disinterested. Your life can often have far less color as a result.

Increase the vibrancy in which you explore money issues and your life will reflect this. This works both ways. It is far less common for a severed money style to not live within their means—these people are instead self-saboteurs.

Self-saboteurs in the high range refers to people who self-sabotage more regularly than not. The distinction is because some of us self-sabotage often, whilst some of us might self-sabotage only once every few years or so.

4. Sorted Quadrant—
High Financial Beliefs / High Financial Actions

Enough of what we don't want. This is the quadrant where we want to be. We want to aspire towards being "sorted" in order to achieve the version of wealth we wish to create, or to maintain the version we already have. Whether it is via self-discipline or from natural inclination, our actions are strong, consistent and dependable.

In this quadrant we have a strong sense of community and we communicate about financial issues openly and well. We have a high level of respect for ourselves and others financially, and we trust and believe in things yet unseen. We also always have a plan B and plan C up our sleeves, just in case we need them.

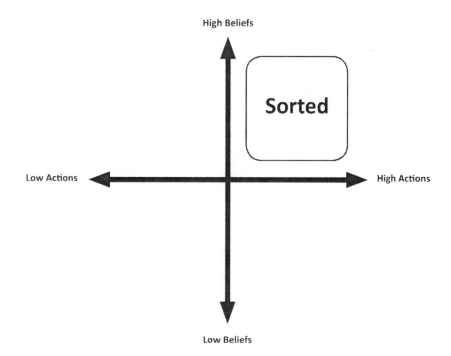

Our consistent actions seldom take for granted the need for Plan A's success. We therefore minimize any downside risk around our finances with our actions, but importantly operate from a place of prosperity consciousness with our beliefs.

If we were an animal, I believe we would be a dolphin. Strong, community based, good communicators, dependable, clever and very loyal. We are able to give regularly, look after ourselves and thrive in a group. We play well with others and are connected to our own purpose.

The money styles in this Sorted Quadrant are:

- **Saver/spender**
- **Spender /saver**

Saver/spender styles save money first and enjoy their life second, always spending appropriate amounts. Some is spent on themselves and some on others or causes. We have naturally come to the sorted quadrant via the stable quadrant, so our natural inclination is to always save.

We have learned to improve the foundation upon which we base our financial beliefs, so we are no longer bound by fear and control. We have learned to operate from a place of high self-worth.

Spender /saver styles spend often, but always within our means. We also save often and it feels like we are "spending our way" to savings. We identify with the concept of saving for our future selves by spending into a savings account. We have found our way into the sorted quadrant via the survival money style. We have had to move through our own belief system and readdress our blind spots around our financial beliefs.

Either of these sorted money styles work well. They work with our natural inclination as a leading style and add the compensating behavior from a place of self-discipline. It sounds quite ludicrous to a survival style that a stable person may need to use self-discipline to spend more, but this can fit. We benefit by learning to live a little more than we currently do.

Diagnosing Your Individual Money Style

The descriptions above will each resonate with you to a larger or lesser extent, depending on which quadrant you naturally operate in. At this stage it is okay for you to either have a good sense of your *specific money style*, or alternatively only a very loose, vague awareness of your *money style quadrant*.

A higher level of awareness about your *financial actions* will unfold in chapter 6. Meanwhile your *financial beliefs* will be more specifically revealed in chapter 7. Both chapters will help you assess where you specifically sit on the respective axes and it will be the *combination* of these that will specifically diagnose your specific money style.

For now, one (or possibly two) of the quadrants is likely to seem more relevant for you than the others. If not, don't be put off by confusion, things will continue to reveal themselves as we progress.

Know that a level of confusion at this stage is of no major consequence. Often survival mode people think they are instead sorted, or vice versa. Sold out mode people often think they are survival or vice versa, and stable mode people often think they are sorted or vice versa. I suggest you do not yet become preoccupied with a need for specific diagnosis. Allow the overall sense to come to you as you continue to consider all the contents of this book. Accept the quadrant that you simply feel is correct for now.

If however you feel really stuck about your own money style quadrant and want wider perspective before moving on, ask someone trusted to give their perspective for you. I suggest they read at least the first 5 chapters though, so they can understand the relevant context when doing so.

A low level of self-awareness in relation to your money style quadrant could indicate a level of disconnection commensurate with the sold out quadrant. If so, I suggest you don't judge this about yourself, but do allow yourself to simply be with it. There is no point beating yourself up about it. You will address issues around disconnection by progressing through the book.

All of this said, it is best for you to have *some* idea of your money style quadrant before reading further chapters. So request help if needed.

Seeing Our Own Inhibitors—
So We Can Find Our Pathway to Balance

The main reason we want to identify our individual money style, is so we can find our own customized pathway to a place of genuine *balance* between our beliefs and our actions.

Once we have genuine balance, we will grow, financially as well as in many other ways. If we don't have balance, we won't. *Maintaining balance* between 1) a depth of loving beliefs with 2) a strength in our respectful actions, is the key to personal growth, financial or otherwise. Over time we learn to move our beliefs away from fear towards love, whilst we learn to take our actions away from recklessness, towards respectfulness.

In order to achieve balance, at some stage we will need to also find the root cause of the beliefs or actions that are inhibiting us, i.e. holding us back. *Fear, mistrust, pride, guilt, low self-esteem, embarrassment*, unhealthy types of *control* and *disrespect* are all examples of financial belief or action inhibitors.

These inhibitors can seemingly prevent us from being able to powerfully address our own personal improvement. We hold ourselves back, often not knowingly. We therefore need to identify these inhibitors and powerfully heal them for ourselves, so we can achieve genuine balance.

In the meantime, know that our inhibitors are the things which either

1. prevent us from having an open mind needed to contemplate that these concepts might be valid, or else
2. prevent us from applying the suggestions needed so we can achieve effective results.

We therefore need to get rid of our inhibitors at an integral, well-healed level because it is not helpful to continue to allow them to run the show. Well, not unless we also want to continue to achieve the same results.

So acknowledging the root cause of our inhibitors, is highly relevant for us to firstly learn and secondly powerfully assimilate to our individual circumstances. This is especially relevant as our results continue to change.

Once we have this specific awareness of our inhibitors and money style quadrant, we have the first two ingredients needed to learn how to shift into the place of genuine balance. This genuine balance is only found within the sorted quadrant.

Why and What to Improve

Generally speaking, survival quadrant people need improvement in financial actions, stable quadrant people need improvement in financial beliefs, and sold out quadrant people can benefit from improvement in both.

That said, all of us normally have both beliefs and actions inhibitors that have room for improvement, regardless of what main money style we operate from. In order to create change and improvement, we need to:

1. determine for ourselves which inhibitors can benefit most from our increased attention. Consider the list in italics above.
2. heal the main root cause/s that first created these inhibitors

Doing these two steps will not only improve your finances but other areas of your life as well. Focusing on and improving/healing your own inhibitors is likely to occur gradually, as your awareness of them changes over time.

The benefits of improving these inhibitors will be far wider reaching than just your financial domain; it will extend to your entire definition of wealth.

JACK AND HIS MOTHER'S MONEY STYLE

Back to Jack and the Beanstalk. There are many metaphors present in the story of Jack and his family, so seek them out and consider how they might apply to your own situation.

Let's presume that Jack has now been at home with his mother for a few more years; he is a teenager in his last years at high school.

His mother is still working, to provide for the family's necessities. Jack spends most of the money from the golden eggs on items that his mother views as luxuries. He is interested in many of the latest inventions and wants to always have the latest model of everything he thinks is cool.

If we were to consider both of their financial beliefs, we might conclude the following about each of them. And these points likely reveal themselves somehow in their financial results, as well as their day-to-day lives.

Jack has always been a go-getter, throwing caution to the wind. He acts first and then works out how to resolve a related challenge later. He operates from a high place of trust and has an acceptance that events can simply continue to reveal themselves. He is motivated to provide for his Mom and he wants to excel at anything she requests of him. He has a short attention span and moves onto the next thing quickly.

He tends to not notice important factors related to his decisions. As a result, some of his decisions with money are highly reckless. He cannot see this in himself and does not yet have any interest to learn. He is still young and such things don't seem relevant yet.

Now that he has a golden egg laying goose, he doesn't really care for knowing what he is spending. He is unconcerned that he has recently spent beyond the golden egg producing capacity and owes money to some people he deals with. Jack knows they will get paid eventually and that things will work out as soon as the goose lays more eggs. He thinks things will be fine and doesn't see that currently he is living beyond his current means. He doesn't realize that some of the people he deals with are losing patience with his financial habits.

Disrespect towards others financially is an inhibitor that will hold Jack back from the success he seeks.

Jack is a survival quadrant money style and yet looking after his mother is more important to him than any amount of cash. He enjoys his life to the max at the same time.

He doesn't think beyond the arrival of the next golden egg and what he can spend this on. He hasn't noticed that the goose is getting older and her eggs are less frequent.

Jack could benefit from seeing what is obvious to others and improve his five financial actions around money. In order to do so, he could benefit from noticing that his high financial beliefs are having a direct impact on his financial actions and long-term results.

If he continues in this reckless fashion, he may become a train wreck. His beliefs around money hopefully will shift, so he can see a higher level of self-interest in being self-disciplined by consistently adopting the five financial actions.

His current beliefs are so strong, he does not yet see the relevance of doing the financial actions. It is likely to be his nemesis, unless he can see this blind spot. He is likely to stay in survival mode while things are going well.

If his goose stops laying golden eggs, he may have a very quick journey to the sold out quadrant. Increased awareness about his beliefs will allow him to improve his actions. If he gets more focused on these five financial actions he is likely to move easily to the sorted quadrant.

Jack's mother has had a lifetime of financial struggle. She often seems to operate from a need to control, which is likely to be sourced in some form of fear, probably relating to her own childhood.

She has however, managed to make ends meet as best she could and has done all she feels she can to provide for Jack, who she adores. But she gets very impatient with Jack often. She has been honest and responsible with her finances and doesn't understand why Jack won't listen to her.

Jack's mom is still able to work and begrudges this a little. She feels she has to work because their financial situation is not safe enough for her liking. She doesn't understand Jack's attitude to spending everything the goose lays and wants him to learn more about her ways. She has high concerns that the goose will be stolen, die or simply stop producing golden eggs. She worries about what they would do if that happened.

She is likely to be a stable money style and seems to have a high need for certainty. Fear is an inhibitor that is holding her back. If her fear was diminished she may well shift quickly into the sorted quadrant. Her high ranking in respectful actions, but *low ranking in beliefs due to her fears, combine to result in a stable quadrant ranking.*

Now that they better understand their money styles, Jack and his mom can begin to choose the aspects to improve so they can achieve their desired version of wealth.

Summary of the Chapter

- A combination of one's beliefs and actions creates a money style for each of us.
- Four main quadrants house the varying money styles: **sold out, survival, stable** and **sorted**. Each quadrant is a combination of beliefs and financial actions.
- Once we know in which quadrant we operate, we can also identify our specific money style.
- Each money style quadrant is characterized by an animal to remind us of our attributes.
- Knowing our money style is needed to know where to improve and shift into a better quadrant (as desired) to achieve better results.
- We often change between the quadrants depending on our current combination of financial beliefs and actions, but we do tend to have a natural style around which we need self-awareness.
- One main aspect is to find *balance* between our beliefs and our actions—sourced in first acknowledging and healing the root cause of our belief or action inhibitors.
- Generally speaking, survival quadrant people benefit most from improving their financial actions, stable quadrant people benefit from improving their beliefs, and sold out quadrant people benefit from improving both. Regardless of our natural money style, we all have some beliefs and actions we can benefit from improving.
- By now it would be good for you to have a reasonable sense of your personal money style quadrant, or even better, specific money style. If you do not yet feel comfortable with your high level conclusions, ask someone trusted to provide their perspective of your quadrant before proceeding to the next chapters.

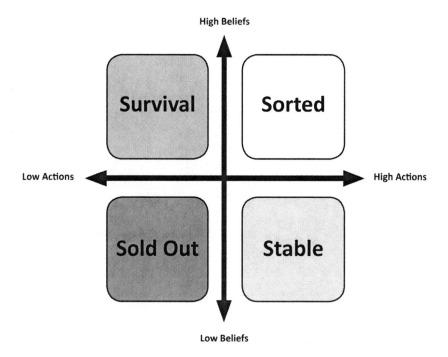

Chapter Five

COMMUNICATING EFFECTIVELY ABOUT FINANCES

K nowing we need or want to shift our money style to another is one thing. Being able to talk about the financial issues to make the shift without reacting badly is quite another! Learning to do this is one of the steps needed to stay in the sorted money style quadrant.

We need the ability to have adult, empowered conversations about all things money without becoming emotionally affected. I know, conversations like these are the ones that divorces are made of. And they can also be one of those times when fools rush in where angels fear to tread. But somebody needs to help us all have better financial discussions, so I figure it may as well be me.

I am always interested in the reactions I face when speaking with clients about their financial situation. Over the years I have experienced a lot of varying personalities and behaviors through conversations about finances and business in general. Some have been more explicit than others.

Money conversations can be highly vulnerable and emotionally charged. Often it is all about perception: some people get really angry over things others perceive as highly reasonable to suggest.

We all know people who fight over money and some who feel like failures because of money. We also know people who gauge their success on money, and some who try to buy happiness with it. And when money works, people feel safe; when it doesn't, they tend to feel vulnerable.

This chapter helps you gain a level of awareness around how to react in a more empowered way when having difficult or vulnerable conversations, so all concerned can focus on resolving the issues. In my experience, finances are one of the top three vulnerable areas that people struggle to communicate about. The other two are health and relationships. While I designed the following communication model to help with financial conversations, it is equally applicable to all three topics. It shows what to make top of mind, so we can respond better when engaging in confronting conversations.

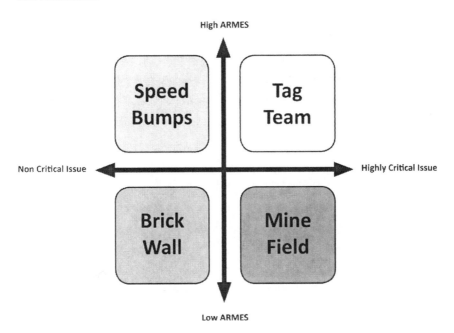

It is only when we notice our emotional reactions, that we can choose to manage or adapt them. The ARMES acronym stands for self-**A**wareness, self-**R**egulation, self-**M**otivation, **E**mpathy and **S**ocial skills. This acronym was first explained to me by behavioral psychologist Keith Randell, my Advisory Board Chairman, and provides a combination of useful skills to help us relate well to others during confronting conversations. When we react emotionally with high levels of ARMES, we can better deal with situations that have activated our negative belief systems.

We all know people who react badly with conversations they find confronting. Some of us are open and willing to express ourselves, while others get angry, punish, manipulate, or control. Some withdraw completely. Many of our reactions are child like in nature, but in the moment we often fail to recognize this.

Remember this model anytime you are having a financial conversation where you disagree with someone. And by the way, it is important we disagree, for if we never do, one of us is unnecessary. I believe there can be nothing more dangerous than a person who blindly follows someone, so I would treat with caution anyone that always has the same opinion as your own. Have a different opinion and be bold enough to express it. It will extend them, as well as yourself.

At times we should disagree with our relationship partner, our advisors, boss, staff, and family; it is through these disagreements we get the opportunity to grow. We need to be able to have powerful conversations with everyone, so we can create a more full picture, and achieve the synergy created from more than one mind.

Why Does This Matter and How to Grow Quickly

When trying to make a permanent improvement in our world, it is easier if we operate from an empowered state and not a dysfunctional one. For example, if you read this book in an empowered state you are more likely to recognize your responses and adapt accordingly. Being emotionally empowered means you can more easily choose to apply the suggestions I am making.

Notice when you strongly disagree about a financial suggestion. Why have you reacted this way? There is a good chance you have more to learn in your reaction than in what provoked it, especially if your reaction is emotionally charged. Your disempowered reactions give you very valuable information about your financial blockages.

Less Empowered Conversations—
Brick Wall and Mine Field Quadrants

Disempowered responses to money topics indicate we are operating in the "Brick Wall" and "Mine Field" quadrants, depending on the importance of the issue. A "Brick Wall" conversation is one where you are met with strong resistance fuelled by one of these disempowered reactions. Because the issue itself is non-critical, the other person does not push the point. Often they simply choose to let it go after feeling like they have hit a brick wall.

The difference with a "Mine Field" conversation is the other party believes the issue is of high importance. They continue to state their case, seek a resolution and try to manage or compensate for the reaction of the other. If one party is operating in the Mine Field quadrant, the other one can feel like they are walking through one, trying to avoid stepping on a live mine at every turn of the conversation. It can take some skill to navigate both people back to an empowered place. Using ARMES will get you there.

If one or both parties are in Mine Field and stay there too long, even divorces can result, both in our personal relationships as well as those with our business advisors. Many relationships cease when conversations about finances are not aligned well enough for effective communication to prevail. Sometimes this is caused by a lack of trust. Or sometimes projections are in play where both parties believe the other is feeling disempowered, but neither actually are. Each person can be simply projecting his or her assumptions onto the other.

More Effective Financial Conversations—
Tag Team and Speed Bump Quadrants

Whatever the cause of discord, the resolution is found by communicating from within the tag team quadrant. We need to return the conversation as quickly as possible to this quadrant to achieve more effective results. Here both parties react with high ARMES responses about issues that actually matter.

As long as good communication prevails, the conversation can get back up into Tag Team quickly enough. Have a predefined declaration process, such as each stating you are feeling okay and refocusing the conversation on the issue, is important, rather than reacting emotionally to the topic.

The tag team quadrant represents a place where the ARMES reaction in both people is high. They are interacting like adults, not children. They regulate their internal responses and take responsibility for any disempowered states. They also shift these, or at least acknowledge them.

A "Speed Bump" conversation is one where internal ARMES reactions are high and empowered, like those in the Tag Team level. A Speed Bump conversation by its very nature is just less important. The speed and ease with which the issues are addressed often occurs faster and more easily.

Recognizing When to Apply this Model

If we consistently apply this model, we are much more like to stay in the sorted quadrant. The key thing to understand most though, is to recognize *when* we should apply it for ourselves. Often we are so instantly affected by our emotional responses that we do not consciously acknowledge our reaction. We are instead blinded by them.

What we should do instead is simply talk about the *financial issues* at hand. As I understand it, we do not actually have conscious choice to moderate our immediate emotional responses—it happens at a core unconscious level of our mind. What we can do is learn to moderate our *logical reactions* to these core emotional responses. Over time, practicing the principles in this chapter will also help improve our emotional responses.

We can all probably list people we know who have disempowered emotional reactions to finances—this list usually includes ourselves at least some of the time. Witnessing an *emotional reaction* about the financial issue, instead of simply *discussing* it, is the clue needed to recognize that we may not be operating from a tag team quadrant.

Assimilating this Information is the Goal

The more we assimilate this chapter's information, and understand when to insert it into our financial conversations, the more we will grow. The best way to do this is to apply the ARMES acronym during your "difficult" conversations:

1. Be more self-**A**ware of your emotional reactions to financial topics.
2. Employ a higher level of self-**R**egulation when noticing your emotional reactions towards yourself and others.
3. Be self-**M**otivated to want Tag Team conversations.
4. Have more **E**mpathy towards another's perspective or circumstances. There is a good chance they may actually have a valid point.
5. Use better **S**ocial skills to communicate in a way that is both appropriate and respectful.

We will then have the ability to discuss financial issues authentically and resolve them promptly with better outcomes achieved.

Mixed Messages: Working Your Way Through Emotional Reactions

It can be frustrating if you believe you are operating out of a tag team quadrant, while others in your financial conversation believe you are coming from a place of disempowered emotional reaction. The messages can get mixed up in the transmission between the parties.

It could be that the other party is projecting emotional reactions onto you that you aren't actually experiencing. This can happen as a result of them drawing from an unresolved past issue because you represent someone from that past situation. For example, they may feel emotionally attacked by you even if you aren't attacking because you remind them of someone who has attacked in the past. As far as you are concerned, you are simply raising a financial issue that is valid. But also remember that sometimes the other party is in fact correct: you might be operating from a place of disempowered emotional reaction, and raising something inappropriate as a result. Being able to genuinely see this escapes us a lot of the time. The quicker we can uncover any blind spots around how we are operating, the quicker we will stay in the sorted money style quadrant.

If you can both contribute to a conversation from a place of flexibility (instead of high rigidity about your vantage point *having* to be correct), then you can move into the Tag Team sector more easily with your conversations.

If you feel you are slipping into a Mine Field space it can help to calmly say, "I just want to keep discussing things from a place of 'Tag Team'", as well as "let's work out the miscommunication we seem to be having." Employ the ARMES principles on the basis both people are aware of this model.

Sticking to the Financial Issues at Hand

Wherever the emotional component is coming from, it can be best to stick to the financial issue at hand rather than focus on the emotional reactions. Steering a discussion toward emotional reactions can sometimes be a very useful avoidance technique (either conscious or unconscious), detracting from discussing the financial issue itself.

This is especially true if someone wants to avoid feeling bad for poor performance, financial ignorance or other perceived negatives. They might take the offensive by shifting the conversation to another's emotional reaction without even realizing they have done so. After all, it is safer for them to do this as it isn't much fun discussing things like poor performance.

Sometimes this type of side tracking occurs because one party does not understand why the other one views the financial issue as important. They presume the only valid conclusion is that the other person is reacting emotionally. Again, I personally find it more useful to discuss the relevance of the financial issue itself, rather than getting bogged down in discussions about any emotional reactions to it.

Noticing our Responses and Learning From Them

All of this said, noticing our responses to financial issues can be a massive clue to helping us understand what might be holding us back within our financial domain. Although it may be annoying, or sometimes even scary, I suggest that from now on you welcome any conversation on financial topics where you feel emotionally reactive.

It can be difficult at the best of times for any of us to trust that a very different perspective to our own is still an empowered reaction. But we can benefit greatly if we learn to give these perspectives validity. A different perspective normally indicates the other party has a different underlying money style. We can learn a great deal from their perspectives as long as they are empowered ones.

Respect in our Financial Interactions

Empowered conversations are focused on maintaining respect. Something as simple as not apologizing for dismissing another's perspective can hold to ransom our own ability to change and grow. We need to be highly respectful towards others so the financial laws respect us back.

Shortcomings either in our conversations or actions can indicate that financial respect towards others is in fact lacking. The universal energies that govern our financial domain will notice this type of disrespect and therefore pay the person back in kind. It may take time to do so, but what goes around, comes around.

Demonstrating high respect towards others allows the energy around our own finances to stay in positive check. Our sense of self-worth is also maintained because we are being true to ourselves. Simply put, if we want to demonstrate respect, we need to be the bigger person and give others the benefit of the doubt that perhaps their views are valid, despite differing to our own. We also need to *actually communicate* to this effect and seek resolution if needed. Otherwise the other party may continue feeling unsettled. Unresolved feelings can negatively influence their actions towards us financially. Without even realizing it, people tend to punish others financially in response to a perceived lack of respect towards them.

We shift money style quadrants quicker once we consistently apply the ARMES acronym in our financial conversations. By doing so we complete one part of the recipe needed to achieve our desired version of wealth.

JACK AND HIS MOTHER'S ABILITY TO COMMUNICATE

Jack and his mother could benefit greatly from discussing financial issues from a Tag Team approach. Despite his young age, Jack has a role in the finances of the household, so both he and his mom should be discussing them. That said, even if he didn't have financial responsibility in the household, they could still benefit from including him in some of the financial goal setting. His Mom would be passing down some valuable lessons by doing so.

Creating a Tag Team approach is crucial, otherwise they are at risk of their financial conversations constantly resulting in Mine Field nagging and arguments. Nobody enjoys that.

Remember that Jack and his Mom have very different money styles, making it even more important to communicate. Jack is a classic survival money style and his Mom has mostly aligned with a stable money style.

It is important for them to recognize that they can balance each other's weaknesses, if they allow each other to do so. Jack is talented and bright, but he also has a typical teenage air of arrogance. If necessary, Jack should read this chapter for himself a few more times until he understands how arrogance might be negatively impacting their conversations. He can still be clever, talented and often always "right" without necessarily being cocky about it. He could also benefit from learning that his communication approach can border on being a bully, even if not intentional.

His mother is not fun to be around and quite tiresome given her constant nagging about the same old financial issues, again and again. From her perspective, she knows no better. Jack could do well to have some compassion towards her but instead gets grumpy in return. He is a teenager after all; he will learn in time. And so will she, as long as they both choose to be open to each other's perspectives. His Mom can benefit from learning to nag less.

A great start to this learning is that Jack and his Mom are fully discussing their financial perspectives now. They need to be able to consistently see each other's vantage point. They begin to understand they are approaching their finances from completely different priorities and perspectives of what is best. In light of this increased understanding, they are able to regulate their internal reactions to each other with money topics. They are more self-aware and they can even discuss mutual goals for their household, assisting them both with self-motivation. It matters not that Jack is a child.

Because they are more willing to genuinely listen and actually hear each other, they are making good progress. This in turn allows each of them to react emotionally much less often. Jack is young and immature. His mother is not. However at an emotional maturity level (in relation to finances), they are not too dissimilar, because until now neither could discuss money issues without being emotionally reactive.

Summary of the Chapter

- Understanding the ARMES acronym helps you manage your emotional responses to conversations around money. Using it will shift you into the sorted quadrant quicker.
- ARMES stands for self-**A**wareness, self-**R**egulation, self-**M**otivation, **E**mpathy and **S**ocial Skills and utilizing these skills can assist in keeping people engaged and connected to the issues.
- Financial dynamics can be highly vulnerable for people and as a result we tend to sometimes react badly emotionally in a childish manner. Recognizing this for ourselves in the moment is key to learning what we might work on to shift ourselves forward financially.
- The goal is to discuss financial issues in a "Tag Team" approach which means highly important issues are addressed in a very adult way, focusing on the actual issues rather than our emotional reactions to them.
- Sometimes we project emotional assumptions about someone onto that person. Discussing this with the person ascertains whether we are correct or whether we are projecting, and allows for a healthy conversation so we can return again to the financial issue itself.
- Notice when you react about financial issues. Sometimes there is more learning to be had from your reaction than from the issue itself.

- By now you will know enough to have a conscious level of awareness needed to apply a high level of respect in your conversations around money, apologizing for your part in situations where one or both of you have entered into the Mine Field sector. If you do not yet feel you have this level of awareness, request insight from others you trust.
- Consider for yourself the extent to which you might benefit from and resonate with the examples provided by Jack and his Mom.
- Your ability to assimilate this chapter for your individual circumstances is crucial to achieve your desired version of wealth.

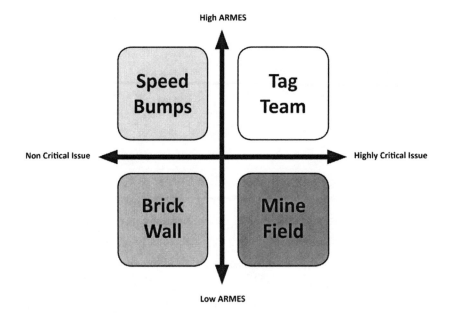

Chapter Six

From Survival
to Sorted

Shifting Your Money Style "Actions"

We now know that we can communicate powerfully by applying ARMES to promote Tag Team conversations. And we know that we want to do this so we stay in the sorted money style quadrant. Unfortunately, despite our best intentions, we seldom have tag team conversations 100 percent of the time. We can create a negative reaction in ourselves even when no else is involved in the dialogue! So we need to always ensure we take action to improve our emotional responses, beliefs and financial habits over time.

If we want to live in the sorted quadrant, a fundamental requirement is to have enough courage to consistently do the five financial actions introduced in Chapter 3. Ask yourself the following questions.

- Do I live within my means? (Every month)
- Do I have a consistent habit of savings?
- Do I have a consistent habit of philanthropy?
- Do I know my financial situation?
- Do I have and operate a budget?

Where Do You Rate on the Actions Axis—
Are You a Survival or Sold Out Money Style?

Chapter 4 taught us that one of the first key questions to ask is "what money style am I?" Especially important to learn is whether you are one of the survival or sold out styles.

Sometimes people simply know they are in survival mode. Failing that, a good way to tell where you would sit on the actions axis is to very subjectively rate yourself on a scale of 1–10 with the above five questions (10 being the highest and meaning you are doing this well).

If you sum the total of your five answers, you can ascertain where on the actions axis you rank. The horizontal actions axis on the model goes from a score of zero, with low reckless actions on the left, and moves towards a score of 50 with high respectful actions on the right.

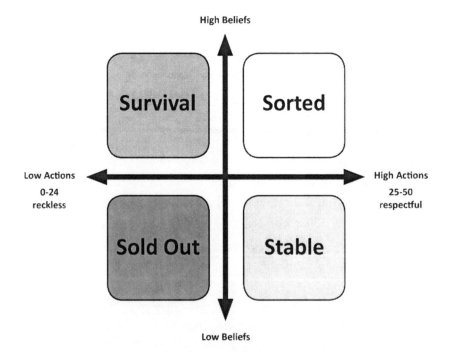

People who operate via reckless financial actions tend to be more disconnected from their finances or responsibilities. The habits of those operating on the right however tend to be more connected and respectful, such as not committing to spending money until they have the cash available first.

Regardless of our money style, we can benefit from focusing on improving our financial actions. Unless you are already operating at your desired level, set a goal to do something to improve your overall actions ranking within the next four weeks. You may be surprised how much magic or ease is created by this.

Some immediate actions you might take include:

- Find a way to make more cash if your expenses are higher than income—such as taking a part-time job or doing commission work—*to live within your means*
- Set up an automatic payment to a savings account of a small amount per month *to improve your habit of savings*
- Set aside a defined amount of time to do charitable activities or make an affordable regular donation *to improve your habit of philanthropy*
- Work out the minimum (and desired) levels of personal expenditure to live on *to have and operate a budget*
- Track all expenditure for at least 21 days *to improve your knowledge of your financial situation*

Now here's some insight. I imagine that most of you will read the above list and think the examples are really obvious, common sense, and almost insulting to suggest. And that they may be SO obvious and easy, that you haven't actually DONE any of them. Rest assured, it isn't until you actually DO any of my (or your own) suggestions that your financial actions rating will improve. Pick the easiest suggestion you think is relevant for you, and do that one first. Then each month focus on improving one or more of the other actions.

Why Bother to Improve Your Financial Actions?

Let's review for a moment why we want to apply these suggestions. Remember this is all firstly sourced in what we want, your definition of wealth.

Imagine if your version of desired wealth included living in a bus shelter. There is a good chance you could achieve that, right? (Authorities willing.) If this was what you wanted, you may not achieve anything more than this. Sometimes if we reach for the stars we might get to the moon. If we instead reach for a rooftop, it can be very difficult to get to the moon. That's fine if that's fine for you; it's your version of wealth that is relevant. No judgment here.

If instead you want to be a billionaire as part of your version of wealth, the fact is you are unlikely to achieve this as easily as if you're shooting for the bus shelter, largely due to your level of commitment. And the gap in your ability to achieve billionaire status will be far smaller if you actually know that this is what you want to achieve.

Other significant factors play a part too. When our combined wants, beliefs and actions are in alignment, the natural laws of the universe provide for us. By using the wider power of our minds, it becomes far easier to accomplish what we are focusing on.

Confronting Our Own Beliefs

Trace your finger from the left side of the actions axis to the right side. You may notice that we need to move through our belief system axis to move across the quadrants. This is because we have to confront ourselves in order to change, and our ability to change is correlated with our degree of wants and our commitment to them.

To shift quadrants and take the suggested actions, we need to confront our unhelpful beliefs. When we do this our useful beliefs need to stay well intact; sometimes it can be tricky to distinguish between the two. The way to figure out if a belief is unhelpful is to ask yourself if it is stopping you doing one or more of the five financial actions. If it is stopping you, then that belief is an unhelpful one. You can use more self-discipline to override that belief with your actions. It is when we improve doing the five financial actions, despite having initial resistance, that we make good progress financially. This is because we are forming new positive habits.

If any resistance you are feeling is sourced in not allowing yourself to do the five financial actions, this is a clue that you are trying to self-sabotage yourself. In contrast, our useful beliefs are the ones that allow us to keep fear and an unhealthy need to control at bay. A belief that enables you to trust is helpful; a belief that prevents you from doing so is not. So we need enough discernment to do both; 1) trust and 2) also take action.

But in general, I suggest you be less concerned about which beliefs are useful or not. Instead just focus on doing the five suggested financial actions and don't overanalyze it.

It doesn't seem logical that sometimes our beliefs will try to stop us from doing the five actions, but I have seen it happen and also experienced it myself. We get confused, justify, or delay. How convenient. It is good to be aware of this yet push on through anyway, until we find the evidence we need to see that the five financial actions do have a positive impact on our financial results.

Whether we take improved financial actions or not reflects how strongly we are committed to what we want. Our financial actions are sourced in our financial beliefs, so focus needs to be balanced across both. It is in maintaining this balance that we stay in the sorted quadrant. Over time this balance between beliefs and actions comes naturally, but until a level of mastery exists, we need to periodically consider for ourselves if we need to perhaps improve either.

Having a Reality Check

Being "real" is imperative if one wants to shift one's financial position. Too often we gloss over the reality of what we need to DO because the topics themselves are challenging. Discussing difficult topics (either internally, or with others) is what helps create the shift, connecting us back to our real selves and our relationship with money.

And let's face it; sometimes it's not easy. One reason is that we have to consider for ourselves that we might fail, or have failed already. Looking at one's financial situation shows courage, honor, and compassion for oneself. Personally I don't associate any of these words with the word failure.

Making Our Wants Necessary

It is important to explore "our wants" a bit more because fundamentally the best way to get someone to DO something is because they WANT to. This is highly relevant to a chapter about actions. I can't make you do these five financial actions; only you can.

With this in mind, the following phrase is intended to annoy you a little. I believe that each of us, right here, right now, has EXACTLY the financial situation we want. Think about this for a moment.

If we wanted something to happen badly enough, we would have "found a way" already. Human beings are highly resourceful people when something is needed. Let's presume that you do not yet have everything on your definition of wealth (well done if you do, or are nearly there). But if not, how come your version of wealth hasn't yet been necessary enough for you?

How necessary are you making your own financial success? How necessary are you making the act of spending less than you make each month? Or from a more positive vantage point, how necessary are you making you earning more than you spend? Where are you selling out? And why does this matter?

Allow negative feelings to surface if they are stirring. These might include feeling judged, proud, embarrassed, dumb, angry, guilty, attacked, or that you want to attack (I might be "wrong" to make you feel bad). You may also feel your self-esteem or self-worth affected. Whatever your reactions, they are all common.

You may instead have little emotional reaction, yet still do not have the results you genuinely seek. Consider for yourself the extent to which you feel disconnected emotionally about your finances. You could also feel a reaction, yet are still "resigned" to results that are less than you desire. Or you may simply agree with my comment, knowing that you have already achieved what you want, or are at least on the path to get there with feelings well intact.

Whatever you feel, notice it. Also know that your feelings are not at all about what I have written. You have simply had an emotional reaction to what I have written. I'm not making that mean anything bad, but there is a chance you might be. Embrace your emotional reaction and learn from it. It provides a clue as to why you are where you are financially. Especially if you are feeling negatively affected. Allow your reactions to settle without trying to over analyze them. Over time your insights will show you which beliefs are unhelpful.

Next steps in the Process to Financial Freedom— Write and Date Your Goals

Now is the time to review your definition of wealth and consider a stepped approach to achieving your financial goals. Not everyone will become a billionaire within x days, so be realistic. Work out how much cash you will need for your current requirements, and how much you need in your future. Also remember that money is only one small aspect of your wider wealth.

Your wants should include your massive, out of reach dreams and your needs refer to managing any downside risk level, necessary to simply exist in life. A "baked beans on toast" level of necessity. Put a dollar value on both these "subsistence" and "above and beyond your dreams levels."

I do not suggest you intentionally live at a subsistence level. What is important is to be able to do so whenever it might be needed. Knowing you can, goes a long way towards not ever needing to. The removal of fear from this dynamic allows the opposite of Murphy's Law to kick in. As long as we are comfortable with the idea of being able to exist at a subsistence level, we seldom need to do so. An absence of fear means we seldom attract the situation.

You have probably already heard, that it's critically important to write your goals down and also put a date on them. Your mind will then start to "goal seek" the activities and results needed to achieve this. It's not complicated. Our minds are incredibly clever; allow them to be. But it's also basic common sense.

I recall many years ago being told about a university study where about 3% of the graduating class (full of very clever, competent achievers) had written down their goals and dated them. Many years later they surveyed the same group and found that those who had written and dated their goals achieved a massive amount of the wealth created. That 3% generated something like 97% of the wealth. There were few other similarities between these people except for the fact they had written and dated their goals. We don't need to fully understand why it works. It just does, and it's not hard. Be specific about what you want, and importantly, add in the desired achievement date.

For some of the critical steps needed, decide on some simple milestones to achieve along the way. Examples are discussed later on. Whether you want a humble existence, or alternatively an extravagant one, your preference will impact the decisions you make and results you make necessary for yourself. So it follows there is a direct correlation between your wants and your financial results, even if the correlation is not immediately obvious to you.

Do not, for one second, think you can miss out the step of writing and dating your goals.

Examining Our Five Financial Actions

There is the simple logic that your financial actions have a direct correlation with your financial results. How could they not? Yet many people self-sabotage themselves through their actions.

For example, in my opinion, the survival quadrant is the easiest from which to escape. Yet it is also the quadrant most fiercely defended by people who sit in it. They keep themselves bound. Survival style folks have a fabulous strength in their very high beliefs about money dynamics. But harnessed the wrong way, these high beliefs can also be their nemesis.

We all have moments where the 'wheels fall off' and we shift back to a less empowered quadrant. This can be overcome by getting a bigger goal. People with strong aspirations just "do what it takes" and also become very teachable if they see something missing from their core information. Albert Einstein said, "We cannot solve our problems with the same thinking we used when we created them."

This is where the five action steps come into play: they are needed to help significantly shift our finances. They should be done together, not in sequence. That said, they are listed in order of importance. But every one of them is a critical piece. It is not a multi choice situation where we only pick a few to our liking. They are all needed to complete the puzzle.

Financial Action 1: Living Within Our Means

One of the main underlying themes of operating from a high actions level is the most basic of financial guidelines: make more money than you spend.

It's easier said than done some months, especially if you are in a business that creates highly unexpected results. If you have ever played monopoly, you will remember getting $200 when you got past "go." This is a "do this or don't get past go" step. At some stage you may choose to stop tolerating anything less than this.

Living Within Our Means—Capital Versus Revenue Items

People sometimes ask specific questions about the definition of living within your means. Especially common are those from people who are asset rich, rather than cash rich. This usually generates a conversation about whether or not living from capital gains on property (realized or unrealized) counts as living within your means. That is, the house has increased in value, so if I sell the house (realized gain) or instead borrow on the perceived increased value (unrealized gain), I can get some cash to pay for my living costs. This then feels like I am living within my means—the question is whether that is correct. Although a conservative answer in a perfect world is normally no, the answer can sometimes be "it depends."

Allow me to be an accountant for a moment and explain the difference between capital and revenue items. Income and expenses are classed as revenue items because they generally have qualities such as reoccurring regularly, are operational in nature, and tend to relate to consumable type issues for the person concerned. In your personal world this would include eating, travelling to work, buying consumables, and rent or mortgage payments for personal living. Generally speaking, your weekly/monthly/yearly living costs.

Expenditure in relation to capital items on the other hand generally tend to be for items more permanent by comparison, (e.g. fixed assets purchases or the capital sums in relation to long term liabilities/loans), and assets often increasing in value over time (but not always as many depreciate in value). Regardless of this, capital items are usually designed to be in existence for the long term (more than twelve months) whether they be assets or liabilities.

General accounting principles suggest that to be financially strong over the long term, we tend to match revenue items with revenue items and capital items with capital items. So as an example, it is smart to match long-term loans with fixed assets, and expense-incurring activities with an income-generating source (i.e. not a capital based source). This is if you want long-term strength to continue to grow.

The "it depends" part occurs when you try to match a revenue/expense item with a capital one. The cost of living is an operational item and therefore would generally be classified as a revenue/expense type rather than being capital in nature. Houses on the other hand are generally capital in nature because they tend to be viewed as fixed assets. So when one "lives" with their personal expenses from the increase in value of their home or other property, there is a mismatch in revenue/capital classification. This seldom creates long-term financial strength, especially in circumstances where the owner lives off the increase in value to an extreme extent.

So generally speaking, it is not usually clever from a long-term perspective to live off the increased value placed on a home, unless your particular circumstances warrant this. This is especially risky where the house value subsequently drops, as many can bear witness to during challenging financial circumstances internationally.

But living from the capital value of property can sometimes be valid. This could be if you are cashing in on investment property during retirement years, supporting yourself due to a serious illness, or for a strategic business investment. The question is incredibly case specific— it should be assessed with the benefit of financial planners who know your full financial situation. The main point is that the answer is normally no, with just the occasional yes.

It is more financially robust to find a regular income source to fuel your regular operating expenses. This means that at an operational level, you are personally doing the equivalent of making an operational profit. And equally this sentiment of making an operational form of profit obviously also applies to your business itself. This is the stronger definition of living within your means and in most cases is the one I would recommend. Allow your capital instead to grow and live off the interest/dividends from investments (which are revenue in nature) rather than the capital sums themselves. But remember this is all very case specific.

That said, we have choices in this regard and my main suggestion is to consider the opportunity cost of taking whatever option you choose. What else could you do with that asset if you didn't want to literally live off it now? And do you have enough assets that this one in question doesn't really matter anyway? This point can be very relevant for some people. It is often a question of degree.

Living Within Our Means— Choices Needed to Improve Operational Profit

If you or your business is not performing to the required operational profit levels, then the choices you should consider include the following:

- How long are you going to tolerate a low profit situation before you either:
  a. Change something about the current income or expenses, or
  b. Change other ways of getting money, via a part-time job or something equivalent?

In other words, refuse to stay in a state of inertia. Move away from relying on capital sums to live on (unless your older stage of life warrants this of course). What other possibilities exist to earn income outside of your current situation? Here's some other questions for you.

- What level of debt is palatable?
- What level of debt is too dangerous?
- What needs to change now, so you are not left "holding the baby" financially?
- How can one receive support without necessarily needing to pay for it?
- What return on investment is expected for your business/situation and how much time is allocated to generate this? If you are living on capital sums to generate business growth, are these specifically related to generating sound future income streams? Or are you fooling yourself in relation to either risks or timing?

Part 2 of this book will deal to these financial dynamics around a business itself. If it is too difficult to make more income, then the other option is to reduce costs. It has to be one or the other. Cash in needs to exceed cash out. Every month.

Living Within Our Means—A Respectful Cash Action Every Day

As part of living within your means, I suggest you do one thing every day that shows a high level of financial respect. Put it as a calendar reminder. This particular point does not center on whether you can afford to do something. Often you could. It is purely about demonstrating financial respect.

For example, I was at the airport one day when my flight was delayed and I was hungry. It would have been easy for me to spend $15 for lunch. Instead I noted for myself that I hadn't done my daily respectful cash flow item. So I chose to stay a little hungry and I bought a roll and some ham from the supermarket next to the destination airport. The $10 I saved was not about the amount of money, it was about the respect I was demonstrating. In my opinion, this habit of demonstrating some financial respect daily is one of the most important things I do.

Note that I also intentionally have conscious actions based around enjoyment and rewards. Often these are linked to achievement of goals and sometimes too "just because I can." It is the balance created between respect and reward that is important. If this resonates with you as a bit weird, that's absolutely fine too. I understand that perspective. I am an accountant after all. That said, the actions suggested are still sound common sense. However there is also an energy around financial flow that I'm starting to teach you to harness at a very practical level.

Financial Action 2: Creating a Habit of Savings

This is one of the easiest of the five financial actions to achieve: it's just a decision away. I don't care who you are, if it was life threateningly important for you to save a small amount per month, you would. So let's pretend its life threatening. Set up an automatic payment to a savings account every month. And then forget about it. The habit is far more important than the amount. Only a few dollars will suffice if that is all you can afford. Here's some points to consider:

- The amount chosen should be easy to sacrifice each month (or sometimes each week, depending on what is easier for you to achieve). It could be very minor.
- It should be paid into a bank account that you cannot access via Internet banking.
- It should be an automatic payment.
- Start out with a low amount and every second month increase the amount, very slowly. When it starts to get too hard to pay every month, stop at that level until that amount seems easy again.
- If you have some months that are really difficult for you financially, make a commitment to reduce the savings amount to the bare minimum, but do not stop the automatic payment. The habit is far more important than the amount. Reduce the amount and keep the habit.

A habit of savings is one of the most important actions steps one can implement. Imagine if you had saved 10% of your income every time you were paid since you were in your first job? I know, I wish I had started earlier as well. For now though, just do something with savings, and do it regularly and consistently.

Financial Action 3: Creating a Habit of Philanthropy

We've all heard of the phrase "what goes around comes around." This is also referred to as the Law of Compensation. Other well-known natural laws include the Law of Increasing Returns, Law of Attraction, Law of Vibration and Law of Success. We discuss these more in chapter 7.

For now, let's consider the Law of Compensation. Making regular donations of varying types is a win/win situation. The recipient of your money or time wins because they receive from you in their time of need. You win because in time this act of kindness comes back around to you. And it does so at an increased level. Hence the Law of Increasing Returns also features.

Farmers understand these natural laws. Plant some seeds and receive whole crops in return. In my experience, the same thing happens with donating time and money. The return you receive only works when the donation is genuinely done willingly without expectation or demand. It needs to genuinely be unconditional in nature.

There is another reason this financial action works. When one can freely pay some money across to others (again even if only a few dollars per month), the stranglehold of keeping your money under your control, which is often created by fear, can at least in part be released. And releasing yourself from fear-based actions in very simple, practical ways increases your comfort levels around money.

From what I've observed, the most important time to remember to donate a little more, is the same time you feel you need money the most yourself. Remember with this it is largely about the habit, not the amount, (so don't be too reckless). Remember too, that it can be a donation of your time or your cash.

For many years now, I have found that money arrives as needed when we can release any fear about whether it will or not. When we can calmly trust all will be okay, money situations sort themselves out (as long as we are also consistently doing the five financial actions).

The irony of this philanthropy action is that it also directly relates to improving your belief system. By doing this action and creating these type of results, you start to build evidence that you can trust and give, rather than operate from fear and control financially. So this philanthropy action allows you to travel up the beliefs axis of the money style model, moving away from fear, and towards love.

Financial Action 4: Knowing Your Financial Situation

As long as we do actually live within our means, then knowing specifics about our financial situation is slightly less important than having a habit of savings and philanthropy. However do not underestimate the importance of this financial action. A clear sign of how connected we are with our finances is whether we know how much money we need to live each month. And preferably know the amount we WANT to live on each month. Lots of people don't know.

Once we know what we are aiming for, we also need to check how close we are tracking against this target. There are many ways to do this for your personal expenses:

- Review Internet banking weekly or biweekly.
- Write down all cash expenditure in a small notebook you carry with you.
- Maintain a spreadsheet or other electronic system. The packages that import daily bank feeds are handy to use because you don't need to re-enter the transactions.

Having awareness of your financials top of mind is critical if your money situation is tight. Your personal preference as to the method for tracking this information is less important.

Financial Action 5: Having and Operating a Budget

From what I have seen, few people have actually worked out their budget so they don't know how much money they need to generate each month to be within it. By the way, for a business owner, your budget should first allow adequate money for taxes. Obviously what you plan to live on needs to be the "after tax" amount. So when doing cash flow planning, we need to think in terms of "before tax" otherwise we risk not consciously allowing for taxes in our week-to-week financial management.

You need to know one number per month, which is the average monthly amount you need to generate before tax to live at the level you want. Once people actually stop and work this out, they are often massively surprised at how high the amount is and just how much it differs to what they initially thought. Once you know the after tax amount, convert this to the before tax equivalent. If need be, request assistance from a suitably qualified professional.

When all of the above financial actions are achieved you will be far more likely to create a positive shift in your financial results.

Understanding the Results of your "Actions"

—— Horizontal Axis "Actions" (from the Money Style Model) ——

From "Reckless"
(Blame Excuse Denial)

through

To "Respect"
(Ownership, Accountability, Responsibility)

transition from the left to right quadrants tends to occur between box 5 & 6

0	1	2	3	4	5	6	7	8	9	10
Commitment of significant funds with no ability to pay.	Commitment of significant funds with little ability to pay.	Expenses exceed income and creditors are impatient.	Ability to pay relies on borrowing (banks, investors, family).	Payment of creditors is often late. No financial reserves exist if income generation fails.	Income versus expenses is almost breakeven, but creditors are manageable.	Prospective debtors are reasonably expected to cover new spend when it falls due.	Money from existing debtors is expected to cover spend when it falls due.	Money from invoiced debtors consistently arrives on time & 30 days before any scheduled spend falls due. Reallocation to more important spend is not needed.	Money from invoiced debtors consistently arrives on time & 60 days before any scheduled spend falls due. Reallocation to more important spend is not needed.	Funds to cover foreseeable spend is already available in a savings account. Creditors are always paid either on time, or earlier. Reallocation to more important -pend is not needed.

The Actions Axis in Detail

I have developed the graduated Actions Axis on the facing page. It rates financial actions depending on how reckless or respectful they are.

When making a decision to proceed (or not) with some spending, we can use the graduated scale to gauge the extent to which the decision will be reckless or respectful. When most of our decisions to spend rank at 7 out of 10 or higher, our financial actions shift us to predominantly being in the sorted or stable quadrants. When most of our decisions rank somewhere between 0–5 out of 10, our actions over time will keep us in the survival or sold out quadrants.

It is the accumulation of our day-to-day actions that determine where we each lie on the actions axis. Sometimes one decision is so significant that it has the effect of changing our ranking all by itself. Take care with the habits created and use self-discipline to apply a higher level of self-awareness, applying spending rules you deem acceptable.

Reckless versus Respectful

Operating well on the Actions Axis is largely about having enough respect toward the relationship we have with our money. And by the way, there is very little else required to maintain the financial actions associated with the sorted quadrant, assuming your belief system is well enough evolved.

People in the sorted quadrant avoid reckless decisions under most circumstances. Respect is the key, but then we don't want to lose the fun in our lives either. Finding a good balance between the two is important.

Be respectful and money will be respectful back. Don't and it won't. It can take time for increased respect to resonate in our results—it's almost like the universe wants to check you mean what you say this time (when you first change your action habits). This is especially so if you have been fickle in the past. This can increase your apprenticeship time, a bit like a probation period.

I am not sure why this is true, but it is what I have observed over my years in practice. I realize this is not an overly scientific comment and is easily open to attack. But we don't always need to understand something in order for it to be true. Sometimes we can be too focused on a need for understanding when we simply need to get out of the way and let the forces that be do their thing. Allow up to ten months for increased respect financially to pay dividends. For some it may take even longer. This is partly due to the length of time it takes for our minds to build new neurological pathways and habits.

Consider for yourself, what aspects of your finances do you currently treat with respect and what aspects could do with some improvement? Improve your concept of respect on some of your financial actions and you are most likely to improve your financial results.

Committing to Expenditure

Think about what normally happens when you commit to new expenditure (commit in this context means you are at a point where you are about to carry through on your decision to spend.) I refer to this stage as going past the "point of no return." Making a commitment directly impacts the pressure you place on the need to generate funds. Take a close look at your current financial situation. Consider which 0–10 Actions Box describes where you normally operate (you might swing between 1 or 2 boxes depending on any given situation).

Note that going past the point of no return can be very subtle. It sometimes occurs mentally, before any actual physical commitment is made. Although these decisions can often be strategically sound, it is still best applied within the context of having access to the required cash. To not do so can place a high level of pressure on the wider dynamics of financial flow within your business. If care is not taken, the result can be lower levels of financial respect for the situation (which is often returned in kind back to you, based on the premise that what goes around comes around. This saying is especially true for finances.)

The desired actions box above (from 0–10) isn't always the perfect 10. The best actions box for your business to operate from depends on the combination of:

- The growth stage of your personal or business goals.
- Your ability to secure extra funding when results end up being worse than originally expected.

For long-term sustainability, one should aim to operate from at least box 6 and between boxes 7–8 consistently as a short-term goal.

Occasional lapses into boxes 3–5 should be acknowledged as being "survival" or "sold out" mode (high-risk) decisions, be infrequent and be combined with time constrained decisions on how to recover into better decisions quickly. Take care to note any patterns forming when operating at box 6 or lower.

Always avoid operating in boxes 0–2. Consider your belief systems regarding prospective income and assess these with a very discerning mind. Taking all factors into account is key (including your values) to gauge impact on your cash flow, operational issues and the marketing/brand positioning. Especially if relying on the prospective income does not actually eventuate.

Decide to improve from left to right along the Action boxes gradually. As much as possible, avoid boxes 0–5. If you are in business, it can sometimes be better to improve "one box at a time" rather than take too big a jump. This is so your business growth itself isn't unnecessarily hamstrung. It's often a balancing act between 1) keeping the cash safe and 2) ensuring enough growth activities are progressing. Consistency will provide improved results.

Decisions for New Expenditure

This Actions Axis helps you decide how to make sensible financial decisions for new spending. This allows you to consider where today's decision will leave you financially in a few months time.

Review each of the 0–10 Actions boxes and decide what Actions Box ranking your desired decision is most aligned with. For example, if as a result of this decision to spend you will be able to just pay for the commitment as the amount becomes due, then you would rate this decision in box 7. Take care when deciding that it is a reasonable conclusion. For example:

- Don't count your chickens before they're hatched–they need to be debtors already invoiced for box 7, i.e. take the box descriptions literally. Prospective invoices/clients don't qualify.
- Consider the time of year and budget requirements relevant for low income months such as over Christmas. Scoring well now

is short-lived and premature if it creates a problem in a few months time.

- Take care not to "over-estimate" the likelihood of "prospective" income actually occurring. If it hasn't happened yet, it hasn't happened yet.

Ranking your decision between 0–5 is likely to perpetuate you being or moving into the "survival" or "sold out" financial quadrant. A decision ranking 6–10 is likely to perpetuate you being or moving into either the "stable" or "sorted" financial quadrant.

Decision making at box 7 or above would be your goal for most decisions as this helps you transition away from the "sold out" or "survival" quadrants towards the "stable" or "sorted" quadrants. There's no accounting for bad luck (which includes things like natural disasters and not low sales or proposal conversions), but the more responsible decisions you make, the better you will manage it. We want to achieve consistent decision making at this level, to help avoid the "reckless" end of the Actions scale.

Delay the mental or actual committing part, until you already have the cash. Take care with the flow on impact from non-cash actions/comments. Sometimes critical paths around business growth can get a life of their own and they can be hard to rein back in. Being reckless at any level can be disrespectful to the universal laws that govern financial flow making it far less likely to have good finances "arrive."

It's better to know the critical path regarding the drop dead dates or deliverables, pulling back if needed. As well as always operating without fear from a high level of financial respect, belief and trust, and changing course if results don't happen.

Do the work first to get the cash results required. Then whatever you want to achieve becomes a no brainer on this Actions scale.

Can it Sometimes Be Worth Going Back to the Survival Quadrant?

I can hear a resounding "yes!" from the survival quadrant people. But then we would say that, wouldn't we? Survival quadrant people love the adrenalin rush of needing to climb out again.

Seriously though, it is a good idea to look closely at all important factors before making a spend decision. Sometimes one of these factors might justify the risk of moving to the survival quadrant temporarily.

I suggest that if the answer decided is "yes, we can be reckless just a little bit", it would be best if it happens for a very short time and the pathway out is an easy one. It takes some skill and helicopter level awareness to navigate the rough seas should the financial weather turn bad in the interim.

Please note: I would not recommend temporary lapses in financial actions if your natural style is in the sold out quadrant. It can be very difficult for sold out people to move back to sorted if they make decisions in the lower parts of the actions scale.

Building on Solid Rock

The extent to which we need to be careful and disciplined around our financial actions is connected to our money style. People who are naturally accustomed to operate as sorted can be likened to people building a structure on top of solid rock.

For stable money style people, applying their required financial actions is like building wealth on a foundation of clay. In order to be stable enough, the financial foundations need to be dug a little deeper than if they were built on solid rock.

Survival money style people are attempting to build their financial foundations on sand in an earthquake zone. It's not impossible, but the foundations need to be very deep and also require some strengthening. Their financial situation can be very shaky.

Building for sold out people is like doing this on quicksand. It just doesn't work. It may be deceptively okay for a short time, but eventually the unstable ground will topple anything being built on top of it.

Our attempts to create wealth follow this building analogy. The strength of our financial building depends largely on how deep and strong our financial foundations are. And there is one thing that ensures this and one thing alone. Self-discipline around undertaking the five financial actions. And more of it is required for some people: those in the survival quadrant need more self-discipline to achieve the same results as those in the sorted. Self-awareness is helpful to know how much self-discipline you need. But it is self-discipline itself that ensures the action is actually taken.

The five key action steps are relatively easy. Our ability to consistently implement them is linked very closely with our own financial belief system. Sometimes we logically understand the steps are sensible, but do not see enough self-interest to actually DO them. We need to notice this about ourselves and find a way to have higher self-interest. Return to your desired definition of wealth to assist with this. If we are not doing the five action steps, this is a big clue that our belief system is not allowing ourselves to escape survival mode. When we improve our beliefs, we help our ability to DO the five action steps. Missing out one of the action steps can be enough for the overall recipe of wealth creation to not to work.

Jack and His Mother

Jack is a young soul when it comes to some aspects of his finances. He is also young in physical years, so has much to learn on many levels. That said, he is a very quick learner and has a significant ability to find his way into good financial fortune, as evidenced by his Beanstalk story.

He does however have an "easy come easy go" attitude which is not overly useful. One of his biggest strengths is an open mind and that he is prepared to try something without having a specific need to first understand or believe it will work.

Jack read this chapter, both loving it and hating it at the same time. He concluded that although he could see the sense in the five financial actions suggested, he might start doing them better next month, or maybe even next year. He does however have a renewed sense of self-awareness around the actions needed and agrees that doing this is likely to begin to change his results.

With an element of reluctance, Jack agrees with his Mom to set goals around his five financial actions. He is beginning to understand that because he is a survival money style, he needs a higher level of self-discipline than others might to do the five financial actions.

Jack's Mom is a stable money style, so her five financial actions are already reasonably good. But she can improve on some of them so she also agrees to set goals around these. She acknowledges that Jack is not as naturally good as her in these areas with compassion, and understands he is not consciously trying to annoy her when sometimes irresponsibile about his spending. Together they are going to work on these five financial actions for their combined benefit.

It matters not that Jack and his mom have a parent and child relationship. All members of a family can benefit from working towards these goals. Different context for varying ages and levels of understanding is what is needed when a family has these discussions.

At some stage it would be interesting for you and your family to digest all the information in this book and discuss a way to make your situation better. If your family members are in survival or sold out mode, making changes to these financial actions is crucial.

Summary of this Chapter

- We need to shift through our own belief system to move into the sorted quadrant. Therein lies the challenge, because our belief system is so very strong.
- Right here, right now we have EXACTLY the financial situation we want. We need to DO the five financial actions before the suggestions in this book will work.
- Write your major goals down and date them. Include mini goals to improve the five key actions within the next 4 weeks.
- Apply the 0–10 actions gradient to your spending decisions so you take a balanced approach to finances from now on, committing to a new spend within appropriate time frames.
- Solid ground, clay, sand in an earthquake zone, and quicksand are related to the four money style quadrants and show the relativity of varying levels of self-discipline needed for desired results. It is

impossible to build a permanent, thriving building on quicksand, and the same is true for your wealth. We need a strong base for it to thrive permanently.

- We need to notice if we are not actually DOing the five financial actions consistently and use this as a clue that our belief system around money could benefit from some help.
- Discuss the impact of this information with your whole family.

Chapter Seven

From Fear
to Love

Climbing Your Way Through
the Financial Beliefs Ladder

We know the five action steps needed to stay sorted financially, and also know that if we are not doing one or more of them, it could be because we are blocking ourselves with unhelpful financial beliefs. In this chapter we will learn where these blockages around money lie. But first we need to check where our financial beliefs sit on the Financial Beliefs Ladder.

Diagnosing Your Place on the Financial Beliefs Ladder

When we refer to the specific details of the Beliefs Axis, we are referring to the vertical axis of the Money Style Model on the next page. The Beliefs Axis starts with 0 at the bottom (fear-based actions) and works up to 10 at the top (love or giving-based actions).

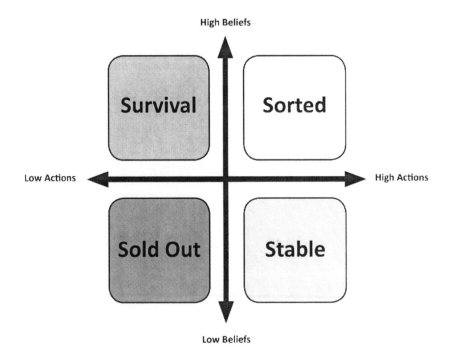

Our belief system will result in us operating at one of the financial belief levels (shown as stages 0–10 in the table on the following page). Changes in our beliefs can occur now or later (6 months–3 years, depending on your choices/growth).

Our beliefs drive the type of world we generate for ourselves. If we want to live in a sorted quadrant, our financial beliefs need to be high, but also in *balance* with our financial actions. Especially if we want to *significantly* shift our financial results.

Read this table from the bottom to the top as it allows you to see more easily the journey from a low to a high financial belief system.

Read through the 0-10 gradient and find the worst one you are currently being. If you are operating at a higher level, but there are relevant aspects of a lower level, the lower level is the one you pick. Traveling up the beliefs axis as our awareness grows is not only possible, but also our duty.

I believe we cannot achieve step 10 unless *all* people responsible for money in our household or business are aligned financially, with a *consistent* absence of fear (most of the time). In this context, one household or

Vertical Axis "Beliefs" from the above model
(climbing the ladder from 'Fear' to 'Love' based beliefs)

Stages 5-10 High Beliefs - 'Love' (giving) based

10	There is a 'knowing' as to one's life purpose and that things are as they are currently meant to be, despite sometimes being difficult. The Financial Laws are understood, welcomed and practiced. Humility, trust, tolerance and patience are consistently 'lived' from a place of 'being.' The goal is to reach one's full potential for the benefit of society and to 'give back' by using one's skill sets and gifts. Fear is seldom present. One is able and willing to access a far wider realm of knowledge and understanding, from both others as well as a higher power, to help manifest their version of wealth.
9	Enjoyment is held 'in the moment', rather than striving for an endless pursuit of wanting more. Achievement is driven and based in wealth generation for the benefit of all. Material things are appropriate for one's income level and are genuinely sourced in enjoyment, rather than seeking status. There is balance between one's own enjoyment and in assisting others financially. An ability to live humbly exists and this has focus sometimes despite improved circumstances.
8	There is consistent alignment of beliefs and very little fear present for financial decision makers in your business or household. Differences of opinion and beliefs are appropriately discussed and reconciled. Connection and focus is present for future based improvements.
7	Continuing personal and business development are acknowledged as critical elements for long term, sustainable wealth creation. Blocks stemming from beliefs and experiences are healed as they arise, and one's "humanness" is both accepted and celebrated.
6	Sustainable accumulation of wealth and what it can achieve for society is celebrated. One's own success is well received and self managed from a place of humility and enjoyment. Dishonorable financial motivations are absent.
5	Belief and trust in one's life purpose is acknowledged and starting to be fulfilled. Financial Laws are understood and applied regularly, with fewer occurrences of fear underpinning beliefs and actions.
4	Sustainable financial progress is desired, but is being prevented by the impact of unhealed past experiences associated with low trust, low respect, fear, pride, embarrassment, guilt, anger, low self-esteem, low self-worth, control, or dishonourable values.
3	Comfort is sourced in the concepts of managing risk and the accumulation of funds, rather than from trusting the combination of sound financial practice with belief in the Financial Laws. Financial decision makers in a household or business, are not aligned consistently enough with their relationship with money.
2	Financial beliefs and expected results stem from low trust, low respect, pride, embarrassment, guilt, anger, low self esteem, low self worth.
1	Money dynamics are stemmed from high needs for control, often underpinned by personal background and fear.
0	Motivations are partly dishonorable, often based in greed and/or focused solely on one's own benefit.

Stages 0-4 Low Beliefs – "Fear" based

business equals one relationship with money, as does one business equal one relationship with money. We need to diagnose the lowest level operating within the key relevant people. For example, you might be operating at level 8, but your business partner is operating at level 4. So your overall rating is 4 because it is the lowest relevant level of the key people in business.

There is also an energy that exists around money and all key people impact it. This energy has a keen eye for areas of trust and also areas of fear, similar to a shark seeking out a drop of blood in the water. This means your results are not only impacted by your own beliefs and actions, but also by those of other key people in your home or business. It can be a hard pill to swallow, I know. It means we need to get all of your key people enrolled in wanting to improve so your results can also be recognizably better.

Making it a Game—Improving Your Belief Habits and Remembering the Five Financial Actions

Regardless of who is involved, we can only change ourselves. So take active and fun steps with your own beliefs and actions. Your approach doesn't need to be mentally dramatic or serious. Lighten up and relax. You now know the five financial actions needed, so just implement them, and make this a necessary discipline.

The path taken to improve your financial beliefs requires high self-awareness. Choosing to operate from a place of *unconditional love, compassion, trust* and a *genuine ability to give* is also important, even if it may sound cheesy. It is through this focus that we access a place of inner calm, giving us more ability for self-love. This in turn improves our self-worth and self-esteem. These changes happen gradually but as we start to notice positive changes and feel better about our self-worth, new evidence to support this continues to show up. Improvements feed each other, helping us ascend the beliefs ladder.

The way to start improved self-awareness is to begin with small risks involving your emotions. Employ some courage to consciously adopt more trusting or giving beliefs, sourced in your core integrity and moral compass. Choose lower risk situations that will allow you to observe that things can work out even better when you trust or give more. We can notice that our previously conditioned assumptions of how events will play out, end up being wrong. Allow yourself to notice that things can actually work out much better than first expected.

Over time I learned that my earlier predisposition towards distrust meant that others were distrustful of me too. Like all of us, I was creating my own reality, even though I was unaware at the time. But as I learned to trust, my results and feelings improved, and others around me were more trustful of me too. I feel incredibly fortunate that I learned much of this early in life. It still takes courage and self-discipline to not revert to fear based beliefs in challenging moments.

Having said this, I am not suggesting that we trust blindly—that would be foolish. We need wide awareness of every factor involved in any given situation. Have sound systems in place to ensure others offer trust and take appropriate actions back towards us. In a business context this would include having good internal controls, regardless of how much you trust someone. This helps prevent you being naïve through inadvertently favoring your trusting beliefs too strongly.

So make improving your trust levels a game. Trust a little more often that things will turn out okay, even with really small things such as your ability to find a new meeting venue, or get a car park. And also with more important things such as generating sales. Or trust that you have good enough systems in place and great customer interactions that will encourage people who owe money to pay you on time. Actively remind yourself that your fears are likely to be sourced in your life's past events, not the people or situation around you currently.

While playing a game of "trusting more," notice what happens to your feelings about finances. They are likely to improve as you find more evidence that things can turn out fine. Also notice an improved ability to talk about financial issues, and have less fearful feelings when you give, or choose to put your money elsewhere. By removing the power that is fuelling your fears, the energy around your finances will be released, and things will work more in your favor.

Once you know which beliefs you want to improve and your action steps needed, and importantly, started working on these, recheck your beliefs ranking in a month's time. Note how much you have shifted on the beliefs ladder. It does take time to form a new habit. Put a date on your calendar to recheck again in 3 and 6 months so you can observe your progress and keep it top of mind.

Ultimately, the desired beliefs box to operate from is the perfect 10. That said, any of the top three provide good outcomes. Whether or not you wish to move up the beliefs ladder is entirely your choice. But remember there can still be issues when belief is high, but actions are not appropriately balanced. This indicates a survival mode person. Regardless of our level of financial beliefs, the five financial actions need to continue. Always remember this.

Finding Your Keys to Spiral Upwards

Some of our financial beliefs are powerful and positive (*financial enhancers*), while other financial beliefs are destructive and negative (*financial inhibitors*).

Think about how often you operate out of *fear* or *control* when making financial decisions. These types of *financial inhibitors* extend beyond our financial domain. Understanding our financial beliefs actually creates a mirror for us to see through to other areas of our life, revealing other areas that may not be working as well as we'd like. We can change only when we can see ourselves clearly enough to identify which beliefs are preventing us from achieving our full potential.

Twenty-five years of dealing with clients, plus my own personal experience, has shown me that hiding somewhere within our financial domain is always *a key* that helps identify our financial inhibitors. These inhibitors prevent us from achieving personal empowerment, so it is important to find the key, identify the inhibitors, and remove them. If you are open to exploring yourself, you will find some of your keys before this chapter's end.

Some people inhibit their financial world via fear-based decisions. Examples of inhibitors include *unhealthy levels of control, pride, guilt, shame, embarrassment, low self worth, low self-esteem, mistrust, and disrespect*. Consider which of these words impacts the way you live now because of a past event. If the inhibitor is relevant in any part of your world, there is a very good chance it will also be impacting your money situation. The inhibitors that are most relevant for you are your keys.

Now is a good time to consider what choice we each have about our emotional responses. Our analytical/logical frontal cortex part of our brain is largely responsible for applying IQ logic in our decision-making. We can also choose to use it when we consciously *respond* to our inhibiting emotions. But the frontal cortex does not create the initial emotional reaction itself. That is sourced in parts of our unconscious mind, found in a far older and largely "auto response" part of our brain.

Sometimes we need emotional healing around events that have occurred in our life. Given that our basic emotional reactions are involuntary, none of us are able to consciously access the part of our mind that controls them. Although this conscious ability to access our unconscious in the moment is impossible, we can improve our automatic responses over time by actually changing our neurological pathways which creates them.

It is therefore important for us to accept that we can only either 1) logically *respond* to our core emotional reactions as quickly as possible or 2) over time do things differently, to actually change our neurological pathways. How these neurological changes actually occur is constantly being revised as research reveals new discoveries. We do know that we can improve our inhibitors permanently, partly because of a change in our habits. This can be achieved via a very simple approach, it doesn't need to be difficult.

We can sometimes benefit from receiving professional assistance to change our a) self awareness, b) healing and c) understanding. Accepting our own humanness and failure helps to provide a sense of inner peace or calm and this can be enhanced further when we remove any resistance or resentment we might be feeling. Reaching a place of inner calm with little sense of resentment, allows the flow of money to travel your way more easily. In the same way things often work better when resistance is low, or there are few blockages getting in the way.

Changing our five financial actions is fundamental to improving our financial inhibitors. These financial actions change our results, but equally importantly, these actions will also change our beliefs over time. This is turn changes our automatic responses through our neurological pathways, which then changes our results, and eventually our actions again. By having a balanced focus on both beliefs and actions, we continue to spiral upwards, towards our desired version of wealth.

Being at Peace With Our Results
and Acknowledging Our Tolerations

Changing our habits can sometimes take unexpected turns. To reach our desired version of wealth, we first need to be at peace with whatever results occur. We need to leave behind the fears that created judgment, blame, denial and excuses, and instead operate from a place of empowered ownership, accountability and responsibility. Stop *tolerating* your financial inhibitors. Mistrust is one example. It can create situations that we do not enjoy, yet bizarrely we sometimes continue tolerating it anyway.

Focusing on Ourselves, Not Others

Because our financial inhibitors are normally sourced in emotional reactions to situations, we need to understand that it is *our reactions* that we need to learn from, not the *actions of others* that we may feel created our reactions.

Our individual keys tend to be actual events, or circumstances, that first created our financial inhibitors. For example, a sense of shame could be linked to something traumatic, big or small. Whatever the event or circumstance, think about an experience where you recall feeling one of your inhibitors and if relevant, seek professional healing assistance to get the issue resolved. Recall the first time you felt fear, guilt, shame, pride, embarrassment, a strong need to control, or all of the above. Heal the underlying issues with these event/s. Some of you will have many to heal, and each one will provide the key to your financial inhibitors. Some may seem insignificant, yet still impact your belief system and self-worth.

Now is the time to nurture yourself. I encourage you not to delay. Apologize to yourself for any feelings that you have been harboring about yourself since these events. There is a chance you may have been berating your inner child for many years, sometimes unknowingly. It's time to love him or her instead.

It is my belief that unhelpful emotions that have been running your life since these circumstances first occurred will have had a direct correlation with your present financial circumstances (unless you are already well-healed). As time progresses, more inhibitors are likely to bubble up too. Properly managed, this is a very good thing. We want to acknowledge, heal and remove all of your financial belief inhibitors. We need to remember that regardless of the particular situation that highlights an inhibitor for ourselves, none of this is about the other person involved. We are focused solely on our own reactions, for this is the place where we shift our beliefs.

In order to find the keys needed to identify our specific financial inhibitors, we also need to acknowledge that we have caused for ourselves whatever we internally experience. That said, we also need to remember we are seldom at fault for the root cause of our responses, especially those that occurred in our childhood. Most of our reactions are highly understandable—no judgment here. But the fact remains that we have created our responses to these past events, and we choose daily whether we promote them or choose a different path to heal them.

Financial Enhancers

Instead of operating from a place of fear, some people know how to reach financial freedom through positive beliefs based in a higher level of awareness, including *trust, faith,* and *belief in things unseen.* Most of these *financial enhancers* are sourced in elements of *love.* People operating at this level have an innate awareness that unlocks the door to assistance from Higher Powers.

Fear has no place here. Control is necessarily present, but only to the extent needed for an empowered sense of commercial best practice, (for circumstances that are commercial in nature). Regardless of the situation, when we employ financial enhancers our beliefs are based in sound moral values.

Using Awareness of Your Own Financial Beliefs to Access Wider Realms of Knowledge

Understanding our financial beliefs does more than place a spotlight on the financial inhibitors that prevent our growth. It also provides a strong clue as to HOW to harness a much wider realm of knowledge to improve our beliefs, our financial enhancers and our results. This wider realm is available to each of us should we so choose and it's often sourced through the concept of a Higher Power.

Our desire and ability to identify with a Higher Power may vary greatly to that of someone else. Cultural, religious and societal beliefs all influence our perspectives, including whether or not we even conceive a Higher Power is a possibility. Regardless of your current view, I suggest you allow yourself the freedom to change your perspective over time and open up to the possibility of utilizing infinite resource.

Key to achieving our desired version of wealth is firstly removing our financial inhibitors. When we remove these, we also remove blockages that prevent us from accessing Higher Power. For example, if we restrict our access to Higher Power because we are fearful, we can better access this realm by removing fear. Or, if we restrict our ability to access Higher Power because we are mistrustful, we can better access this realm by improving our levels of trust. And so on, through other financial belief inhibitors such as guilt, pride, embarrassment, anger and disrespect. Remove your inhibitors, and you can more easily access assistance from places *other than our own logical thoughts*. Until we do this, our inhibitors will keep us bound within our existing financial paradigm.

For some people, the concept of a Higher Power has little or no resonance, either at a spiritual or energetic level. For these people, the context of a Higher Power may be as simple as seeking expert assistance from external advisors who know more than you about a particular topic. Logical, left-brain, practical assistance from other people can assist you in achieving your goals. This is one very simple and logical context of how you could interpret the term Higher Power.

Although valid, it is not the definition of Higher Power that is most useful. I'm referring to accessing source energy, infinitely stronger than all of us individually, to request help in receiving what we need to achieve our desired version of wealth. For each of us, our ability to meet, know and access this realm differs, and often changes, over time. I intentionally choose source energy or Higher Power to describe things of a spiritual nature to include all spiritual, religious and cultural belief systems.

Accessing Knowledge Beyond Our Own Logic

In both the logical and spiritual contexts of the term Higher Power, the common element is that we wish to seek assistance from a source outside of ourselves. We want this when we learn we are unlikely to reach genuine success on our own.

To seek assistance from some other place always requires us to first reduce our financial inhibitors. For example, we seldom ask for help if we are operating from a place of mistrust, so logically we first need to be more trusting. This holds regardless of where the help is coming from.

Get a Bigger Goal and Get Out of Your Way

Why is getting a bigger goal relevant? Big goals create strong focus. When we have stronger focus, we can more easily embrace our financial belief inhibitors. We might still feel some of them (e.g. fear, pride, guilt) but we keep doing the required actions anyway, until we truly change. We find a way to heal our past, have courage, and apply compassion towards ourselves and others, so we can strive forward.

By doing these financial actions and embracing our inhibitors, we get out of our own way. Building confidence as we go, we take small bite-sized steps toward what we desire. We still make mistakes, yet learn to accept its okay. We still have blind spots too, but learn to shine light on them, moving forward with increased awareness and self-acceptance. Along the way, our self-esteem and sense of self worth improves as well.

Your Purpose

So, do the planet a favor and get a bigger dream. Also consider your life's purpose. What would you like it to be? Often we need assistance to understand what holds us back from having this conversation with ourselves. A topic like your life's purpose allows your inhibitors to surface. This is a good thing.

There may also be an emotional block stopping you thinking about this. If you are experiencing anything negative, it may be a big clue as to what part of your belief system is inhibiting your financial success. For now, just think about your inhibitors and "be with them." No need for drama or significance.

Freedom From Fear and the Impact of this on Our Purpose

In order to achieve our purpose, we tend to need freedom from fear. Some of us have learned that operating out of a place of fear or control keeps us perceivably safe. But doing so also keeps us bound. It is helpful to check out then the *extent* to which we operate out of fear or a need for control.

With relation to control, I'm in no way discrediting having sound values, systems, and process, and adhering to best practice business controls. Sometimes though, we hide behind these controls as a justification. The real issue can be a need for control sourced in fear. If so, what exactly are you afraid of?

Having a healthy relationship with our own fear, judgment and failure can be an interesting transition. The ability to be with ourselves in these moments can enrich us as much as in our moments of success.

I think we should all have a goal to achieve complete, unadulterated freedom from fear. To know that whatever life throws at us, we will be able to take it in our stride, because we already have everything we need to do so. This takes self-leadership, and leadership takes courage.

Courage is not doing something in the absence of fear. It is doing something despite the fear. After all, it's not brave unless you're scared. The irony is that by pushing our comfort zone and finding evidence that all is still okay are the very things that help remove the fear. It makes life so much more enjoyable.

Why tolerate a life with fear? I'm not discrediting the reasons that first created the fear. Sometimes these are massive and totally understandable. Just get some help so you can learn how these feelings can stop influencing our beliefs, actions and results, financial or otherwise. Stop tolerating anything that is holding you back. It costs you too much.

Keeping Our Financial Beliefs
and Maintaining Financial Actions

Fear often manifests in a need for control, but over time, you can learn to release it. You may resonate with a concept of a Higher Power helping you do this by providing a powerful sense of safety. Or you may not.

Other people and their expertise might instead provide you with the safety you seek, or you could simply achieve it by yourself. Personally I believe it is far easier when we do not try to achieve it alone.

Removing fear and the need for control so we grow our financial belief system is a great thing. But we still need to remember that appropriate *balance* between our beliefs and our actions is needed for long-term financial success.

How to Diagnose the Cause of an Imbalance Between Financial Beliefs and Actions

Seeking out the causes of an imbalance between beliefs and actions helps us achieve financial success and our preferred version of wealth, and gets us to the sorted quadrant. Once we have reached a level of mastery in achieving balance between our financial beliefs and actions, we can allow ourselves an unconscious (or automatic) level of awareness needed to maintain the balance.

Until we have reached this level of mastery, we will need to occasionally stop ourselves consciously to diagnose the cause of any financial unrest. Consider any imbalance, especially if you are a survival or stable money style. These styles have a natural tendency to be out of balance—survival money styles score high on beliefs but low on actions, while stable money styles score low on beliefs but high on actions.

A balanced money style is one where both beliefs and actions have similar scores out of ten. We therefore benefit from looking for areas that create low scores out of ten; these are the ones tipping the equilibrium. The easiest way to check whether you are operating in balance between your beliefs and actions is by looking at the money style model again. Get your Actions score from the Actions axis in Chapter 6, and your Beliefs score from earlier in this chapter.

Remember that our financial beliefs inhibitors include unhelpful ratings in *trust, respect, self-worth, self-esteem, pride, embarrassment, anger, guilt, fear, values, knowledge, and control.* From Chapter 6 we know that things that inhibit our financial actions include: *not living within our means, not regularly saving, not being philanthropic, low ratings in financial knowledge, not operating a budget, low ratings in trust, respect, self-discipline, values,* or when our actions are being driven/prevented by *fear or control.*

This list of inhibitors is provided again to help you consider what factors are involved in balancing your beliefs inhibitors and actions inhibitors. For example, do you *trust* people with your financial information or money commitments? Do you feel *guilty* about anything money related? Are you *fearful* you won't have enough money to live, or for example you might lose the house? Are you *angry* (resentful) your finances are not working out the way you deserve? Which of these issues is relevant for you? Whatever words resonate most, they are your *financial inhibitors*, while the events that created them are your *keys*. You will have more than one inhibitor and they are likely to reveal themselves at different points along the pathway of your desired version of wealth. How are these inhibitors affecting your beliefs, and how are they affecting your actions?

Remember your version of wealth, especially if you have causes you wish to support in some way. Remember too, the honorable impact you could make to these causes if your current income was ten times, or a hundred times, or a thousand times what it is now. Use this as a motivation to find and improve your inhibitors.

Your Financial Currency and Self-Sabotage

One such place our inhibitors can surface is within the concept of our financial currency. People tend to trade off emotional things that are important to them and in doing so, effectively create a currency based on those emotional needs. We tend to get our core needs addressed first, and then for the rest of our needs, we trade via some version of money or barter system. We have many core needs including:

- security or certainty
- a sense of belonging or connection
- self-actualization, being significant, or wanting to grow
- wanting to give

Our financial currency will always feature somehow in our financial world. It is the aggregate of

1. our emotional currency, plus
2. our actual cash

Together these derive the total currency we use as a means of exchange for our work.

If someone wants security in their life for example, they may be prepared to earn less money if it also feels more certain. The certainty element therefore has an intrinsic monetary value. So too do all of the other types of currency. If someone really wants a sense of belonging, they may even volunteer for free in order to gain this. That person's currency, a sense of belonging, is therefore valued very high as they are prepared to forego all cash to get their emotional currency satisfied.

Our definition of wealth should recognize our preferences around financial currency. We are likely to regularly fulfill this emotional currency in conjunction with earning actual money.

If we operate from a place of wanting to give to others for example, we may also do things for free, rather than charge. Often this is a good and honorable thing, but sometimes it can also create a cash flow problem. Self-awareness is needed for any activity that places an unhealthy level of emphasis on our emotional currency instead of a tangible means of exchange. The easiest way to recognize if our emotional currency needs are at an unhealthy level is if it detrimentally impacts your financial well-being and safety, or that of your family. For example, sometimes we are so good at helping others that we negatively impact our own family's financial well-being.

We can therefore sabotage our financial efforts with an inappropriate emphasis on our financial currency. Survival people tend to align with wanting to grow and to give to others, and stable people tend to align with certainty (but often may not fully recognize the places this occurs for them). Sold out people can bounce anywhere and are rather erratic with the application of their financial currencies. So their chance of self-sabotage is high. The sentiments of giving and growing or being stable themselves are obviously sound. It is when there is excessive focus that self-sabotaging can occur. Especially for Sold Out and Survival quadrant people.

So, Who Am I Being in This Moment?

Consider for yourself if in moments involving financial issues (including either money or time), you might be self-sabotaging as a result of the strength and degree of your financial currency.

One of the main concepts I try to adopt (but given I am human, doesn't always happen), is that when things go wrong, I try not to consider anything external as the cause. Blaming is often a projection anyway and is usually not useful. Often I need to look no further than my own financial currency for the cause.

It is most important to focus on *who am I being* as a person to have attracted any situation into my life. I then ask myself how can I be more grounded, more centered, or more connected, so that I do not attract this type of situation again.

Sometimes the lesson being taught reoccurs often. We need to consider that this may be because we have not listened closely enough in the past. Someone else's perspective may be that we are being judgmental, arrogant, uncompassionate or such like. We may be. Or we may not be.

Our Inner Calm and Staying Teachable While Learning to Be in a Place of Zero

On some levels, another's perspective doesn't matter because it is more useful to focus on operating from a place of stability and calm. This is easier when we remember that our intent, life purpose and results are not reliant on another person's opinion.

But I imagine you would agree that we should still do our absolute best to stay teachable when hearing another's opinion. We all continue to learn forever and the last thing I would want to do is appear arrogant or dismissive of others' views.

Our lessons tend not to be about the person delivering the "message" via their comments, actions, or the situation—it is about us. Stop and consider how we can be different, so we don't have negative reactions about others' interactions towards us. Work this out and you will move up the beliefs ladder more quickly.

We need to recognize we cannot change anything about others, regardless of who they are in our life or we are in theirs. The only way change can really occur is by changing ourselves. The person we are being in the moments we are irritated or pushed to the limit is very telling; it is not how somebody else *acts,* but more how we *react* that matters most. I know this is easier said than done.

People in our lives are sent to teach us things and sometimes they do so by igniting responses in us that we do not enjoy. My mother used to remind me often that patience and tolerance are virtues. We all understand that, but sometimes struggle to apply it. The results we achieve financially will reflect our ability to accept these virtues. I suggest you read this last sentence again.

The Hawaiian cultural practice of h'oponopono is based on the concept of keeping ourselves in a place of zero and not reacting badly to the circumstances or actions of others. It's a way of staying grounded internally and not attaching any meaning to events or interactions. This doesn't mean being disconnected from our issues or experiences, just that we recognize events occur because of the person we are being. This recognition assists us to react more often in a positive way. We have a choice as to whether or not we want to change. When we change who we are being, remove our blockages, and improve our beliefs, it normally results in rewards flowing more readily.

Being in a place of zero is a similar concept to operating in a balanced, calm way. The trick for each of us is being able to create this in ourselves at any given time.

Seeing Balance between Financial Beliefs and Actions

To better understand the balance needed between financial beliefs and actions, a quick exercise can help create some metaphors.

Place your hands flat together horizontally, fingers touching. Look at them with your right hand on top and then rotate them to have your left hand on top. Keep rotating between the two showing on top, creating a naturally flowing figure 8 motion.

You will notice that an easy, balanced look occurs when you keep your hands moving. It is only when you stop that one hand is given preference visually. Notice too that when you stop, there seems to be more pressure on your muscles, and that the exercise takes more effort. One hand represents your beliefs, the other your actions. Think about how you use your hands every day. We naturally favor one hand, while the other would need more practice to achieve the same level of competence and skill.

Managing the balance between your financial beliefs and actions is similar. There will be some things that come naturally to you and some things that need more work in order to get the equilibrium right. And as either your beliefs or actions improve, the other may need refocus for balance to endure.

There is another way to view beliefs and actions, but this time in unison instead of favoring one over the other. Rather than placing your hands in a horizontal position, hold them vertically, (like a visual of praying or showing respect to a martial arts master). By changing your perspective, you can now easily see both beliefs and actions (one hand representing each) at the same time. And you can do so without any need to constantly move them. Neither is shielded by the other.

Imagine that they are not two hands, but rather parts of one combined being, your life. Viewing your hands in this slightly different way, there is less effort and yet far better ability to see all that is needed. Your hands themselves have not changed, just your awareness in the amount of effort required to see all. You can be still, viewing both your beliefs and actions without needing to spin your hands around to see all sides.

Similarly, you can master the combination of both beliefs and actions at such an integral level that you can BE still, despite feeling like the world is sometimes spinning out of control around you. Your moving hands in a figure 8 motion means you can see both your beliefs and actions yes, but this part of my metaphor represents the busyness of doing things.

We can actually pull back from our busyness and allow our intuition to see another metaphor. This time it is a movie of our business or life. When we are able to be still internally, we can see our own movie happening frame by frame, seemingly in slow motion. It can have wide-angle cameras from within ourselves and our own knowing, and also cameras from the outside looking in. This can happen at the same time others rush around us in fast forward mode, sometimes spinning without purpose. It is when we are too busy that we don't stop to enjoy our life, or forget to watch the preview of our own coming attractions. These previews are available to all of us if we just stop for a moment to look. They are called our goals, our causes, our legacy—what we wish to create for both ourselves and others.

The best lens to view our own movie through is one of calm equilibrium, found midway between our strong beliefs and actions. That's where we can be still, watching our legacy unfold and our future arrive before us. This stillness brings calmness with it, a state I believe is very attractive to the Universe's Financial Laws. It helps them continue to favor us.

Harnessing Universal Financial Laws

The Universe's natural Laws are highly relevant for financial success and achieving our goals. I am not a quantum physicist, so cannot explain how they work at a scientific level. I am also not an electrical engineer and cannot tell you exactly how the lights in our houses work. I just know how to flick the switch. When I do this, the energy flows. The same applies to the Financial Laws. We don't need to understand the ways such things work in order for them to just work.

Harnessing the Financial Laws improves our experience of trust, respect, patience, tolerance, humility, anger, pride, guilt, and embarrassment. This in turn impacts our self-esteem and self-worth, and helps us open the floodgates of the universe so that we can be provided with what we need to fulfill our goals, vision and purpose.

To achieve long-term benefit, I also believe harnessing these Laws from the perspective of honorable pursuit is important . You would have heard of some of these Laws:

- The Law of Compensation.
- The Law of Increasing Returns.
- The Law of Attraction.
- The Law of Vibration.
- The Law of Success or Abundance.

These Laws are very intangible in their application and also highly interdependent with each other. Understanding *how* to harness these Laws is both an art and a science. Some elements need very heart-based (right-brain, intuitive) principles, and some need very head-based (left-brain, logical) principles.

Many of these laws are in part the basis of some religious teachings. But they are not necessarily aspects of religions in their own right. They reflect sound justice and the natural order of things. If you want to apply a religious context, more power to it, but you do not need to in order for the Laws to work. The light switch will work either way.

Personally I think the Law of Compensation is the most important to understand and apply consistently. The Law of Compensation is best summed up with the common phrases "what goes around comes around" or we "reap what we sow." It is similar to the concept of karma.

Let's use the New Zealand banking system to illustrate. There are a number of nationwide trading banks but only one centralized clearing house. ATM machines from any bank work for customers of all the banks, throughout the whole country. So we can literally deposit into one bank and use any other bank's money machine for withdrawal. The Law of Compensation, a bit like karma, acts in the same way. We give or bank good things in one area or to one person, then receive goods things in return from a completely different source.

One of my mentors loved the saying, "the Law of Compensation, although slow, is very thorough." It basically means that we receive as a result of what we give—in time, cash, sentiment, values, wealth, and love. But we do need to employ patience, trusting that this Law will result in everything being just as it should be.

A significant aspect of this Law's effectiveness is about who we are being in the moments we give. This is a significant aspect of the Law of Vibration. If we are settled in ourselves and are giving unconditionally with our gifts (whatever these may be), we are much more likely to receive in kind. But it doesn't necessarily mean we receive from the same source to which we originally gave. In my experience, more often than not it's different.

The Law of Increasing Returns suggests the amount you receive in return will be far greater than the effort initially exerted. Some religious texts refer to this concept as things coming back tenfold. One important aspect is that whatever you put out comes back, the good and the bad. It can sometimes take a while, but it always does. It's like the universe wants to test our resolve by withholding from time to time before we are given back.

Sometimes it's also that you or your partner is not yet ready to receive. When the "receipt" is in relation to finances, sometimes the principle of one household = one relationship with money impacts timing because the universe makes you wait until you are both ready to receive.

We have a choice in those moments to resist, get resentful and do some emotional version of argue or blame; or we can accept our circumstances, be patient and, importantly, continue to take actions that forward our game. Employing a constructive mental attitude of high respect and tolerance is important in the interim.

Such things are always exactly as they should be. There will be a reason why we are not seeing immediate results, and we don't necessarily need to question this. All is revealed in time. I believe it is quicker to just go with the flow while continuing with our five financial actions. This approach is certainly less stressful, and also maintains a level of calm, so our financial domain is open to rewards flowing to it. It's important to remember that these Financial Laws are all very interdependent on each other.

You have probably heard of the Law of Attraction. This is based on the concept that if you want something, focus on it and a pathway to achieve it will present. This concept works for whatever we focus on, either positive or negative. Personally I believe the other Financial Laws are also needed to create overall financial success.

There have been many books written on the Laws of Success and the topic generally is very wide. These books often refer to relevant things like writing down goals, having a positive outlook, going the extra mile, believing in things unseen, and having appropriate levels of both self-discipline and self-worth. Achieving your own version of wealth will need to employ these fundamental Laws of Success.

Applying these Financial Laws consistently requires us to be emotionally empowered, centered and grounded. We need to demonstrate a genuine high level of respect towards the Financial Laws so we generate a sense of worthiness to receive. It is when we are worthy that we receive in a permanent, sustainable fashion. One fundamental belief I hold is that when we remove our emotional blocks (our financial inhibitors), the Financial Laws have an easier job assisting us with our goals. The light will switch on even if we don't know how it works.

Respect Towards Others, Ourselves and the Powers that Provide

Respect is a fundamental ingredient for permanent success and to ascend the financial beliefs ladder. We need to demonstrate respect as best we can—towards others, ourselves, and the powers that provide for us. We have to show respect when consistently doing the five financial actions too. By being respectful about "all things money," we will be respected back in kind. The opposite is also true.

Consistency in our respect reminds us we are 100% responsible for our own perspectives, thoughts and actions. Issues involving money are no exception. We need to respect ourselves enough to consistently recognize our financial responsibility. People who operate with a high level of self-respect do not let themselves off the hook around issues of financial commitment.

Holding Financial Boundaries Despite Having High Beliefs

Most people want to operate out of a place of trust or high belief and also from a place of genuinely being loving towards others. Some of us can also benefit at times from tempering our giving sentiments, putting boundaries in place to prevent others from taking advantage of us financially.

We each need to decide what boundaries we are prepared to set and maintain. We also need to decide what level of variation to agreed financial terms we will tolerate. We want to engage from a place of love and compassion, yet still ensure appropriate boundaries are in place.

Sometimes this requires a commercial focus to ensure safety of our own situation. Alternatively, if appropriate we can consciously choose to tolerate a situation that differs to agreed terms. But if we do this, sometimes we might be selling ourselves short to avoid confronting conversations. It is best to learn to have these conversations anyway.

When a situation occurs that is different to the previously agreed arrangement, our individual core operating values will take centre stage. Each person is likely to have an aspect of loyalty feature, along with factors we consider acceptable, and factors we do not. Sometimes a resolution is reached where everyone is comfortable. Sometimes rifts are created. Either way, individual boundaries should be maintained.

Our belief systems are impacted by these types of leadership issues, as are our financial results. Our leadership style impacts our ability to influence and achieve results from others and this in turn impacts our finances.

Improving Our Ability to Influence

One key insight I have had to accept over the years is that if I do not have the results I seek, it is because I do not have enough influence over myself and others to achieve them. This can be difficult to accept and takes a very pragmatic perspective to not make it mean anything negative about ourselves.

If I do not yet have enough influence it means I am not yet being the person I need to be to achieve that level of influence. It is seldom about what I am saying, but who I am being. In these moments, the first thing I do is look in the mirror. Sometimes I need to buy a bigger mirror.

It doesn't matter whether or not the other person involved in the situation understands this. From your vantage point, it is not about them. But the person or situation has been sent to teach us something about ourselves. Learn from this. This issue is sourced in our beliefs, because it is our beliefs that underpin the person *we* are being. The other person can choose to apply a similar approach if they wish, but whether they do or not is of little consequence (except to themselves).

There is normally a financial message or clue being shown to us from within our issues, situations and financial interactions. When we wake up and pay attention, we can see our financial inhibitors playing out within these circumstances. One example could be you are applying an excessive amount of pride in your interactions. This in turn might impact your results because of an inability to receive assistance from others.

Once you have seen the message that is being shown to you, it can be far easier to apply compassion for yourself, compassion for the situation and compassion for the other person. Being an impatient person myself, tolerance and patience are values I sometimes need to engage at a conscious level, rather than from a level of unconscious, auto response. We all have goals that set the bar higher than what actually results. If we fall short of our own standards, we should still re-engage or reset our intent.

When we employ compassion towards another's perspective, we are more likely to be operating from a space that creates influence. This is because we generate empathy and understanding towards another's situation and issues more frequently end up in win/win situations.

Freedom to Lead, Freedom to Fail.
The Other Side of the Looking Glass

At the core of our desire to influence is often a motivation to seek freedom for ourselves and others. Freedom comes in many forms, including financial freedom. We also seek freedom from another's control or criticism, freedom to choose, freedom to achieve or fail, freedom from fear or disease, and freedom to simply think and act as we wish. When we experience any type of freedom, we usually have a sense of immense satisfaction.

Sometimes the thought of freedom conjures up images of being footloose and fancy free. This could be a good thing. But sometimes viewing freedom in this way could lead us to abdicate our responsibility, causing us to fall short of our own goal to contribute to the betterment of society.

We can achieve freedom as well as honor our responsibilities. I am not suggesting we abdicate these; behavior that dishonors our commitments is not desirable. Honor is important to remember because it's presence or lack thereof impacts how we lead. The degree to which we employ honor in our interactions can impact the way and extent to which we fail and also how we deal with conflict or undercurrents.

As a business leader, I have learned that actively *seeking out* opportunities to lead well is very important. I kick myself when I realize that my childish, fear, or control-based behavior resulted in missed opportunities to lead well. But it happens to all of us sometimes.

Being fair, consistent, just and honorable about an issue can be a deal maker or a deal breaker. It's best when we can be real with ourselves and acknowledge when we have made a mistake. To me, there is nothing so off putting than a person who leads in a way that is reactionary, or out of a need for control or fear, rather than from a place of freedom, where others are able to fail under appropriate circumstances and supervision. We learn when we fail. Why deny this for others?

The irony is that when we stop and see these elements through the other side of our looking glass, there is massive freedom achieved. This occurs when we release judgment, drama or significance and simply let it go. Part of being human is our ability to be with failure. After all, we all experience it to varying extents. Understanding this as a leader enables us to lead better.

Stop and reflect about the issues raised in this chapter. Heal what needs to be healed, grow what needs to grow and love the parts of you that need to be loved.

THE WAY FORWARD FOR JACK AND HIS MOTHER

Jack and his Mom are now good at discussing things in a tag team fashion. They still have moments where their toys get thrown out of the cot, but there is a noticeable improvement. Despite this, they could still benefit from creating a shift in their financial beliefs.

Jack's mother could benefit from discussing the original cause of her fears because they are impacting her ability to trust in things that are not yet occurring. She could also benefit from focusing her mind to live in the present more, rather than worrying about the future.

Issues around her relationship with the concepts of "Trust" and "Fear" are the two main financial inhibitors impacting her money style. She found these two keys by considering some events in her past that she only now realizes still impact her emotional wellbeing. She can now see that these two issues from her past still play out in her financial domain.

If Jack could understand why these two keys are relevant for his Mom, he would gain helpful insight. He would then be able to see why this has resulted in her wanting to regularly save some of their household money and manage their financial situation with a great deal of caution.

Now that she understands the five financial actions, Jack's mom wants to donate to their chosen causes. Making shifts in their level of understanding and actions means Jack and his Mom's combined household financial situation would improve for both of them.

There would be more overall balance between their beliefs and actions. For all the strengths they have individually, they each have significant weaknesses, so they would benefit greatly from working together as a team.

Together Jack and his mom commit to an action plan and a way to communicate moving forward. This in itself immediately aids Jack's mother with her fears and she is able to have heightened awareness of where she has been operating previously. A helpful by-product of this is she is better able to trust that things will turn out fine.

Neither of them are "broken" in any way, they just have had some blind spots. These blind spots are now clearer for each of them. Jack loves his mom and now understands why his actions have scared her in the past. Given his core motivation is to provide for her, he is wanting to change some of his habits. He is quite mature for his age and also very competent.

―――――――――――――

We will find out how Jack and his mother are getting on in a later chapter. In the meantime, consider if there are any similarities between them and yourself.

Summary of the Chapter

- Diagnose where you think you might normally operate on the beliefs axis. Consider the same for others in your household or business who have responsibility for money issues. Once we know where we operate, we can choose if we want to shift.
- Consider what financial inhibitors might be relevant for you and seek help to remove or heal these so you more easily access assistance from your preferred version of Higher Power.
- Get a bigger goal, consider your purpose for being on the planet, and get a vision around this. Dare to be bold. Get help with the specific steps needed to realize this vision.
- Consider how you could demonstrate more respect for your finances and how to stay more grounded and to be in a state of zero.

- Understand your financial currency and consider where you might self-sabotage as a result of your current beliefs getting in your way.
- Find your balance between financial beliefs and financial actions so you can be in a place of stillness and calm while you achieve your goals.
- Examine for yourself how your beliefs and actions might be improved to better harness the universal Financial Laws.
- Still hold boundaries about your finances as needed.
- Explore your freedom to lead, your freedom to fail and your ability to influence.
- Other people close to us can assist in highlighting our blind spots for us if all parties can approach the topic in an appropriate manner, similar to Jack and his mother.
- Stop and self reflect about the issues raised in this chapter. Heal, grow and love the parts of you that need these things most.

Chapter Eight

TRAPS FOR YOUNG PLAYERS

How to Get Out (and Stay Out) of Survival Mode

Survival Mode Revisited

The interesting thing about survival mode people is that they keep thinking things are financially okay (or soon will be). This chapter is about getting you present and making sure you haven't "slipped back" into survival mode without realizing it.

You may not yet be connected enough to your personal money style to see the relevance of this and apply it to your own situation. Instead you are skim reading, thinking this all relates to someone else you know. If there is any struggle at all around your finances, stop and realize I am talking directly to you. Not your spouse, friend, family member, or colleague. You.

I am laboring this so we can move you through any perspective similar to "all will be fine." Yes, this is a fabulous attitude. But it can also restrict your results unless you are very careful to be aware of your financial actions.

The survival quadrant is the easiest to escape from, but also the easiest to return to. Before we know it, we can be back where we started. We are forever the lemming, climbing our way back to the top of the cliff, playing up there for a while, then throwing ourselves off the cliff again for no apparent reason. We rely on being able to swim in the waters below. A few simple key strokes and our credit card is maxed out, or a few quick comments see us committed to something from a place of emotion and belief, rather than one of sound business or financial practice.

We each have a choice about whether or not to follow the five financial actions suggested. Will you require they be done? Or will you appoint someone else to make doing them a necessity? It is better if it is you. Otherwise you are at risk of abdicating responsibility.

Imagine you have a really big mirror with the word RESPECT all around it and you look into it to see the impact of your actions. Are you treating your financial situation with enough respect? The underlying theme of all of the five financial actions is to be more respectful. This means respectful to yourself, respectful to those around you, and respectful to the powers that provide for you. Equally importantly, all of these five actions are designed to gradually move you further and further away from reckless financial actions.

Every financial decision we make can be categorized as mostly reckless, or mostly respectful. The decision itself is therefore either a survival mode decision, or a sorted mode one.

Recognize the survival mode decisions you make versus the sorted mode decisions. Use the 0–10 gradient of the financial actions axis to guide you through which quadrant the decision sits in. Over time we would want most decisions to be sorted quadrant decisions.

What Happened Ten Weeks Ago?

Survival mode people are rife with high beliefs impacting their financial situation, ten weeks down the track. Often they don't impact immediately. Our cash flow, or lack thereof, is only ever a symptom of past actions. This is one reason why we can feel really annoyed when we finally change our beliefs and actions: for a time we still suffer from the consequences of our prior actions and beliefs. Knowing this will hopefully keep you in the game.

Nothing changes if nothing changes. There is never a good time to start improving our habits, except for right now. We are *always* too busy, or too broke, so we may as well make a start to change today. Make looking after the things that will happen in ten weeks time necessary, so you can get beyond subsistence operations and operate for your future.

As the saying goes, "the best time to plant a tree is twenty years ago. The second best time is today." If we don't start now, we won't get the results in ten weeks time. Or twenty years time. A year from now, you may wish you had started today. Do this in bite-size chunks so that we eat the elephant one bite at a time. When we start, we begin to break the cycle of survival mode results.

We begin by doing *one* thing today to improve your financial actions. And do that one thing consistently. Then once that is easy, we pick the second thing. Consistent, small, incremental improvements are all that is needed. It is all we *ever* need, as long as we actually DO them.

The choices we made ten weeks ago may have been conscious, or they may have happened by default. But whatever we decided ten weeks ago, it is relevant now. Think about it. Learn from it. Decide whether in hindsight it was a good thing or not so next time you have this information in your conscious awareness.

How Do I Know if I'm Operating in Survival Mode Right Now?

We fairly regularly change which money style quadrant we are operating in, depending on the combination of our financial beliefs and actions in any given moment. We are not always aware of our quadrant at a conscious level. It is important though that our money style becomes as clear as daylight, especially for survival or sold out mode people.

Some people instantly identify with the phrase survival mode; they actually feel like they are in that space—so there's a clue! Others may not realize they are playing in the survival quadrant. Here are some key survival mode traits to help you figure out if that's you:

- You cannot currently pay debts as they fall due.
- You have a level of anxiety about upcoming commitments.
- If you are in business, it is not profitable at the moment.
- You have high belief systems in place about your business and it's purpose/worth/benefit to others and often (but not always), about yourself as a person.
- Partly because of your high beliefs, you do things like commit to new expenditure before there is a definite way to pay for it—sometimes doing so with little prospect of payment.
- You don't have a high level of awareness about how much money you need and how much you actually spend, or on what.
- You are good at taking risks, and you genuinely believe they are always "measured risks," for the benefit of the business and its growth. You focus on the benefit more than your ability to pay.
- You make commitments and then do not keep them—for whatever valid reason.

Sounds like you? If so, depending on the extent of relevance, there may be a good chance you have been playing in the survival or sold out quadrants a very long time. You may also believe that your answers to the above are justifiable and right.

And they may be. At least some of the time. Your internal belief system is likely to be driving this situation, using its many strengths. And like all of us, also its weaknesses. Once we have a heightened and more consistent level of awareness about ourselves, we can make a choice as to what changes we want to make.

What is Key to Getting Out of "Survival Mode"

Can you relate to the concept that the causes or reasons for our biggest strengths are also the very same for our biggest weaknesses?

For example:

- People that are goal focused get results, but can also be more likely to alienate themselves from others if they are too driven.

- People that focus on "keeping the peace" won't deal with the issues needed to grow or improve their situation because they avoid conflict. Everyone is happy with them, but they are less likely to get results.

These examples show how the same personality trait can have both positive and negative outcomes. And it's the same with our financial dynamics: positive and negative financial results can show up from one trait too. It's not complicated. People in survival mode basically have an imbalance between their wants, beliefs and actions. Survival mode people's financial beliefs are stronger than their financial actions. And by the way, one might be strong in taking many actions but if they are in survival mode, there will be at least one of the five financial actions that "let's the side down."

The universal laws that impact finances will brutally punish someone who does not have their actions both in check and balanced. The opposite also holds true: rewards are massive when financial beliefs and actions are balanced.

I have consistently noticed that things start to improve financially for survival-based clients when their financial actions improve—it is then easy to shift the energy around their results (as long as they believe this can happen). Obviously some of the improvement is purely at a logical level, due to someone being better at living within their means or having an improved habit of saving, but that's not all of it. It's about an improvement in their actual *relationship* with money.

Having Enough Self-discipline to Get Back to Sorted

Any relationship can get old and stale; sometimes you just have to stay focused on wanting to improve it until such time as it naturally becomes fun again. Your relationship with money is the same.

Employing self-discipline to return to the sorted quadrant needs to be undertaken consciously. As part of this conscious effort, we can train our minds to alert us whenever we are about to take a survival mode action. Our unconscious can easily become a finger tapping us on our shoulder. Once the survival mode action is clear within our consciousness, we can remind ourselves 1) about the importance/preference of our overall goals, 2) the level of respect we want to have with our finances and 3) to give ourselves an opportunity for a more balanced decision.

Choosing to operate in the sorted quadrant is a moment-by-moment decision. That said, making a survival mode decision doesn't have to be always avoided or viewed as scary. Fear dissolves once you believe that no matter what happens, you have enough skills to always adapt and live within your means.

In fact, I would recommend reducing your expenditure to a level of bare existence every now and then. The purpose of this is simply to know that you can. It reminds you that you are a resourceful person and can deal with any level of income. One way to demonstrate this is to have a week of very cheap but healthy dinners. Get creative.

You could go a week without basic services as well if needed. I'm not saying you should, I'm just saying you could. To know you could if needed is very empowering. You could practice natural disaster procedures for a few days as a family game, just to see what you would need in the real event, and learn how much money you can save in the process.

Once you know you can survive under stressful financial circumstances, the concept of fear around "risky" financial decisions is far less binding. This is the sole purpose of the exercise—to learn that you can survive, if you need to.

If you are still scared to occasionally make a survival mode decision, review your personal definition of wealth. What are you more committed to? Being in survival mode, or realizing your dream? Recognize you are on the path already, and be more patient. Just be cautious and take care with your decision-making.

Thinking about downside risk is not necessarily a reckless focus, or one based in feelings of low trust. We manage risk because it is important to have our eyes wide open, and our decisions are both conscious and empowered. It is also important to have a robust plan so you have an agreed timeframe for being back to living within your means.

And always, always, always have a plan B. My plan B has always been if it all turns to custard I can get a job somewhere. I can't imagine myself ever being employable again, but it is always an option as long as

I allow humility and the absence of pride. Not ever wanting to do this has also been a source of motivation for me. Having an advisory board in place where I need to report profit results is also a good motivation to not return to survival mode too. We each have different strategies that work.

Making Choices to Honor our Worthiness to Thrive

Occasionally I make survival mode decisions so I can see how quickly I can get back to sorted—and to check I actually still can. That part is about not professing to teach something unless I can still do it myself. One other reason is I love the challenge, so I allow myself some crisis on occasion. It is not something to be recommended.

Sometimes I have misjudged and have had to roll my sleeves up and work really hard to recover from a situation financially. It has always served as a good reminder and I have learnt a lot from these moments. My actions have never been wasted—I have always grown through it.

Occasionally the roll of the dice has been very risky and I have had to dig deeper for my own level of belief in things unknown. But, I can tell you this. When we reach a place where we know, no matter what happens, "all will be okay," it's a good place to be. We want to get you to that "all will be okay" place too.

At times people resist even the possibility of this level of inner calm. They seem to prefer a consistent level of crisis and fear. Or without realizing it consciously, they inherently want to stay in survival mode. Why? Is it possibly because you don't feel worthy? You are worthy. If it's because you love the crisis, remember that you can fuel your adrenalin habit in areas outside of finances. Come to New Zealand and partake in our adventure tourism. Or set a different goal and tackle it from an empowered place of high achievement drive. You do not need to stay in survival mode to satisfy any crisis type cravings previously learned.

What do you need to change so your actions show you truly believe your core worthiness? Your actions need to be in alignment with the outcomes you logically believe you deserve. They need to be aligned with your self-worth. All money styles should reflect on this.

Breaking All the Rules and Making
Survival Mode Decisions Anyway

Try to recognize in the moment whether a decision is a survival mode one. Make the decision knowingly, after weighing up the options and risks. Consider your other options and make an informed choice with awareness of potential outcomes. Sometimes knowingly entering into a survival mode decision is still appropriate, as long as you have awareness.

Awareness allows you to manage the downside risk, and this is the most important part. It is not expecting the downside risk to actually happen. It is about acknowledging it as a possible outcome, not feeding that thought, and knowing right from the start such an outcome can be dealt with should it come to fruition.

When you make your next business or personal financial decision, decide whether you can utilize what you learned from your last survival mode decision. Include sold out mode decisions too. The only real difference between them is that sold out mode decisions involve more fear, control or mistrust, and tend to be even less empowered.

Survival mode decisions are not always bad. For example, making incremental changes, with some element of failure, can be far better than no action at all. And a flawed decision can still have far better consequences than if another had been made, or no decision altogether.

Regardless of what actually happens, we want to be able to look back and feel that given the circumstances present at that time, we would still have made the same decision again. If instead we want to kick ourselves for our decisions, we need to learn from this. Have your eyes wide open and take a balanced view from the possibility of your future looking back. Allow the possibility of less than favorable outcomes factor into your current decision. Do not allow this perspective to command the decision, simply to temper it. Manage the situation so you allow for negative outcomes in a sensible and appropriately balanced way.

If in the fullness of time we go into blame mode about any aspect of that outcome, it can sometimes be because we have forgotten the circumstances present when we first made the decision. So mentally take yourself back to that time and consider at what point you would have made a different call. We can then use that information to adapt our decisions next time something similar presents itself. This review needs to be done consciously and we need to remember our lessons learned.

When we make the same mistakes over and over, it can be because we forget there is a delay in how decisions made today affect our cash. A ten-week time period is a good timeframe to consider for business owners, as well as individuals to a degree. Credit card payments, holidays, children's birthday parties, special events, actions taken in anger, forgetting to save money, and forgetting to save tax can all impact our finances 10 weeks down the track, even earlier.

Survival and sold out mode people are most likely to get caught out by such issues. Use the decision gradient in chapter 6 to decide where the decision you are making right now sits on the 0–10 scale. Then remind yourself where you want your decisions to sit.

And again, some survival mode decisions are okay—it just depends on the overall costs versus benefit analysis. What are all the pros and cons, and which of these are more important? Taking risks and then being wrong is not necessarily a bad thing. Businesses would never grow if they didn't take risks. There is a definite art in discerning the right level. Survival and Sold out mode people should request wise counsel from a few stable mode people, allow their opinions to settle, then take action.

Reviewing your Five Key Actions & The Futility of Comparison

Above all else, survival mode people should check in on the five key action points. In fact everyone should do this. It's just more important for survival and sold out people.

The second most important point is never, ever, compare yourself with others. If there is one thing I have learned from being in the incredibly privileged position of seeing my clients' real financial situations, it is this. Of all those people that look good, smell good, and sound good, half of them are usually broke. The other half is normally doing okay financially.

Unless I had seen their tax returns, I wouldn't have been able to tell which was which. Often they had the trappings of success. How tiring it is for those pretending to live within their means, when actually they are not. I have been there too and know it is not much fun. How long do you want it to continue? I suggest you just do your five key actions and do them every month.

Also related to the looking good aspect, learn from those that have actually done what they are teaching, including those that have failed and gotten back up. Most people are fundamentally kinesthetic learners, those who learn from doing, and I believe business owners are even more so. Until we have actually had an experiential understanding of something, we find it difficult to internalize and integrate. If we intellectualize it too much, we feel immune from needing to do something. Sometimes we believe our talents exempt us from the laws of the universe. In these moments a humility check is needed, and the universe seldom hesitates in sending us one when needed. Who are we being to attract such circumstances?

Which of My Actions is "Out of Balance"

Actions needed to manage financial dynamics shift one towards higher levels of gratitude, humility, and respect. And by the way, it isn't necessarily respect towards another person, or to oneself, which is relevant. It is about financial respect towards the forces that provide whatever one asks of them, when done in the right manner and intent. To provide context, ask yourself the following questions, either now or later. But do remember to come back to it if you don't complete now.

1. How much income do you need at home each month? $_____
    Do you know with certainty (i.e. it's not a guess)   YES/NO

    Calculate your personal expenditure amounts if not and if you are a business owner, also get the equivalent before tax amount calculated—this is important so you don't end up with a tax bill year end.

    What else don't you know about your finances that would be good to learn?

2. Do you live within your means NOW?   YES/NO

    This does not mean your future, it means now. Things relevant for financial actions need to focus on your current situation, while items relevant for your beliefs are forward- looking to your future. Prosperity consciousness or scarcity consciousness is based much more in your beliefs than your current actions. Have an *attitude* of prosperity consciousness at the same time as undertaking actions that are highly respectful for your current reality.

3. Do you have a regular habit of saving (regardless of amount)? YES/NO

    It can be $5 per month. It is the habit that makes the difference, not the amount.

4. Do your savings get "dipped into" whenever you run out of cash? YES/NO

    If yes, change your answer at question 3 to NO if you had put YES. The easiest way to keep the savings habit permanent is to have an automatic payment set up to a savings account in a different bank and do not have Internet or ATM access to it. Recognize your weakness and don't allow it to "take you out" when temptation arises.

5. Do you have consistent actions to give back financially to others? YES/NO

    If any of the above is answered NO, change what you are DOING. Set a simple goal around improving this. Check how you are going in four weeks.

6. Do you have and operate a budget?   YES/NO

A budget doesn't need to be restrictive, the point is to have one that allows for whatever you want and need. The point of it is to prove you can live within your means.

I believe the main reason people stay in survival mode is because fundamentally our beliefs won't allow us to move out of it, until we choose to change them. Despite sometimes not consciously seeing the value, we need to try something we haven't previously done—that can sometimes be difficult for us. It's best to just trust and consistently improve on our 0–10 ratings for the five key actions steps.

We operate so often out of habit. My chairman who is a business psychologist tells me this is around 88% of the time. But when people are truly present to the cost of their actions, they can always break a habit. What is staying in survival mode actually costing you? In terms of money, time, relationships, fun, and health? Understand the cost and use it to motivate you to change your actions and improve your beliefs.

Yet some people still resist. Why on earth would they not at least *try* everything suggested to improve their financial world? Where are you blocked? Is it around a lack of trust in things you have never tried? Or perhaps you think it will be a waste of time if it doesn't work? But what if it does? Are you more committed to the results you are currently achieving? If so, why if your results are not what you want them to be? Think more about your self-interest and just start some change.

I suggest some people think the above is just too simple. For example, everyone can live within their means if they want it badly enough. There are always some extreme examples, but some people simply choose not to increase their income or reduce their expenses. Or both. Sometimes weird stuff like pride can get in the way of creating a life lasting change.

At the end of the day, we have a choice. Don't let what you cannot do get in the way of what you can do. Work on the things you can change. I know what I would choose, but then I have gotten through to the other side so I have a different vantage point. My looking glass probably has a different perspective. I still travel back and forth between quadrants on occasion, so I am no different to you in that regard.

Suggestions for changing what you are DOING to Live Within Your Means

To Increase Income/Cash:

- Work at it! Consistently follow all leads for income opportunities (and yes, with a high level of belief. That's crucial).

- Consider getting a part time job to supplement your income—can take a lot of humility to do so in some circumstances.
- Consciously know and improve the imbalance between income and expenses.
- Get advice from others on how. Don't let cost get in the way; work out a way you can get best bang for your buck. Lots of advisors give free time (for example we offer free 5pm meetings) so thinking you cannot afford advice is seldom a good excuse. Make a request.
- Set up an automatic payment to a savings account at a different bank. Most people can forego the price of one coffee a month – start with that amount. Have one less coffee. Or some other coffee equivalent.

To Reduce Expenditure

- Track it! Buy a small notebook and write everything down—sounds anal but it is designed to get you present to what you are spending. For at least 21 days, track everything you spend, and then share with your partner—your spending will reduce simply by being more conscious. I've heard it said that anything we focus on improves by at least 10%. By the way, this is good to remember when dealing with staff issues, but that topic can wait until later.
- Set targets for your expenditure. Don't be too miserly; be realistic and respectful to your situation.
- I get this is obvious, but shop around. Never pay full retail; wait for sales and ask for discounts.
- Intentionally trim your expenditure.
- Have food menu plans and make a game of who can cook the cheapest healthy meal.
- Separate your shopping list between luxuries (including alcohol, cigarettes, chocolate etc. if relevant) from "must have" items. Cut down on the luxuries (especially the above ones) and be kinder to your body in the process—a win/win. Wait a minute, can I just take a moment and acknowledge to myself I have just suggested people

reduce their chocolate consumption! Phew, and we think we know ourselves! (I quite like chocolate.)

- Avoid paying by cash—temptation is too great to have cash in your wallet to just spend. Different if you are a Stable money style, but avoid this at all costs if you are a Survival style.
- Freeze your credit card—literally. In a small bowl of water that needs time to defrost before using. Oh, and best not defrost it in the microwave, this can mess it up.
- Set an appropriate budget for entertainment, so you still feel prosperous.
- Keep a $100 bill in your wallet (or a few of them) but never spend it. This helps with both your prosperity consciousness and reducing fear around not having enough cash. If you are a survival mode person, you might notice how often you want to spend this, just never do it. You will need more self discipline until you operate in the sorted quadrant.
- Save small amounts regularly for special upcoming events or for things you don't know about yet. It feels good when money is readily available when wanted.
- Consider very carefully whether to go into debt for anything except things that increase in value (take care you are not overestimating your business investment with this comment).
- Reward yourself, often, for sensible spending choices. This may sound counter intuitive so remember that rewards don't need to involve money, or much money. Get creative.

Training your belief system that it is okay to do things differently can be really hard for some. There are so many reasons we can use to tell ourselves it is not possible and justifications occur at our very core. We all have blind spots, so we need to work on improving our overall beliefs in order to achieve the five financial actions.

Living within your means is a prerequisite to getting sorted. So too is having a high level of respect for your financial situation—regardless of your current circumstances. Adapt each month if circumstances change. Make it necessary, but don't turn this into feelings of scarcity. Just be real about your ability to live within your means and make the tough choices when needed. Increasing income is always an option if reducing expenditure is unpalatable. Give yourself a time limit and if you have not increased your income within it, reduce expenditure instead.

Remember the model below. Trace your finger along the Actions axis from left to right —it is not until we shift *through* the vertical "belief axis" that we can move from Survival to Sorted. Which of your beliefs is so strong it's holding you back from being Sorted?

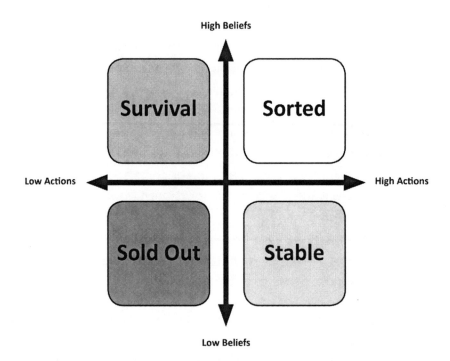

How does this tie back to your version of wealth? And remember that money is often *only one* aspect of wealth. Which of your beliefs about money is self-sabotaging you from achieving your other desired aspects of wealth?

Those of us who are naturally survival mode people need to regularly review our situation in relation to the five financial actions. Ideally this should be at least quarterly, even when you feel you are at a mastery level of competence. And even monthly until then.

Slipping backwards into survival mode is so insidious that we need self-awareness to be always top of mind. I suggest you set up a quarterly calendar reminder that automatically occurs forever. This is helpful from a "prevention is better than cure" perspective. Self-discipline and self-awareness allow us to stay safe. Sometimes all we need is a simple reminder.

How to Enjoy Your Life, Your Whole Life: Balancing Rewards Between Your Current and Future Selves

Sometimes when we start to get really good at the Five Financial Actions, we feel torn between honoring our commitment to these and enjoying ourselves in the present. What do I mean by this? Well, we might feel like we are so focused on living within our means and having a habit of savings for our future, that we sacrifice our enjoyment on luxury items that we could purchase now. Or the opposite can also be true: we might feel guilty for wanting to enjoy ourselves now, instead of reducing debt or saving for the future.

Do we go for a holiday, reduce debt or save for our retirement? Where is the balance to be found? The worksheet below walks you through how to find that balance when making a spending decision. It is especially important when we are a different money style to our partner.

It can be very helpful to agree with your partner to a set of rules that keep you safe from your own random spending. So too is remembering to reward yourself appropriately so you enjoy your successes along the way, and acknowledge them.

Do this worksheet now or later, when you genuinely want to change your results. Compromise and discuss with your partner from a tag team approach as described in chapter 5.

Questions: Your Now Versus Your Future

1. How do you want to be able to reward yourself for your achievements? Be creative and include aspects that might not cost much money, yet still acknowledge your success. Some ideas are at the end of this exercise.

2. Using the 0–10 Actions Scale (from chapter 6) as a guide, what spending rules would I want to consistently adopt so your decisions fall into an appropriate box? For example,

   a. You might agree all spend decisions on luxuries need to be able to fit into the definition for 8/10 or better on the Actions Scale.

   b. You might agree to have a rule to always maintain a habit of savings per week in preference to spending on luxuries, but you are okay if the amount reduces to $x per week savings as long as you both agree.

   c. You might agree that luxuries can be purchased only if $x can still be allocated to reducing debt.

   d. You might instead declare a war on debt and agree all other things need to wait until your overall debt is down to $x

   What rules do you want to agree to? Remember to compromise and tag team

3. What qualifies as a necessity purchase? Make a list and agree this with your partner. Compromise until you have a shared list.

4. What qualifies as a "luxury" in your world? Make a list. It is important to distinguish between your view of luxuries versus necessities. Agree to this list with your partner.

   How much entertainment, alcohol, cigarettes, sports etc are viewed as necessities in your world and at what spend level do these type of things tip into the luxury category each month or week? Compromise until you have a shared list that fits within your means.

5. What dollar amount is significant enough to require a discussion with your partner before spending occurs? Agree with your partner the level that is needed in order to need to consciously assess the 0–10 Actions axis ranking. For example, you may know that spending less than $100 does not need to be consciously considered because this is a minor amount for your budget. However it may be a significant amount if you spend this amount often.

   Agree what the word significant means in your spending. You might agree that you can spend up to $x per month, no questions asked, either of yourself or each other. If it is more than this value, you might need to agree first and it might need to qualify as at least an 8/10 decision on the Actions axis 0-10 guide. Work out how to have these conversations in an empowering way by focusing on the priorities you share for your current and future goals. This is not to be confused with an exercise in controlling one another or applying blame.

6. Still using the Actions Axis 0–10 scale as a guide, if you rewarded yourself with one of the ideas you listed in question 1, where on the Actions Axis 0-10 scale would the spend on that chosen reward lie? For example, if existing money owed to you will just cover the reward expenditure needed, then paying for this reward would be a decision that qualified as a 7 on the Actions scale.

Would this spend decision therefore align with the rules you have agreed to? If not, find a cheaper reward that you still feel good about. This ensures you reward yourself with things you can afford, instead of only considering the reward from the perspective of what you deserve.

A similar thought process is to give yourself the same reward, but in a cheaper way. For example, still have a holiday, but do it at or near home instead of flying overseas or interstate. Going to local tourist attractions with day trips here and there can feel like a really good holiday at half the expense, especially if you can include some free activities in the mix.

7. Should the money that you would use be reasonably allocated for a different cause? If yes, what? Which use of this money is most important and how might you afford both? Put your ideas below and if only one of the uses for your money is affordable, note why your choice is more important so you feel settled about it.

8. Considering your answers to all of the above questions, does spending this money on this issue seem like the right answer? And if it is a significant dollar value, do you both agree on this? YES/NO
    Negotiate in an empowered way until you have a shared view. Compromise.

9. Are there other factors you think you should consider when making this decision? For example has the reality of your financial situation changed such that the rules you originally put in place now need amending?

This might be because one of you earns less or more now, a result of changing family circumstances, or such like. The point is not to blindly follow the rules previously put in place if your circumstances change.

10. On a scale of 0–10, do you feel you have the right balance between your enjoyment now versus saving money for your enjoyment later in life? What rating 0-10 does your partner conclude?

Once you have considered your answers, depending on the significance of the purchase, remember to discuss your thoughts with your partner and make the decision together. Setting up the rules and then applying them helps remove any perceived guilt and allows your decisions to feel empowered and well justified.

After completing this exercise, choose specifically how and when to reward yourself. Your decisions are likely to conclude some should happen now, and some later.

Your rewards tend to feel even sweeter after having done the exercise because you know you are operating in alignment with the rules previously agreed. As long as we are honest with each other while answering the questions, feelings of guilt and anxiety tend to dissipate. This exercise done well can enhance your relationships to a point where all parties are in the same boat, rowing in the same direction at the same speed, together.

Ideas For Rewards

We all know that we feel really good when we reward ourselves. But they don't need to break the bank. The following is a list of inexpensive ideas for yourself—if you are an employee, some of these will need your employer's approval. Expensive rewards can be easily added per your own preference and ability to afford them.

- Schedule a date with your loved one
- Hire a DVD and have a family movie night
- Take a paid day off work—vacation leave or if self employed, schedule it into your calendar
- Have a long lunch
- Leave work early
- Go to a movie with friends or family
- Have a round of golf
- Visit family or friends
- Go fishing or hunting
- Have an afternoon at home without the kids
- Get your family to let you have a sleep in
- Get your boss to let you have a sleep in
- Pay for a housekeeper
- Go to the gym
- Go clothes shopping to a certain dollar value
- Donate money to your favorite charity
- Go out for dinner
- Go to a show
- Have friends around for dinner
- Take the kids on their favorite activity
- Pay for family to come visit
- Have a night in a hotel with your loved one
- Have a massage or facial
- Increase your food budget temporarily and buy your favorite luxury food
- Have takeaways for dinner
- Buy your favorite wine or beer
- Give a loved one a gift
- Buy something you can easily afford but have often wanted
- Visit a tourist attraction
- Go to a sports game
- Have a party
- Cook your favorite meal
- Ride your horse

JACK AND HIS MOTHER

You will recall that Jack is the person in their household most likely to play in survival mode. Because his mom is a stable mode money style, she is well able to help Jack understand the types of actions he could benefit from most. Jack does his best to keep an open mind. Together they work through this chapter and the worksheets to set goals about these. Jack is getting much better at living within his means, but he still has some work to do on this front.

Jack's mom has realized that she is worrying too much about their future and identifies with the concept of rewarding themselves in simple ways. She makes her own list of rewards so they can draw from this as they achieve their incremental goals for their five financial actions. She includes examples that are motivational for both of them.

They both practice living humbly every so often to remind themselves they are well able to do so. Jack's mom considers for herself how she might operate with higher self-worth and creates a sense of self-nurturing from a space of compassion and understanding.

Summary of the Chapter

- Periodically check yourself to see if you are operating at high levels of financial respect. This is especially important for Survival or Sold Out money styles.
- What happened financially ten weeks ago? This will most likely be impacting you now.
- Make good financial actions necessary—who does this for you? Is it you, or someone else?
- Buy a really big mirror about the financial aspects of the word respect so you can recognize the signs of survival based decisions.
- Choose enough self-discipline to get back to sorted.

- Know that you are worthy enough to thrive financially and take actions that are commensurate with high self-worth.
- Learn how to know when to break all the rules and "go survival" anyway, setting a time frame to return to Sorted.
- Complete the worksheets to assess your five financial actions and to balance rewards for yourself between now and your future.

Chapter Nine

SEVEN STEPS TO WEALTH CREATION

Where Are You Now? And How to Get You Where You Want to Be.

Now is the time for everything discussed so far to be brought together, so we can navigate through the specific steps of wealth creation. We will also recap what the word wealth means for you. And remember, it can be as wide a meaning as you wish. Firstly though, let's check in on our hero Jack.

Jack met Jill, and now its 20 years on...

I am bringing you into Jack and Jill's future now so that you can see how things are progressing for them. Looking at their future helps us learn from their experience, as well as aids us in making choices now that will benefit our future selves too.

A bit later we will learn what Jack and Jill originally set out to achieve. You will find they are very good at running their business, but they seldom addressed aspects of their personal finances together. We will see what impact this paradigm has been having, and later learn what created it.

JACK AND JILL'S DESIRED VERSION OF WEALTH

Rolling Jack's story forward 20 odd years, we are at a time when Jack has a family of his own and has long been in business. He has a lovely wife Jill and two children, Thomas and Sarah. His elderly mother is still alive and they take an active role in caring for her.

Jack has matured since chopping his first beanstalk. His family and various businesses are thriving. However there seems to be a lack of balance in his world. He is not having as much fun as previously. He is certainly not experiencing as much adventure as he was in his youth, and he sometimes misses this. He has some unmet expectations.

Jack wants to recapture the feelings of his youth. Jack and Jill both want to work on achieving certain goals within the next 3 years, some of them immediately. You might resonate with some of these too. They want:

- More harmonious relationships with each other as well as their children Thomas and Sarah.
- To continue caring for Jack's very elderly and sick mother.
- One weekend a quarter away without the children, somewhere affordable.
- Continuous personal development and to actively push their own boundaries.
- Training time for Jack to do a marathon with his best friend.
- To focus on a healthy lifestyle.
- Time for Jill to meet with her friends once a fortnight.

- To watch every game of sport played by Thomas and Sarah.
- An overseas holiday every second year for two weeks.
- An absence of fear in their world.
- Take home cash of $350,000 per annum, increasing to $750,000 per annum. They want the increase in their take home cash to go 100% towards their personal philanthropic goals.
- A strong connection with their faith.
- Savings per annum of $30,000 and debt reduction per annum of $30,000.
- A voluntary management role at their local school.
- The ability to engage with anyone about anything, in an empowered manner.
- To set up and manage a new community centre and fund for underprivileged kids in Jack's home town.
- To sponsor three African children and visit them every three years.
- To finish the start up phase all of their four businesses and have profits from these donated to their chosen charities.
- To help their children achieve their goal of becoming business owners.

Despite being married for 15 years and together 17, this is the first time Jack and Jill have ever properly attempted discussing personal and financial goals. Previously they found the topic very charged and never got past go. Even now they fight over their preferences, but make a commitment to work things out. Jill is very strong-willed and doesn't like situations lacking certainty.

Jack remembers fondly being taught some financial skills as a teenager. He hasn't yet worked out why things are different now. He also remembers discussing financial issues with his mother years ago, but his focus became side tracked somewhere along the way. Reading this book has reminded Jack of what he learned, but is not currently applying.

Jack recalls that he is a survival money style and Jill has worked out she is in the stable quadrant. Both recognize they had periods living in sold out as children and dearly don't want their children to experience this. Jack already knows a great deal of this information but 1) he needs to be reminded because his current results are less than desired and 2) he isn't actually doing what he logically knows is best.

The following is a strategy to help them achieve their goals.

Creating permanent wealth

Jack and Jill want permanency in their results, so they made a commitment to apply the following principles to their discussions and situation.

- Operate with sound values/good intent.
- Be consistent with themselves and each other.
- Employ an appropriate level of self-discipline.
- When focusing on beliefs, they will also consider their actions.
- When focusing on actions, they will also consider their beliefs.
- Be empowered, not disempowered, in interactions with others.

Here are the steps they went through to achieve these. On the next page is a graphic summarizing these steps.

Step 1: First Tier Actions

Jack and Jill reviewed the five financial actions and subjectively ranked them on a scale of 0–10. Here is how they fared along with what they desired their rankings to be in four weeks.

SEVEN STEPS TO WEALTH CREATION

Step 7
12 Months expenses saved
Belief/Actions Process Never Ends
Accessing Power
Adapt / Change /Grow

Step 6
Review Beliefs Again
Release more control, fear
Live in the Now, embrace financial situation
Be in state of Zero – no meaning

Step 5
2nd Tier Actions
Lead- Be, Connected
Balance – Wants, Change/Adapt
Financial Base, money style
"Fail" quicker/smaller
Lead/Manage to the "issue"
Consistency /Growing a "team"
Allow others to "fail"

Step 4
Maintain 3 months
operating expenses in a
savings account
Find a way to find a way

Step 3
Working on your beliefs
Diagnose 'beliefs axis' placement
One household= one relationship with money
Harness the financial laws
Acknowledge your 'currency'
Honorable pursuits

Step 2
Maintain 1 month's
expense in a
Savings account
Find a way to find a way

Step 1
1st Tier Actions – live within
your means. Habit of savings
Habit of philanthropy
Know your finances
Budget

		Now	Goal – 4 weeks
1.	Living within our means	6	8
2.	Habit of savings	7	7
3.	Habit of philanthropy (time & money)	10	8
4.	Knowing your financial situation	4	8
5.	Having and operating a budget	0	10
	Total	**27**	**41**

They agree to do the following within four weeks:

a. Work out a budget and plan the steps to improve their rankings.

b. Provide less pro bono work to customers—currently they do large amounts of work at discounted rates. They agree they will peg this back to move their habit of philanthropy from 10 to 8. They recognize some imbalance was from just one step ranking too highly.

c. Have more intention to live within their means, only taking out a set amount of cash each week.

These three actions will improve their relationship with money over the next month and will be a very good first step towards taking back control of their financial situation.

Both Jack and Jill have had their heads buried in the sand, hence their lack of awareness or focus on goals. They resonate with the concept of being an ostrich and can see this has resulted in being somewhat Sold Out.

Once the three actions have been achieved, they are ready for the next steps.

Step 2: Always having ONE MONTH'S personal operating expenses

Jack and Jill need to "find a way to find a way" to maintain one month's operating expenses in a savings account.

For some people this is significant. In fact for some, just living within their means is a massive change from current circumstances. Some people have never done either, so it can be a really big achievement and paradigm shift.

Setting the goal for a month's savings is key and doing it in bite-sized, easy, steady-as-she-goes steps. It is important to ensure step 1 is also maintained throughout the entire process of moving through these seven steps. Do not underestimate how easy it is to slip backwards to a place of not living within our means. This is especially so for survival and sold out mode people.

The seven steps of wealth creation are like a game of snakes and ladders. And the steps are sequential. All prior steps need to be maintained, or else we cannot progress to the next step. It is important to not mentally beat ourselves up if we slip backwards. Instead we just pick ourselves up, dust ourselves off and start to climb the ladder again.

People sometimes tell me they don't want to put money into a savings account because they want to put everything back into the business. I want you to understand that this is a survival mode mentality. It is okay to do this, but generally only if you want to stay in survival mode. The goal is instead to achieve both savings and reinvestment.

Putting all your cash back into the business can omit issues around risk management. It places a great deal of pressure on everything working out okay and this needing to always be the case. None of us can predict the future to this extent. In order to build a robust financial safety net, we need to start saving.

Start with a goal of having a week's expenses in a savings account. Then aim for two weeks and then four. Know that I am all for reinvesting back into a business. I just believe we should achieve both results. This creates strength and it is within this strength that we are able to adapt quickly and have enough cash to make wise financial choices.

For Jack and Jill, a lot of this was already in place previously. Circumstances have meant they slipped backwards; they just need to regroup. They now have a goal and plan to increase their income incrementally. They will budget, track, and reduce their expenses. This will increase their awareness and make their savings happen easier.

They are being "real" about living within their means and are having a competition week once a month to see who in their family can make a healthy dinner for the cheapest price. The kids love it and it draws their family closer.

Step 3: Working on our BELIEFS

Jack and Jill have diagnosed where they believe they may be operating on the beliefs axis. Jack thinks he is at stage 4 and Jill feels she is at stage 3 so the combined relationship is stage 3 as the lowest common denominator.

They have considered the underlying cause of their financial dynamics. Jill's is sourced in an inability to trust other people and lower self-worth ratings. Jack's financial issues are sourced in an underlying fear and a need for control in order to feel safe. He also does not feel highly worthy to achieve and receive financially. His significant childhood events to fend for his family impacted his feelings of safety and also his worthiness to receive money. The couple now recognizes that some of these issues are impacting their relationship with money and therefore their financial results. This is a significant level of self-awareness for them.

They have considered their financial currencies and believe that Jack's main driver is to give to others, while Jill's is certainty. They now know to take care to not "trade off" their cash via these currencies too often. They have a much higher level of understanding of each other's needs, motivations and aspirations and are more supportive of each other's belief systems.

For the next month, they have agreed what to do and then they will review and assess what has worked well, and what needs some adjustment. They will seek advice if needed. They also acknowledge that while this is what they intend to achieve, their actual results may differ. They know they are more likely to achieve these goals by agreeing to them up front, compared with not considering them at all. They acknowledge their results will largely depend on their level of commitment.

This is what they agreed:

- To remove a high level of emotion from their financial decisions.
- To work on their need for control and allow some risks to play out (at an appropriate level of risk).
- To work towards trusting the unknown more, and consciously considering the issues when fear arises for them. To find ways and evidence to attempt to build belief instead.
- To practice giving freely without condition but within their budget, and not overreacting if others mistrust or misinterpret their intent or actions.
- To stay True North to their honorable values, regardless of the opinion of others.
- To stay aligned about their finances and discuss them regularly so they are able to benefit from each other's understanding.
- To choose to not be mentally "taken out" by each other, if one of them is having a bad day around achieving any of these goals. Instead they will commit to helping each other get back on track.
- To enlist the support of their children and align them with the family goals. (It is harder for them to back off if they tell their children they will achieve something.)
- To accept (without a need to understand) that they have a combined relationship with money. They will "take one for the team" if they don't understand the relevance of any issue and simply go along with it anyway.
- To focus on being true to the Laws of the Universe. They understand their financial results will be impacted by who they are being in terms of the following:

◊ Law of Vibration: being at peace with one's own thoughts and actions.

◊ Law of Compensation: what goes around comes back around.

◊ Law of Attraction: we attract what we focus on most.

◊ Law of Increasing Returns: seeds planted will return bigger crops.

◊ Law of Success or Abundance: the habits of success including working conscientiously with strong intent from a place of sound values, competence and high beliefs to achieve one's goals.

- To focus on honorable pursuits to give and avoid dishonorable pursuits such as greed. To apply courage to maintain this.

- To acknowledge their "financial currency." To work to their strengths and allow the other to compensate with theirs.

- To be adult in their discussions. They will manage their responses if the other has disempowered, childish, or negative interactions.

Step 4: Always having THREE MONTH'S
personal operating expenses in a bank account

Jack and Jill are doing really with their goals. Their next step is to maintain access to three month's worth of operating expenses in their bank. They need to find a way to achieve this. They brainstormed together as a first step to working this out.

One thing they are learning is the distinction between:

- Respectful actions around expenses (which is different to having a scarcity- based consciousness).
- Prosperity-based beliefs for income generation issues.

They have learned to apply a different financial energy for different types of decisions. They apply respect in spending, but prosperity thinking for income generation. They learn to not mentally spend until they have received the cash. To mentally (or even worse, actually) spend before money has safely arrived, is one of the biggest trademarks of the survival quadrant.

Self-discipline and genuine non-judgmental support from Jill is the main thing that helps Jack around this. He has a blind spot, wanting to spend often, so Jill helps him see it so they can live within their means. Jack helps Jill with her blind spot and fear about taking well-managed risks. There is a balance reached through the conversations they have together, and over time they are able to have these conversations without tension. Soon enough, financial conversations are an empowered, every day topic with a tag team focus.

Step 5: Second Tier Personal/Business "ACTIONS"

Jack and Jill have been doing well, and although they found it difficult to reach three months savings, they've made it. They feel more empowered and excited about their goals.

This step is more about working together as a team rather than the amount of cash they have saved. They are beginning to trust that no matter what life throws at them, they will be able to deal with the financial aspects together. Although this is a subtle change, when they stop to realize this, they see it is a significant one.

Now they have a reasonably solid personal financial base, they are really getting focused on reaching their aspirations. There is a trade off between keeping three month's cash available and applying some of it towards their goals. They navigate this balance by agreeing together which issue is most important at any given point in time. Should the three-month savings need to be dipped into, they ensure they have a solid plan to get it back to three months worth within reasonable time frames. They acknowledge that dipping into the savings would make them slip down the wealth steps and their financial stability would be impacted. Armed with this knowledge, they choose wisely.

Once they are at this step, Jack and Jill start to have a higher level of recognition with their leadership, both in their personal lives and their business. They focus on the following that can be applied to either a business or family context.

A. ***They make a decision to lead and get connected to their relationships****—with each other, their team, and their finances. This means they:*

- Start by always asking themselves "who am I being" in this situation, and why? What is the cause: what about this is about me, not about the other person.

- All of their decisions link far better with their defined values—they use their values as a basis for decision-making. They teach their team (staff and/or family) how to apply these values in decision-making. This provides a higher level of consistency across the team and enforces their brand experience in their businesses.

- They now have a higher level of awareness of "what does my customer want" (and what they are prepared to give.) And why. They understand that the word "customer" relates to all their relationships in business, at home, and in life—"customers" are everyone they interact with.

- They really start focusing on building their team (both at home and work) and understanding other people's views better. They ask their team members their preferred leadership style. They adapt often. Jack and Jill start to release control, incrementally.

- They are learning to "meet them where they are at" (customers, staff, suppliers, network affiliates, family, friends). This means allowing people to have their own opinion, think differently, and change (or not) per their preference, readiness and timing. Once they have genuinely acknowledged where the other person is operating, they still do their best to compassionately extend them.

- They realize they need to focus on growth so they don't inadvertently die. As the saying goes, we are either growing or going.
- Consistency in decision-making is something they are both very good at now.
- With defined boundaries in place, they now hold them, both at home and at work. Not all parties they deal with understand the need for various boundaries. They hold them anyway, respectfully.

B. **Building from a place of "balance."** *They apply this balance mantra to allow for:*
- Their "customer" wants.
- They consistently promote the concept of wanting to change/adapt/innovate.
- Systems/documentation are refined and areas for improvement are starting to be documented regularly at the time things change.
- Their financial base takes into account the need for enjoyment as well.
- The underlying money styles of each team member are well understood and their strengths and weaknesses are compensated by each other.
- Jack and Jill start to focus their actions on the sequence of "Think it, Plan it, Skill it, Drive it" so both their personal world and business grows in ways that are safe and achievement driven. Everyone in the team applies compassion and support to everyone mostly of the time.

C. **Fail—quicker and smaller**
- They recognize the ability to deal with failure lies in acceptance of mistakes, themselves, their ideas, their planning, their training, and the execution/implementation of these.

- They constantly improve via a cycle of change/adapt, change/adapt, change/adapt, incrementally learning via failures that are bite-sized chunks. They intentionally risk failing, so they can learn most and adapt the quickest.
- They remember to train well, so failure is minimized.
- They embrace their own humanness around failure, and also others' failure.
- And for all of the above, the standard they set for the concept of failure is that it is to be learned from and not repeated unnecessarily. They also learn from the failure of others, trying their best to avoid failing in the first place.

D. Always lead/manage to the issue/policy/procedure

- They are trying to always manage the same way, regardless of the person involved.
- To honor the above mantra they go so far as to change the policy if needed, creating a basis for consistency across different decisions.
- They understand that consistency is one of the biggest keys to permanent growth and also for sticking to their values. They focus on keeping/growing a good team and understand this level of consistency and fairness is a critical element of a good team's longevity. They apply this from a sound basis of integrity.

E. Allow others to fail

- Risking their brand/family situation beyond their control has been a challenge, especially for Jack who has a need for control underlying his survival mode style.
- He recognizes though that there is gold in the risk, so that their brand can create its own "life" (beyond just themselves). They both start releasing control and allowing this to happen.

- Understanding the analogy of "never touch the butterfly's wings in moments they are learning to fly," they see that interfering can prevent the butterfly from flying forever. Instead they start guiding from beside their team without "touching." This means "crossing the street" with team members when they need assistance, watching but letting them "cross alone" when ready, and finally trusting they are fully competent without watching at all.

- Remembering to delegate, not abdicate, they ensure they have the right people on the right seats, doing the right things. And because they do, delegating is easy. They trust a good result happens because they have earned that trust. This trust continues to be honored, but sound processes are still in place to check delegated tasks are completed appropriately and in a low risk manner.

This step of second tier actions has taken quite a long time for both Jack and Jill to master. Despite some challenges along the way, both their business and their personal lives are much better for it. So too is the enjoyment level of most of their staff, as well as their own children.

Some staff needed to change jobs when it became obvious their values were misaligned or their competency levels out of step.

If Jack were viewing the step in isolation, he would be at a different stage to Jill. But together they are supportive and their finances are as a result improving.

Step 6: REVIEW your Beliefs again, moment by moment
Jack and Jill feel significantly better about their finances by the time they have completed step 5. They acknowledge that like all of us, there is a high chance they may travel back down the seven steps if their decision-making and mental attitude doesn't

stay focused, empowered and committed to achieving their version of wealth.

During this stage:

- Both consciously release more control and have a higher level of belief in things unseen.
- Jill is far less driven by fear in everything she does, especially in financial aspects, but also in other areas of her life.
- The more they improve and grow, the more willing they are to look at themselves first as a starting point for situations involving conflict, dissent, or judgment. They are more aware that how they listen to others is mainly influenced by their own projections.
- Both generate a higher level of confidence and acceptance of their financial situation. They clearly see the impact of their choice in the past and the impact of decisions today on future results.
- They are present to living and loving in the "now" instead of worrying about the future. They do this from a place of responsibility about their future. There is a balance between their present and their future.
- They are enjoying what they already have and also striving for more enjoyment. They are doing so without an actual need for material possessions. Their happiness is not dependent on them, nor do they strive for them. They simply and happily enjoy their life to the best of their current financial ability. This does not mean an absence of material possessions, more a contentment about their current position at every stage.
- Jack and Jill are learning how to stay better grounded and be in a state of zero, a place of no meaning. They consider who they are each being to have attracted any given situation into their life. They don't judge or condemn each other for getting anything "wrong." They

know things are what they are for a reason; they don't necessarily need to understand the reason but more simply be with it. Importantly, they also know they can learn to change and grow at will.

Step 7: Always having 12 MONTHS personal operating expenses.

Reaching the upper stages of your defined wealth can be similar to excelling in martial arts: the higher levels can take longer to achieve than the first few. Good things take time and there is always a reason for this. Now, Jack and Jill have learned to be humble, patient and tolerant most of the time. They have good periods and not so good periods and regroup as needed.

They have been rewarded with many aspects of their version of wealth. There are a number of items still to achieve, but they know it is simply a matter of time before these occur as well.

They have learned many practical ways to increase income, reduce costs and maintain strong beliefs around their results. They achieved 12 months savings by building savings gradually. They took an easy approach to everything, with small incremental steps, simply deciding to "make it necessary." They consistently focused some of their time to future-based improvements, also remembering to improve their "operational now."

They are benefitting from this future based approach. Sorting out their personal budget is key, as is sorting out their business so it can better fund their personal life. They remembered that the best time to plant a tree was 20 years ago. But given they hadn't done that, they also knew the second best time is today. The tree is for their future, helping it be easier when they arrive there.

Jack and Jill continued to save a portion of everything they earned. Importantly, any savings they made they did not touch except for a predefined purpose. They made it a rule that those particular savings were for their future goals and they patiently wait for these to come to fruition. This brings immense satisfaction.

The couple realizes this process of alternating focus and improvements between actions/beliefs, actions/beliefs, actions/beliefs is an ongoing one, never changing as long as they want to stay in the sorted quadrant. They are proud of their achievements and have made a significant dent in their debt.

Their focus is firmly on the concept of adapting/changing/growing as life throws things their way. Maintaining higher levels of respect and gratitude towards their financial situation is important for both Jack and Jill. As a matter of best practice, they occasionally consider whether they have balance between their own enjoyment and the good they could achieve for other causes. They also ensure with each other's assistance that their financial activities and attitudes are based in honorable pursuits to give, not dishonorable pursuits of greed.

They both know that this process would still have worked even if they were alone or had another for support instead of each other. Keeping it simple has been an important factor. Magic has been created, and they still do not truly understand how it happened. They acknowledge that this magic is found in the concepts of balance and respectful financial actions, as well as belief in things unseen.

They willingly want to continue regardless of which parts created the magic. Having increased awareness and trust in the powers that provide for them is a shift in both acceptance and understanding. Their life is still not without challenge. Challenge and suffering is a necessary and valid part of all life. But their challenges are dealt with jointly from a place of financial empowerment.

On occasion they will make a decision to dip into their 12-month savings when it seems strategically sensible. They know that if they do this they will ensure a solid plan is in place to rebuild their savings quickly. Over time their goal is to have even stronger cash reserves available so they can more easily realize their vision and definition of wealth. They want to ensure continued flexibility in their decision making and timing.

Everything they do is from a place of co-creation (or collaboration) with other experts and colleagues. They focus on allowing the experts to be advisors while they make the final decisions. They consider all factors and allow synergy from a number of different sources to achieve a far better overall result.

Jack and Jill have learned a lot over this time, at different paces and levels. At times they were surprised with what each could learn whilst allowing the other to learn slower, or at a different depth. It wasn't as if either had any choice about it. All was as it was meant to be. And they each learned to accept a different pace and understanding to enable them to get to their destination together, relationship well intact.

Now that they have read part 1 of this book, they are ready for part 2. Instinct tells them it wouldn't hurt to read part 1 again. Jack and Jill both know their lessons learned from part 1 will be highly relevant for how they run their business going forward. It is also highly relevant for them personally. They feel encouraged by what they can teach Thomas and Sarah.

Summary of the chapter

Navigate through the seven steps of wealth creation to achieve your own version of wealth.

Step 1: FIRST TIER ACTIONS

    a. Living within your means—this is the most important action

    b. Habit of savings

    c. Habit of philanthropy

    d. Knowing your financial situation

    e. Having and operate a budget

Step 2: Having one month's personal operating expenses the whole time

Step 3: Working on your beliefs—diagnosing, acknowledging the cause, harnessing the laws of the universe, understanding your financial currency

Step 4: Maintaining three month's personal operating expenses in a bank account

Step 5: SECOND TIER PERSONAL/ BUSINESS 'ACTIONS'

    a.   Make a decision to lead - get connected

    b.   Build from a place of "balance"

    c.   Fail, quicker and smaller

    d.   Always lead/manage to the issue/policy/procedure

    e.   Allow others to fail

Step 6: Review your own Beliefs again, moment by moment

Step 7: Maintain 12 months personal operating expenses the whole time.

Adapt/change/grow. Access your source of power.

Part II

LOOKING AFTER
YOUR BUSINESS

Chapter Ten

Start as We
Mean to Go On

The Basics of Business Value

We rolled forward 20 years in the last chapter to see Jack and Jill's progress in their personal world (which for the most part, was before having read this book). They then set off to achieve their desired version of wealth by applying what they learned from this book. As I understand it, they are progressing very well. We might meet them again in subsequent stories.

We now roll the clock back again to find out how Jack and Jill got their business to a prosperous stage. We start with Jack who is much younger and still single.

JACK'S EARLY BUSINESS UNDERSTANDING

Jack has helped his mom for a few more years after killing the giant. He is most of his way through college and has asked for help to understand what areas to focus on for business. He has heard that planning is good to do and wants clarity as to what he should do to ensure he will sell his business later. Jack has a short attention span and expects he will get bored of a business quickly and want to diversify often. Let's help him out.

There is good reason I spent part one of this book focusing on you as an individual. I wanted to show you the types of things you might achieve personally. But equally importantly, your business will only thrive once you understand the financial issues you are personally bringing to it.

Throughout this second part, when I refer to your business, nearly every tip or reference is equally applicable to your individual role as an employee, or as a family member responsible for financial or leadership aspects. Consider both scenarios.

Your Business is a Mirror of You— How Well Are You Leading?

Your business is a mirror because as small business owners, its results tend to be a reflection of ourselves. It is also a reflection of other key personnel, owners and managers. Our business tends to grow when we grow, and stagnate when we stagnate. Whether we understand it or not, our business and ourselves are energetically related. We therefore need to look in the mirror to see where our business issues might be.

If things are not working out well, it is good for us to ask how can we lead better. Who are we being in the quieter moments that influence our team to either grow or to resist change? We all make mistakes, some of them significant. And sometimes our teams forgive us, while sometimes they carry a grudge. Although a case can easily be put forward that this is a reflection of them and not you, it's powerful to look at ourselves first and examine our own role in what transpires.

What Aren't We Doing Yet?

The best place to start understanding our business better is to see who we are being in our moments of leadership. To ask, "what *aren't* we doing yet?" We may not be doing anything wrong; we just may not be doing enough right. What is missing, where are the gaps? I have certainly put my hand up in the past and acknowledged my shortcomings.

Aside from yourself, the business also reflects your team. So once we have looked at ourselves, we should lead our team to do the same. Their self-awareness and desire for growth is important as it also helps the business to grow. Have staff agree with this concept and your business will be better for it.

If we are not growing, we are slowly dying. This sentence applies to both our business and ourselves. Personally, I would prefer to live each and every day of my life fully rather than be stuck in a rut of slow death and frustration. And it's the same for your business. Just like a person, it needs to be fed, nurtured, and have well maintained boundaries via good systems. It also needs to be supported.

Starting with the End in Mind

If you were to roll your life forward a number of years, what story would you like to tell about your business and other aspects of your world? How big is your business vision? More importantly, do you have a plan to execute this? This business vision should obviously be complementary with your personal vision so both can be achieved in harmony.

Whatever your business vision, one aspect of it should include a variety of options for exiting it. Knowing that plans are likely to differ once the rubber hits the road, it is more preferable to have an exit strategy, than have no plan at all.

What Story do you Want to Tell?

We all have different motivations for wanting to build a business, and also for wanting to leave one. Any reason is not necessarily better than another. But it is important to know your why for having your business, and also your why for exiting. Do you want to make lots of cash, move onto more exciting things, retire, reduce risks, or simply change direction to gain more variety? What legacy do you want for your business past your personal tenure?

The reasons for leaving can impact the best method to exit. Part of your "why" can be nurtured by the simple concept of having a "story" (sometimes solely in your mind) of the way you want your exit to happen.

How will you feel if you shut the doors, walking into retirement with nil cash return? This might be fine. If not, we need to help prepare you. And please do not underestimate the possibility of shutting your doors. Statistics show a significant portion of business owners are aged 55 or over. And a high percentage believe selling their business will be a significant part of their retirement planning. To give you context, more than half of New Zealand business owners are in this category and many western countries have similar statistics.

One inherent problem is that there are less people being born who are genuinely interested in buying. In addition, generations X and Y are less interested in owning their own business compared with generations prior. Demand therefore outpaces supply and many business owners are not likely to get the price they want, or even any price at all. Only the best businesses will sell. Or at best, the prices will drop significantly.

So from the perspective of starting with the end in mind, let's examine the basics of business value so your business is one that can be sold.

Asking the Right Questions—As Simple as Our Fairy Tale

Asking the right questions is critical for assessing business value. We need to gauge the business's risks, return, growth potential, systems, reliance on certain people/situations/seasons, and its need for capital. Your future lives in these questions.

Let's return now to Jack and the Beanstalk for a good metaphor on business valuation. You will recall in Chapter one my son asked me why Jack hadn't gone for some help to get rid of the giant, so he could play on the beanstalk as much as he wanted. This thought process is strongly connected to the way businesses are valued.

We Inherently Know What Makes a Business Valuable

Let's first consider all the characters in Jack and the Beanstalk. We have Jack, Jack's Mother, a Cow, Magic Beans, a Beanstalk, a Giant & the Giant's wife, and the Golden Egg Laying Goose.

Remember these characters. For now, let's check in on two different types of similar businesses.

1. McDonalds. Started by Ray Kroc, over time the company has become a worldwide presence with high value, both at an individual retail outlet level, as well as their head office.
2. A corner takeout business, the original version of McDonalds.

Without knowing any specifics about these two businesses, which business is likely to cost more if you wanted to buy it? Most people say McDonalds. The reason is because it has more inherent value, even if people aren't sure exactly why.

Why do we inherently suspect McDonalds might be more valuable? Here are some common themes:

- Better systems, processes, a more streamlined business
- Better branding, advertising, IP, locations, business ideas
- More certainty and therefore less risk (of many natures/types)
- More capital to develop and grow as desired
- The competency levels of the owners may be different
- The drive/ambition/reasons for growing a business was different
- Better return on investment

Whether or not someone wants to sell their business in the future, improvements in the above list have a direct impact on the business value—and often more importantly, the results enjoyed from it along the way. This list impacts the value placed on a business by a prospective purchaser.

Improved systems, return on investment, lower risk, more capital, and excellent branding positioning all enable a business to "make more hay while the sun shines." Even if you don't want to sell long term, it is a smart idea to get the business to a position where you could if that's what you decided.

JACK AND HIS BEANSTALK

Let's go back to the fairy tale. Each of the characters can represent one of the items on our list below. Unscramble these two columns and match each character to the appropriate business value on the right. The answers follow further on in the chapter.

Column A	Column B
Jack	Systems, processes, the business itself
Jack's Mother	Branding, IP, business ideas
Cow	Risks
Magic Beans	Capital
Beanstalk	Return on Investment
Giant & Giant's wife	Business owner skill set
Golden Egg Laying Goose	The why, drive, ambition

What is Most Important in Business Value— Symptoms Versus Cause

Consider for a moment which two items in column B are most important for improved value. Lots of people think of the following:

1. Better return on investment = more reliable cash in your hand each year
2. Better systems, processes = a business that is systems dependent, not people dependent.

These are important if you are focusing on results. However they are symptoms of something more crucial. Searching into the *cause* of business value, we also consider the underlying reason that improved systems and better return on investment significantly impact the business value. Anything crucial to a business's value should be what you review the most.

One crucial element is having enough capital to fuel growth. Being undercapitalized is one major reason for business failure. And it is equally important to have both appropriate direction and good systems and processes in place. But again, these are all symptoms.

The real *cause* of value is around risk. When business risks are high, the value is low. When business risks are low, the value is high. Improved systems & processes, coupled with more certainty and better return on investment, results in lower risk. When we remove the risk, we increase the value. Having enough capital to weather any unexpected storms also reduces business risk.

It follows that managing risk has a direct inverse correlation with value. The higher the risk, the lower the value. When risk is well managed, it can be one of the easiest things to improve business value. So risk needs to be assessed.

What type of risks should you review?

Reviewing risk should always involve professional assistance. A great team to assess risk should include a commercially focused certified public accountant and lawyer, coupled with an insurance or financial advisor focused on risk management.

Key person risk in small to medium sized private companies is a major risk. It should be well managed via appropriate insurance cover, shareholder agreements, and buy sell agreements, or the equivalent.

SWOT analysis and PESTE analysis should also be considered. SWOT stands for Strengths Weaknesses (internally, in the business itself) and Opportunities Threats (around external factors). PESTE stands for risk consideration for Political, Economic, Social, Technological, and Environmental issues.

Other standard due diligence should be carried out by a qualified professional too. In preparation for a potential sale, your accountant should at a minimum review the following, otherwise your sale may fall through.

- The past 2-3 years of financial statements to see if the returns suggested are valid.
- Check source data such as external tax assessments and work papers to confirm reliability of information.
- Review existing customer contracts, supply agreements.
- Review transactional information, records.
- Review operations, procedures and manuals, and compliance against these.

Whether or not this extends to a formal due diligence at time of sale depends on the scope and agreement of the engagement. The bigger, riskier the business, the more likely a formal due diligence is necessary.

Understanding the Value

Now, back to Jack and the Beanstalk. Here is how the characters match up.

> Jack = business owner
> Jack's mother = the why, drive, ambition, and also the inner critic of the owner, or bystanders
> Cow = capital needed to start/grow a business
> Magic beans = branding, creative ideas, IP
> Beanstalk = business itself, its systems, processes
> Giant and Giant's wife = risks
> Golden Egg Laying Goose = return on investment

Using this story as an analogy for your business, when assessing its value you and your advisors would look at:

- How "magic" the magic beans are—it is best when they are different or special (ideas, branding, IP). What does your business have that is different and magic?
- What giant (or smaller) risks are looming. How are you going to manage these and what help do you need?

- See how strong the beanstalk systems are, including how much bigger the business can grow, and will it stay as strong when it does?

- How important is Jack to the story (could somebody else do that instead). How easily can Jack (i.e. you) be replaced with another person, gradually over time?

- How much cash cow capital is needed to fuel growth? When will this be needed and how are you raising the funds?

- What type and degree of golden goose return on investment (ROI) is at the top, if the beanstalk is to stay strong? Is this return on investment worth the effort? Or would you be financially better off to get a job? What needs to change so that ROI changes? It needs to change if we want the vision to happen. If this doesn't resonate, you need to get more connected to the vision. Get a bigger "why" and commitment.

If you can get rid of the giants, the value of the business will increase because there is less chance you would need to chop the beanstalk down. Hence your ability to have certain, reliable reward while you still play on the beanstalk. Or, you can let someone else play on it instead when you sell. The stronger the beanstalk, along with better treasure and lower risk of giants, the more valuable your business is.

One word of caution. Take care not to have the beanstalk growing too close to your home. That in itself is a risky business if it needs to be chopped down. Ensure your home is well protected from your business.

Being prepared for exit

The main reason a business owner will successfully sell is because their business deserves to sell. To achieve a premium price, it will likely rate well in the above list of attributes.

The main benefit however can be the rewards earned along the way. The best businesses provide great return on investment as the risks are incrementally being reduced. Make small changes, often. Stay focused on the future, always.

All of this does not happen overnight. Preparation, execution and milestones are needed to create the overall combination desired. Once a decision to exit occurs, improving the above is a necessary part of any exit strategy (if achieving an optimum price is the goal). It's a different story if getting out at all costs is the goal.

Key Things to Do Now to Prepare for Sale

To maximize your sale price and increase the chance of selling you should:

- Have a plan for exit 3–5 years out so you can execute your plan well in time.
- Work out the critical path of key steps needed to realize your vision.
- Manage the profit growth to be sustainable and appealing to an investor.
- Develop sound systems and processes to create/maintain simple but effective operations manuals.
- Remove the dependency of key people, growing competencies with others over time.

If there were only one business tip I was allowed to share in this entire book, it would be this. Make constant, small, incremental and focused improvements to prepare for the next time a current problem occurs. It is not until we make changes now for future issues that our future will have fewer problems than we face currently.

People can get so stuck in dealing with their present that they forget to spend just a little bit of time now to improve their future. This small step will eventually do just that. Big changes can sometimes also bring bigger risks. So making smaller changes will also manage the downside risks better.

Ways to Exit your Business

There are various factors to consider:

Who to sell to: an external independent party such as a competitor or aspiring business owner. You can also sell to employees. Or grow so big you have an Initial Public Offering (IPO) The option you choose relates to your "why."

How much to sell: you might exit completely or have a partial sale of your shares, keeping some involvement yourself. There are pros and cons to both, depending on your preferences. These include tax benefits, a gradual approach to ensure goodwill transfers well, minimizing risks of handover, and other inherent risks.

Continued Investment /Management: do you want to have a manager involved in your business and keep ownership? This can sometimes occur by intent, but sometimes by default if there are no willing buyers at desired sale levels.

Once you have answers and a plan to manage these, you will need to develop your critical path for the steps and milestones needed to get there. I show you how to do this a little bit later.

In the meantime, know that an important aspect of this chapter is to align you with the concept of being able to create your own Independence Day. You can choose whether to actually take it; it is not compulsory. What is most important is to get your business into a place where you have that choice. This creates a strong business that is very valuable and sought after. There is a sweetness gained when you continue to work within your business purely by choice, and are able to focus on the areas you enjoy most.

Scheduling Jack's Independence Day

Jack is nearly finished College and is contemplating what type of new businesses to promote following graduation. Jack resonates with the idea of having an Independence Day and right from the start chooses to set a personal goal. He wants to have a great business story to tell (other than a fairy tale). He believes that aiming for his own Independence Day will help him achieve his vision and create a business worth selling.

Jack wants a situation where he exits his business on his terms, with a successful sale. He can see that many businesses will not be in this position unless they focus on factors that make a business valuable. He knows that a big draw card for an external investor will be a business capable of operating well without Jack. This would means lower risk and therefore higher value. At the moment, he doesn't need to choose how he will exit his business. What's important is being able to exit in the future if he wants.

Exiting his business should be a choice and on his terms, not anybody else's.

━━━━━━━━━━━━━━━━━━━━━

Part of my job in this book is to help business owners be compelling in the execution of their plan, so they won't be simply shutting their doors.

Summary of the Chapter

- Your business is a reflection of you and your key personnel. All of us should therefore be seeking to grow personally in order for our business to do the same.
- We need to start with the end in mind and know what story we want to be able to tell if we rolled our life forward a number of years.
- The fairy tale of Jack and the Beanstalk provides a good analogy for the fundamentals of understanding business value.
- Of the main business value characteristics, reducing risk (getting rid of the "giants") is the most important to address. This is partly because it can be the root cause of two of the main symptoms improving value: 1) return on investment and 2) your business being systems dependent, not people dependent.
- There are varying ways to exit your business, so your vision should allow for the options you prefer but also include other options for factors unknown.

Chapter Eleven

THE JOURNEY TO FINANCIAL FREEDOM AND LEVERAGE

Combining Business Competencies With Business Values

Now we know the fundamentals of business value, it is timely to discuss the importance of *combining* sound values with best practice business growth principles. Much of this topic is sourced in the concepts of leadership and team creation.

The Guardians of Leadership and Team

What type of leadership are we bringing to our lives, whether in business, or our personal life? There are many different types of leadership and most of us probably believe our style is really effective. For the most part, it probably is. But sometimes we can benefit from an outside perspective.

Guardians, leadership and team are three words that are interesting to place in the same heading. I did this because of their strong interrelationship. It is important to honor all three in both ourselves and others.

Guardianship

You may recall that I was taught as a child that it is our duty to reach our fullest potential for the betterment of society. My dad also taught me that if we can help, we should. These concepts together create a guardianship effect, and give rise to us taking a team leadership role, regardless of whether we have actually been appointed the official team leader.

An element of leadership exists whenever we decide to assist other team members. Nothing much is ever achieved on our own, and given we are born with a duty to do our best for society, we should always make team goals the priority whenever we can. I love the saying "all it takes for bad things to happen is for enough good people to do nothing." We can achieve so much more together than alone.

Leadership

A key question to ask when wanting to grow our business is "how are we leading?" Are we supporting, empowering, teaching, guiding, apologizing when needed, embracing our own change and also changes in others, and promoting the fact that so-called failures teach us? Are we helping team members reach their fullest potential and doing the best we can to assist them, even if it means they may then move on from the business? Do we look in our own mirror and request every other senior team member do as well, before pointing the finger of blame elsewhere?

Or instead are we leading from a disempowered place of control, fear, criticism, condemnation or complaint when we think about a team member? Or worse, when we actually interact with them? This is not a question of strength. We can be strong under any leadership style, albeit in different ways.

Sometimes our team members may think we are taking a disempowered approach, even when we are not. So how do we deal with this type of misunderstanding? Are we open, transparent and empowered enough as leaders to have real conversations with our team so we resolve issues? Or do we shrug them away and think everything is just their issue to deal with? How loyal and committed are we as leaders towards our team members? Are we respectful when we disagree with their opinions, or actions, or performance? Or are we disinterested, disconnected, controlling or something similarly disempowering when we deal with varying expectations?

Team

By the way, if you were a team member, who would you sooner be led by? A supporting, empowering, teaching leader, or the controlling, criticizing, condemning one? Who would you respect? Who would gain your loyalty? If you don't care, know that most people do. And since team members are actually our customers too, if it is important to them, it should be important to us as well.

It's pretty obvious who your team would prefer dealing with, isn't it. Most of us don't even realize when we are responding in a disempowered way. We just know we are feeling irritated, angry, or sometimes even stupid, scared or rejected. Sometimes though we aren't fully conscious of how we are acting or feeling.

We need to be highly aware of our thoughts and feelings in order to lead well as appointed leaders, team members, customers or advisors. Especially when leading by example. Every day we are afforded opportunities to lead. And all of us probably mess these up more often than get them right. But when our intent is true, our team usually know.

The word team means different things for different people. In our homes our team includes everyone living there, or hanging out frequently—including stray teenagers—pretty much anyone who is close enough to be given chores or turn up without an invitation. Team always includes us too. At work, team includes you, your staff, contractors, clients, suppliers, and affiliates. Basically anyone who you deal with regularly. They are all part of your wider team.

One of the most valuable outputs of a good team (besides effective performance and creating more sustainable results) is the strong loyalty it can develop. Loyalty is a precious quality that is so very subtle. It can sometimes take significant events and periods to build, and also be easily diminished. For loyalty to endure, it is vital to discuss issues with your team, and apply a wider view to consider all factors and team preferences (as well as your own). Do not underestimate the value of loyalty. When some form of loyalty is present in team members there will be more alignment with your business vision, greater staff longevity, less need for retraining, and more commitment to competency and achieving desired results. Disinterest, disconnection, contempt, disrespect and lower commitment levels tend to occur when loyalty reduces. This can be despite your best efforts to promote and maintain loyalty. Some people simply cannot stay empowered, preferring instead to operate from a place of mistrust, victimhood, or some other disempowered space. Fundamental to the development and continuation of healthy, loyal relationships are the values we apply when dealing with people, plus our ability to communicate in a real and empowered manner. Sometimes the road is a challenging one when the other party finds it too hard to consistently operate in an empowered manner.

We can only do our own part in this though. Despite our best and well-intentioned efforts, it does take two to tango. Gauge your results from the perspective of your ability to stay empowered and apply compassion in times when others cannot. I know from personal experience that it can be sad and disappointing when others operate from a disempowered place. But such a situation needs to be well managed so you do not allow your own goals, business or personal, to be sabotaged as a result. There is a mental strength needed to stay true north towards both your values and your goals. It is easy to trust and be empowered when things are going well. But when others act in a disempowered manner, it can test your resolve at a very molecular level. Stay true north anyway. Besides being the right thing to do, over time it will also help create loyalty.

The Source of Your Freedom

Loyalty is one of the fulcrums for the source of your freedom in business. Consider how much freedom your business currently offers you. Some of us are at a stage where our business does not generate money unless we are there doing the work. Some have staff to do the work, but they are not senior enough to be left in charge. Some of us have more choice around this, but are still needed in emergencies. And some of us have people that deal with the emergencies as well as we would. Consider where your business is at to help distinguish how much time and money freedom you currently have.

In order to achieve freedom, or leverage, we need to be able to appropriately influence others well. This includes having quality relationships with those close to us, an essential part of most people's definition of wealth. There is little solace in achieving other aspects of our desired version of wealth at the expense of our relationships.

Create a great team and freedom will follow. Permanent freedom follows when we lead well. This is because good leadership creates influence, and influence gets you more business and better results. While other things also create influence, most can also be placed under the label of leadership and loyal relationship building. None of us are good leaders all of the time, especially if under pressure with competing demands. And sometimes we mess up simply because we don't realize the way some people interpret our words or actions.

We need four cornerstone pillars if we wish to develop strong freedom and influence in business. These are:

1. Resilience
2. Honor/courage
3. Compassion
4. Loyalty

These are shown in the Guardians of Leadership model on the next page.

The purpose of this model is to demonstrate the aspects needed to achieve more financial and time freedom in our life, to create choice. Consider where in your life there is an absence of choice and whether or not this is okay. Then make a decision whether to add any of these aspects to your personal definition of wealth.

1. Resilience Pillar

As business owners we need lots of resilience. People who have not grown their own business from inception find it difficult to appreciate the resilience needed to keep paying the bills in financially tricky times. We have probably all had periods in our business where things have not been overly healthy.

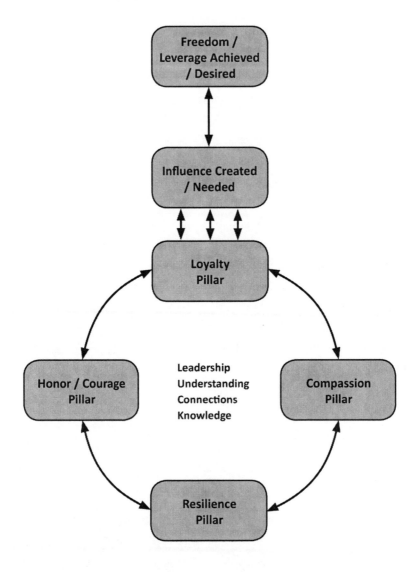

Resilience gets us through these times and helps us recover, or adapt from misfortune or change. We also draw on resilience to trust and believe that things are as they are meant to be and will work out.

At a Resilience in Business seminar I attended, the main speaker cited resilience as being the most important quality present in the world's top 1000 CEOs (as measured in a study undertaken over a number of years). He also mentioned a very high percentage of these world class CEOs had come from dysfunctional backgrounds. Those analyzing the results had worked out that because these CEOS had learned resilience early in life, they had climbed their success ladders faster—in a weird sort of way it seemed to me that their dysfunctional backgrounds had given them a head start on everyone else.

I'm not trying to discount or discredit any dysfunctional experience you may have in your present or past: my point is that our life skills can serve us well when we seek out the ways to do so, viewing them from a place of empowerment, as well as from a place of healing. Having the ability to "sway in the wind" with whatever turns up is critical to growing a business, as well as surviving any challenges. Resilience allows one to maintain sound values (shown in the model under the broad headings of honor/courage and compassion) even when the chips are down.

As the model depicts, these sound values together with resilience help create loyalty, loyalty creates influence, and influence creates freedom and leverage. Without resilience and operating sound values, business freedom is seldom sustained over the long term.

2. Honor/Courage Pillar

Honor and courage are obvious needs for a business owner, yet we sometimes falter creating them. The word honor covers a lot of specific values such as integrity, honesty, respect, and the like. If we want long-term success, we need a long-term perspective and to employ appropriate values. Especially when dealing with money issues.

It takes courage to ensure honor is maintained. I love Winston Churchill's quote, "Courage is the first of all human qualities, because it is the one which guarantees all of the others." This is why courage is right next to honor in the model, guaranteeing it.

It is easy to be honorable when things are going well. It is when things are challenging that it takes courage to act honorably. Here are some thoughts. Do we honor our financial commitments? Do we communicate to people if we do not? Who do we take for granted financially? Why is that? Have we checked that our perspective is aligned with theirs? How recently have we checked? Their view may have changed. In my experience it is easy to miss this and I have made some mistakes that I needed to learn from.

The most difficult time to stay true to one's values is when finances are challenged. It is fundamental to maintain communication at these times, especially to those closest to you. Money issues are very vulnerable for people and some people find it very difficult to discuss them. I suggest we do our best to have compassion without negative emotions when discussing money. All is possible through honorable communication, as long as our actions are consistent with words. This can be difficult to maintain when there are so many changing variables in business. Always stay in communication about money, regardless of changes in circumstance that impact your ability to deliver on your intent.

It is courage that guarantees the honor needed to stay true to our original intent, regardless of circumstance. It is courage that places a "not for sale" sticker on our values. Sometimes finding the courage to be honorable is easy; other times it tests every inch of our fiber.

At times our intent can be true, but there is a time lag as to when we can deliver. Communicating this and not taking people for granted is fundamental. We all make mistakes, but it is how we deal with them and put them right that counts. We need to learn not to make the same mistakes over and over again.

3. Compassion Pillar

We need compassion for everyone we deal with—or do you disagree? And why is agreeing or not important? If you disagree, consider for a moment the place from where you are operating. Do not judge yourself; just notice. Is being in this place serving you well? What are you getting out of being there? And most importantly, what is being there costing your relationships, emotionally, financially, spiritually? I fundamentally believe that if we want true freedom, we need to operate from a place of compassion towards others as consistently as possible.

We also need a lot of compassion for ourselves. As human beings we all make mistakes. Sometimes people mentally pummel us for making them, and sometimes we do the pummeling. Having compassion suggests an absence of judgment. Sometimes we also need to request compassion and understanding from others towards us.

Judgment doesn't help anybody. It serves to alienate. Yet we all do it sometimes. Some of us package it as "jumping to conclusions." The point is to contain it, move on, and shift quickly to compassion. Communicate and do so with integrity. It's only through doing this that we earn the ability to influence and obtain our own version of freedom. A lack of integrity will come back to bite us in the butt very quickly.

4. Loyalty Pillar

My experience as a leader in all aspects of my life concludes that loyalty comes from combining resilience, honor/courage and compassion. This is because of who we are being when we combine these.

Creating loyalty in others is not a conscious intention. With the right people around you, it just happens. This is especially so when we are presented with challenging situations. Character is not made in a crisis, it is simply revealed. When we are consistently resilient, honorable, courageous and compassionate, regardless of our circumstances, we can stand tall. It helps us earn trust from those who are able to trust.

Being resilient, honorable, courageous and compassionate encourages others to do be the same. But only if you are genuine; people can smell it when you are not. If your intention is to truly help people, most will want to help you back. And over time their loyalty will grow.

If any of the resilience, honor/courage and compassion cornerstone pillars are perceived to be waning or missing, loyalty tends to wane too. People only need to *think* they are missing to reduce their loyalty. This can be disappointing, but all we can do is focus on being genuine with our intent and actions.

When we demonstrate loyalty towards others for the benefit of their business ventures, we can also benefit ourselves at the same time. When allow ourselves an opportunity to freely give towards another human being, we also receive acts of loyalty back somehow, at some stage in the future. People who do not align with this sentiment seem to be lonely and disempowered. I have a great deal of compassion for those that cannot genuinely give or receive support. In my experience support communicated towards others is always well received.

Influence

Influence is the first cousin of loyalty and critical for freedom. People who have the ability to influence have the ability to achieve whatever they wish. Our leadership in times we are trying to influence needs to be sourced in the four cornerstone pillars, or interactions won't be received as genuine, or have a long-term effect.

So can I make one point crystal clear. None of what I say is intended to promote any form of manipulation, control, or sneakiness that a disempowered interpretation might conclude. All of which I speak needs to be genuine, real, authentic. Treat the world from a place of integrity and your business endeavors will eventually be repaid in kind. It is a sad situation when an authentic gesture is received from a place of mistrust. But the fact remains; we cannot control the responses of others.

We know that we have formed the four cornerstone pillars well when we have long term relationships that are both mutually respectful and beneficial. Conversely, we have deficiencies in our ability to create and maintain them if our relationships crumble under duress. For example, a lack of loyalty, especially when accompanied with an absence of open communication, is a big clue that people around you think you haven't applied the four cornerstone pillars well enough. They most likely don't trust you.

Putting to one side that this may simply be due to their own issues, what are you not being to have attracted this situation? I believe we need to focus less on them and more on us. How we can be different? Take care to not over analyze it though. Just be aware of your role in what is happening and learn as much as possible from the situations life is presenting to you. What situations are being given to you so you can learn to apply more resilience, honor, courage, compassion, loyalty and influence? There will be lessons occurring for you (if you want to see them) within many facets of your life.

Core Competence

A number of core elements need to be present for the above values to help create solid foundations and consistently improve results. One of these is that the cornerstone pillars need to coexist with a high level of competence in the delivery of your business offerings. There is little point running around being nice to people if we cannot deliver on the promise of our core business.

It is the combination of all of these factors (resilience, honor/courage, compassion, loyalty, influence and core competence) that I believe provide freedom over time. We also need to have an appropriate amount of LUCK as part of that competence.

How to create LUCK in business.

Competency is created by effectively applying four business competencies:

1. Leadership
2. Understanding
3. Connections
4. Knowledge

This creates the acronym LUCK. Have another look at the Guardians of Leadership Model. Notice that the four cornerstone pillars visually surround and protect the four business competencies above. The four cornerstone pillars are your guardians, helping to grow and nurture your competence in business, while also ensuring you do so with an appropriate degree of moral fiber.

I have seen different variations of LUCK. For example some people use Location Understanding Connections and Knowledge. I'm suggesting Leadership instead of Location because it is more pertinent to achieving better results. But location is also valid, as we need to be positioned well to allow business opportunities to present themselves, and have good places/ methods to reach our market.

We need to understand the relevance of *combining* the LUCK business competencies with the four cornerstone pillars, and why it is through their combination that our results are impacted. This is quite intangible and as a result can be difficult to measure. Strength and longevity is developed through the balance of these factors, and this is incredibly valuable.

The combination creates a high degree of magic or gold within your business. How well you see this depends on how aligned you are to the concepts. Some of you will think the points above are incredibly obvious and will already have experienced massive benefits from similar application. Others may disagree with me, or simply not see the relevance.

These points create gold in your business from the real synergy created from combining LUCK with the cornerstone pillars. This is turn creates a multiplying effect on the amount of influence you bring to a situation and results. When we quantum leap our influence levels, we can create amazing collaborative or co creative results. This occurs through the combination of various people providing inputs from widely varying skill sets, as well as widely varying connections of their own.

Creating More Freedom

This is important if we want more freedom or leverage and marginally less important if we do not. Simply put, if we want more freedom than we currently enjoy, then we need to have more influence than we currently experience. If we already had more influence, we would have already achieved different results. I know this because any business relationship or negotiation you might name can have better results, should one be able to influence better. Suppliers, customers, staff, bosses, colleagues, and network affiliates can all achieve better results with stronger abilities to influence.

Influence can occur in many areas. For example, a good thing about social media is that discussions can open up about business owners who operate at low levels of competence and cornerstone pillars, as well as about business owners who are great at what they do.

Transparency in Feedback

We are often in situations where we need to give feedback. If we are transparent in this feedback, a real conversation can ensue. It is difficult to fully manage any misunderstandings that occur sometimes and often foolish to even try, unless all parties engage from an empowered place. Those that stay true will shine. People will learn to listen more accurately over time as their awareness and empowerment grows. Feedback is helpful so we can learn and adapt as relevant. But that is all the attention that feedback normally needs. Adapt ourselves if relevant; brush it off if not.

Achieving, Together

We need to be really good at our core business competencies in order to achieve the overall LUCK we seek. Each of the four business competencies requires that we are good at what we do. To create a depth and strength in our leadership, understanding, connections and knowledge requires that we are highly competent. Failing this, our ability to create loyalty and influence will diminish rapidly. We cannot fake our competence long term. Luckily, we do not have to possess all of this competence needed all by ourselves. I believe it would be foolish to try.

None of us know enough by ourselves to run a thriving, growing business. We need a really good team who can deal with various subject matters. I deal with many experts and personally prefer finding those who are exceptional at their chosen craft. It makes everything so much easier when we need to access the leadership and the knowledge needed. Dealing with exceptional subject matter experts also helps with the connections and understanding factors, because competent people deal with competent people—and they also tend to know many others.

Sometimes the people we deal with can also have a role in your business akin to also being a guardian for your leadership, supporting your elements of LUCK with a similar essence to the four cornerstone pillars. These people are gold. I am very grateful for the ones within my realm.

Playing a long term game – Not Taking People for Granted

The Guardians of Leadership Model works when we want to create long-term permanent success with our efforts. Good things do take time. Some business relationships take years to nurture in order to build adequate trust. And importantly, it seems that when resilience, honor/courage, compassion or loyalty reduce, so too does our ability to influence. I believe that most times, this tends to be because of reduced trust.

Be especially careful about issues involving money and "taking people for granted." Remember that we sometimes miss what is obvious to others and it is therefore important to address issues consistently. Stay true north to your policies, especially those involving money, and avoid a change in approach based on your perception of someone else's situation. Half of whom you think are flush with cash will not be. We just can't tell which half. So it is best to be consistent with money regardless of the person.

Over the years I have gleaned that people who alter financial behavior towards someone based on their perception of the other's financial situation tend to be operating in survival mode. I believe this type of approach to their financial circumstances is one of the dynamics that actually holds people in that mode. I have made this mistake myself when I have been in survival mode. But I can also tell you that as soon as I recognized what I was doing and became more consistent across all commitments, my financial situation started to improve quite dramatically.

- To play a long-term game honorably, I suggest that if you are in survival mode financially you:
- Stay in communication with all parties about timing or current circumstances. Be genuine.
- Pay all creditors, on a pro rata basis if need be, so everyone gets something until you can pay people in full on time, every time
- Carefully consider how to reduce your own expenditure to pay your creditors—acknowledge to yourself that their debts should not fund your lifestyle. If you have outstanding debts, you may not deserve luxuries yet. Live within your means. To do otherwise can be viewed by some as a form of theft.

The energy around your finances shifts when you apply the above because it draws on fairness and consistency. To communicate using these terms can be helpful. Remember to be genuine and communicate from the other party's perspective.

Summary of the Chapter

- Guardianship, leadership and team are all central concepts to ensure permanency and prosperity in business and society generally.
- The Guardians of Leadership Model explains interrelationships to achieve freedom/leverage.
- The source of our freedom is through an appropriate combination of sound values and best practice business growth principles. The four cornerstone pillars are resilience, honor/courage, compassion and loyalty.
- Loyalty from others is a by-product of the other three pillars. We need to be loyal towards others in order for relationships to have a solid basis upon which to be nurtured and create influence.
- To generate LUCK in our business we need Leadership, Understanding, Connection and Knowledge, in appropriate portions to ensure a highly competent and consistent business delivery.

- The four cornerstone pillars surround, underpin and protect, as guardians, the generation of LUCK in our business.
- Once we have enough LUCK and strong loyalty in our business, we will build influence with all relationships that provides the gateway to freedom and leverage.
- Consistently playing a long-term game is especially important via money issues. Communication is key to ensure we do not take people for granted.

Chapter Twelve

From "Mission Impossible" to "Mission Accomplished"

Getting Better Leadership and Knowledge into your Business

The Leadership Team Effect

Having great leadership and knowledge forms a powerful combination when growing a business. It's important to realize that you don't need to personally possess all the leadership and knowledge skills yourself. Too often, we feel we need do things without assistance from others.

No business owner can grow a business alone. We all have attributes that hold us back from being more successful. Sometimes it's money style, sometimes it's our leadership style, or sometimes it's the extent of our overall business knowledge.

Now that we understand your money style can impact your business results, the next step is to understand the relevance of combining your leadership and knowledge. The leadership and knowledge of all team members creates a leadership team effect, as shown in the next model.

Applying this model, learning how to grow our business involves determining whether we need 1) a better understanding of our money style 2) an improvement in our leadership style or 3) an improvement in our overall business knowledge. We might need all three. To determine this, we need to:

- Diagnose the combination of leadership and knowledge we currently operate under (high or low for each)
- Assess which need most help
- Find the easiest path to get the best results with least effort
- Work out how to get your business into the "mission accomplished" quadrant quickly.

Step 1. What Are Your Knowledge Gaps?

Make a list of all tasks needed in your business so it can successfully operate without major mishap and encourage strong growth. This helps you define your knowledge axis.

This list should include tasks that relate to:

- strategy
- marketing/branding/sales
- client service delivery
- people management
- wider team building (e.g. including advisors in your team)
- systems management
- operations/production management
- finance
- administration
- governance
- legal
- risk management

List the tasks under three headings:

1. entrepreneurial tasks
2. business management tasks
3. core operational tasks

Next put a:
- * next to things you want to continue to do in your role.
- + next to the things that are critical for you to do.
- K next to anything that you believe you need some help with to understand how to up skill yourself.

This is the list that we will help you delegate later. Some delegation is likely to be to internal staff and contractors/advisors, while some might be to varying external advisors. If need be, get someone good in business to help you create your list.

Take a very subjective look at your desired list of all knowledge needed in your business and rate each point on a scale of 1–10, 10 meaning that knowledge in this area is already very high, whether this knowledge be found in yourself, your staff or your advisors. This gives you some indication of where you would rate your business overall on the above knowledge axis. An average score of 0 is at the far left and 10 on the far right. Your answers give you context for where you might want to improve and how big a knowledge gap exists.

Step 2. What are Your Leadership Gaps?

There are many varying leadership styles and one is not necessarily better than another. As long as you can maintain a stable effective workforce and get sustainable results from your team then your leadership style probably matches the needs of your team/personnel reasonably well. If you feel either of these is lacking, there may well be a leadership style in your business (somewhere senior, not necessarily your own) that is counter productive to what your current personnel want/need. Sometimes it may simply mean you need a change in your staff. It's important to discern which is actually correct.

Make a list of the attributes of a great leader. Thinking of all the people who have led you will help. If you liked their leadership style, write down the exact qualities they possessed. If you didn't like their style, write down the opposite of their traits (i.e. the qualities you wished that they had). What is most important is to have a style that matches your own personality, as well as the needs of your team. Ask your team for their perspective. Their list is likely to be a reflection of themselves and their own attributes, good and bad. But it is good to understand their preferences.

As you did with the knowledge list, next to each attribute write either

- * next to leadership things you want to continue doing
- + next to things that are critical for you to do.
- Put L by the leadership aspects you want to learn how to improve.

Again, ask a good businessperson their opinion on leadership attributes that are important for a successful business. And once you have read chapters 14 and 15 on team building and delegation, revise your list again as necessary. Your list is likely to change over time as you, your business, and the leaders within it all grow.

Take a very subjective look at your desired list of leadership attributes. Rate each point on a scale of 1–10, 10 meaning the particular leadership aspect is very high within your business. Taking an average result across all attributes will indicate where you would rank on the above leadership axis. A score of 0 is at the far bottom and 10 the far top. Also get your staff to complete this exercise. This can be quite telling and, for some, takes courage. It is important that you include leadership traits important to them and rate yourself and others accordingly.

The next step is to consider the steps and sequence of how to improve both leadership and knowledge gaps you have listed. This is where skill is required in deciding the areas to focus on first. Sequence, cost and timing should be considered once the steps themselves are detailed. Request assistance from a mentor who has working knowledge of leading within your industry, and consider the expected return on investment from what they charge with your commercially and strategically focused Chief Financial Officer (CFO).

Creating the shift with least cost and most ease

Over time, consistent, small and incremental changes create magical results in your business. Gentle changes also mean major risks are unlikely to surface. Cherry pick the knowledge gaps that you see as the easiest to improve, taking a highest value/least cost approach. You might choose something as easy/cheap as learning more helpful reports from your new accounting system, or attending a half-day sales training course. The main point is to focus on some form of new learning consistently.

Sometimes a major change can also be done with least cost. In these circumstances, ensure you also do a SWOT (Strengths, Weaknesses, Opportunities and Threats) analysis of the intended change.

Attitude and Time for New Learnings

If you think you are too busy to have a consistent approach to new learning, or to find time for improving your business generally, have a reality check. There is never a good time, so it may as well be today. Every week, do something that forwards your game from a new learning perspective. Depending on your role in the business, you may have a significant learning component in your standard week. Create a war against being stuck in a rut.

I accept that sometimes the least cost, easiest knowledge point may not be the most important change for your business. But this exercise is about creating an intentional habit so that new learning occurs regularly, and that over time, everything learned is highly relevant for helping your business thrive. The points you have already detailed for yourself are important gaps. So everything you do should create relevant improvements.

We need to connect with the importance of doing things now to improve things for later. Nothing in our present or future will change unless we change our current paradigm. Otherwise it is way too easy to put things off.

Chunkier knowledge issues should get addressed in order of importance. For the items that are going to cost enough money to make you cringe even a little, I suggest doing the following:

- rank each one out of 0–10, with 10 being very important.
- Compare each one in turn with the next item and decide which of the two is more important—mark the more important one with an x. Keep going until all items have been marked and then rank them by the number each item has been marked, highest to lowest.
- Compile a 90-day plan that includes a schedule for improvement in the more important knowledge areas. The issues will fit under the following categories:
  1. strategy/marketing
  2. team/HR
  3. systems/operations
  4. finance/compliance/risk

Focus on the gaps in these areas first.

Combining Leadership style, Management style, Money style and How it All Ties in With Growing your Business

Growing a business can either be approached from:

1. the top down, a strategic brand focused approach
2. from the bottom up, tactical widget building-block approach

Both strategic and tactical approaches should carefully ensure holistic, robust and safe growth strategies.

From a tactical, bottom up approach we would consider the following:

1. Financial base. This incorporates your money style to ensure you have:
   - A strong financial foundation so your business doesn't topple once it grows
   - An awareness of the level of self-discipline needed for your financial actions. Survival money styles need deeper more stable foundations than stable money styles to achieve similar results. And stable money styles need deeper more stable foundations than sorted money styles. Stronger foundations create the strength needed for long-term financial success. Increasing your self-discipline in money actions is what creates the depth, and therefore stability, needed to grow your business safely. Sold out money styles do not have stability so cannot create a strong financial base until they first choose to change.

Once we have a strong financial base, we also need:

2. Strong systems and operational processes
3. An appetite to consistently change and adapt
4. A top down, strategic approach that focuses on the "whys" and "needs" of the customer

The attached model shows how these areas tie together.

Focusing on our "Why" and "Needs" strategy, as well as a habit of change, supports our leadership style to thrive and inspire. You may notice

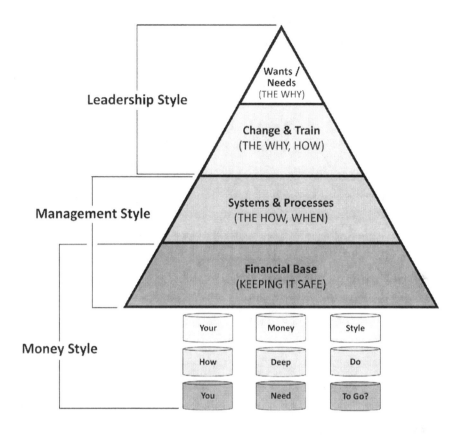

that there is overlap between the four main levels. This overlap helps ensure balance in your business or personal world.

When we lead well, we inspire and help the business and people within it to change, grow and flourish. This differs to when we manage well, which is when results occur on time and within budget. Good management ensures boundaries are well maintained and personnel have appropriate, clear expectations. Both leadership and management of the business can also be impacted by our money style and associated behavior. The combination of leadership, management and money style has a direct correlation with our business results. Improve in these areas and your results will also improve.

This model applies to your overall strategy and tactics, but also applies to any individual issue needing some decision-making. Consider the four areas (customer wants, training/change, systems/processes and financial base) equally to see if any of them need more focus or resolution than the rest. Don't forget to also consider changes in your leadership, management or money style to improve results with either macro or micro management issues.

Making your Strategy Happen
"On Time" and "Within Budget"

My chairman is a business psychologist who specializes in brain research. He uses a phrase "think it, plan it, skill it, drive it" to consider any business issue, strategic or tactical. The sequence and the steps themselves connect in with our core behavioral styles and skill sets. "Think it" uses our creative, imaginative skills, "plan it" our analytical skills, "skill it" our social interactive skills, and "drive it" our achievement drive skills.

All four steps are critically needed for growing business. And importantly, the steps you would naturally skip out are likely to be the ones where you lack skills. For example, if you are not very analytical, you are likely to find it difficult to plan and might naturally avoid the "plan it" step altogether. As the saying goes "when we fail to plan, we plan to fail." If we want to be on time and within budget, there will need to be a plan, despite any of our own failings.

From my CFO perspective, if I was a small business and had to choose between being on time or within budget, most times I would pick the latter. This is because limited resources will have a significant impact on cash flow if timing is wrongly calculated. Whether or not "within budget" is better than "on time" is highly case specific. The main point is you should know which of the two deliverables you can afford to adjust. Some things are so time critical we need to accept cash flow overruns. But apply caution if it's difficult to afford.

Building Your Critical Path for Business Growth

We need to create a plan for steps needed to ensure your strategy is achieved and tactics successful. Here's how to do this.

Step 1: List items that need changing in your business from a knowledge perspective. Include items at a strategic, tactical or operational level so your business is taken from where it is now to where you want it to be. Include personal things.

Examples are:

- Review your brand positioning
- Achievement of minimum sales targets of 'x' units or 'x' dollars
- Hiring a bookkeeper
- Update cash flow budgets for new sales levels
- Book a holiday
- Giving yourself a pay rise of 'x' dollars
- Review your tax planning structure
- Rollout new product/service
- Develop marketing plan
- Have 'x' percentage of your tax bill saved
- Work out how to increase production to 'x' units per day
- Have 'x' dollars available in a savings account
- Get 'x' overseas customers secured
- Complete legal contracts for 'x'
- Negotiate new lease
- Train manager in 'x'
- Register company in 'x' state or country

Step 2: Sequence your steps into logical order. The way to do this is to put each step individually onto a square of paper, and order them until the sequence seems correct. This is a very effective kinesthetic exercise. Request perspective from your advisors and team as relevant.

Step 3: Date each step for achievable and acceptable timeframes.

Step 4: Implement the plan. Know that sometimes the sequence is more important than the timing. Allow the deadlines to be fluid, as long as the sequence works. That said, some milestones are too important to miss—for example an important trade show or a really big tax bill.

There will also be some critical success factors that need to be addressed as a matter of priority. Once you have the main critical path, you will need to update it regularly. It is likely to alter significantly over time to achieve the business's strategic goals. Check this every 90 days and reset your priorities for the next quarter.

JACK'S CRITICAL PATH

Returning to our example, it is currently ten years after Jack cut down the beanstalk. He has a beanstalk centre. Jack's attitudes have changed over the past few years. Jack has become mindful to ensure the continued wealth for his family, including his mother and new girlfriend Jill. He also wants to share some of his good fortune with others.

Jack defined his version of wealth, including activities he would like to be involved with at some stage during his life. This is his list.

- Keep his golden egg laying goose healthy and safe
- Develop other income streams in case his goose gets sick or stolen
- Learn how to invest better
- Holiday overseas twice a year
- Export his beanstalks internationally
- Breed golden egg laying geese
- Pay for better medical care for his Mom
- Donate beans to third world countries
- Create an adventure tourism business for beanstalk climbing competitions
- Research and develop the qualities of magic beans
- Donate baked beans lunches to poorer schools
- Start an education foundation for kids learning to cook with healthy vegetables
- Negotiate a peace treaty with giants bullying a neighboring city
- Buy enough farmland for mass beanstalk production and bean harvesting

Jack's aspirations are high aren't they! He is blessed with an ability to allow things to unfold gradually and to address relevant steps as needed. For now he is focusing on two main outcomes in his next 12–24 months.

1. Continue keeping his goose healthy and safe
2. Continue operating his first beanstalk centre

Jack has luckily studied horticulture at college and this is where he met his new girlfriend, Jill. She grew up on a chicken farm and is interested in animal husbandry. They believe they can start to test their golden egg laying reproductive theories within a few years.

They agree Jill will work in Jack's beanstalk centre whilst Jack arranges beanstalk climbing competitions for college students over summer.

He has listed out his leadership gaps and knowledge gaps and can see merit in shifting his business to the mission-accomplished quadrant.

Jack's Knowledge Gaps

Despite operating for two years, Jack doesn't have a marketing plan to include strategy, tactics, and marketing channels. He needs to:

- Model the cash flow needed to get past their initial start up phase
- Understand the best insurances—they suspect they may not be well enough covered
- Put in place better health and safety practices, especially in the beanstalk climbing competitions via higher safety certification. Luckily courses are available as beanstalk climbing is becoming popular in neighboring towns.
- Research and install best practice stock management, payroll, procurement, financial and reporting systems.

- Ensure good tax structures are in place for future growth.
- Seek and better understand options for funding their business during stages of high growth.
- Learn legal implications should Jill end up having a long-term relationship with him. At present she reports to a different manager. Most of her current job consists of walking up a nearby hill to fetch pails of water for the beanstalks.

Jack does not yet truly see the impact of his own survival money style on his business. The way he deals with money, his low attention to detail, and his commitment to the five action steps all need improving so the business can thrive. This awareness will continue to evolve over time.

Over time he will also learn to what degree he needs to employ self-discipline to maintain balance between his beliefs and actions. For now this is a blind spot for him.

Jack's Leadership Gaps

- How to manage a team of people.
- How to be more discerning in his decision-making and take appropriate advice from other experts.
- Understanding and predicting risks, especially the gigantic ones.
- Understanding and applying employment law better so he can discuss performance issues with staff in a more empowered way.
- How to plan better to avoid "fighting fires".

Jack wants to shift to the mission-accomplished quadrant within six months, requiring a high level of commitment. If Jill was already more involved, it would be beneficial to have her perspective and buy in too. Her role may change over time and all things about this structure can be adapted. It is still early days for their relationship.

In the next chapter we will learn how Jack decides to get assistance with his leadership and knowledge issues, as well as how to work out the sequence and priority to improve these gaps. At the moment, Jack's business is operating in the mission critical quadrant. Although Jack has a massive amount of local knowledge on beanstalk growing and harvesting, he lacks some significant leadership awareness. This makes his vertical axis rating low.

Summary of the Chapter

- In order to operate your business in mission accomplished, you need good leadership and knowledge. Most business owners have gaps in these.

- List out your perception of leadership gap and knowledge gaps within your business. Pick them off one by one and improve them incrementally.

- Identify what gaps need to be dealt with by you and which ones should be delegated to experts.

- Learn to create "the shift" from one leadership/knowledge quadrant to another, with least cost and most ease.

- Apply your leadership style, management style and money style to your business issues to achieve your overall wealth.

- Build your critical path and be focused on the sequence and timing needed of each milestone. Review via 90 day planning cycles.

Chapter Thirteen

Stepping Up and Taking Charge

When to Get Advisors on Board and When to "Do it" Yourself

Cost Versus Benefit/Risk of Return

Having trust and belief in what advisors say can be tricky for us entrepreneur types. We need to believe their advice will create results, otherwise it is not worth our money. I look for solid return on investment in order to justify any spend on advisors. If I am not certain I will receive more value than what it costs, I seek evidence there is a sound chance of at least five times my cost available in returns. If I absolutely believe the advice will provide my desired return, I will seek it every time.

How easily we believe is influenced by how much pain we are in, how much we trust the advisor in question, and whether or not we have the cash to spend. That said, any resistance is normally about the trust. If we want something badly enough, we can normally find the cash.

We need to factor the following into our decision:

- the amount of money we can make or save by using the advisor.
- the likelihood our results will be better by using them.
- the amount of time that will still be needed from us even though there is an advisor on board.
- the likelihood our results will be better if we did the task ourselves.
- whether we even have the skills required.
- the time we would need to do the task ourselves.
- whether we have the time required.
- what the timing requirements are—is there enough flexibility for the issue to wait until we can do it ourselves?

Compare your answers to the above points when deciding whether to hire an advisor or not.

Pay Peanuts and Get Monkeys—
Receiving the Right Advice is Gold

This is so true isn't it! I like working with people that are exceptional at what they do. When an advisor offers advice that is like having a hot knife going through butter, I allow them to lead that aspect of my business and return to the areas best suited to my skills. As they are highly competent, I have the utmost belief in their abilities.

I have learned to accept and receive advice from many experts over the years and I believe I know how to distinguish the best. One thing I have noticed is that everyone has an opinion. This is great and I try to welcome them. But I do not take all their advice all of the time. I am discerning depending on the subject matter, and their experience with it.

Where someone provides me with an opinion that appears off their topic, I always note their idea to myself. This is regardless of whether I personally like it. It could turn out to be sound—it may just be that the packaging and context need changing. Let's say one of my team or my clients has a marketing idea. I already have very experienced marketing advisors. I hired them because they have exceptional discernment around our wider strategy and always bring other considerations I hadn't thought of to the table.

I might really love the marketing idea raised by the non-marketing advisor, thinking it a no brainer. But what do I know? I have lots of instinctive marketing knowledge, but I am not an expert. So while my instinct is relevant, it is not the most relevant opinion. Not yet. I would always run the idea past my relevant subject matter expert first to see what they think. And every time I do this, I receive some perspective I hadn't considered. Importantly though, the decision rests in a different place to the advice. Being the person legally responsible for my business, most final decisions rest with me. But not all.

My business is at the stage now that a good number of marketing meetings occur without me. So these concepts are applied by others. It is still very important that I lead, but not necessarily manage. I delegate, rather than abdicate, my responsibilities as the overall business owner. I am still provided with a marketing report and have regular meetings to debrief. I also attend anything that is strategic in nature rather than tactical. I delegate basically everything I can, but still make it my business to know my business, regularly.

Knowing Our Own Strengths and Working to Them

If we each knew our strengths and worked to them, we would be happier in our roles. There are still some aspects of my role that I know are critical for me to be cover. There are also some aspects that would be really dumb for me to do.

The easiest way to focus on our strengths is to write down everything we do in our role, then work out the bits we don't like. These are normally the parts we suck at anyway. And the really fascinating part is that people actually exist who enjoy doing the bits we hate. It's a beautiful thing.

Making Your Advisors a Revenue Centre

Our advisors should make or save us more money than they cost, sometimes over time rather than straight away. As an advisor, I do a quick calculation on the value of my time versus a summary of the things achieved for clients. My assessment may differ to the client's, but at least we are both focused on value rather than price.

Quotes, Fixed Prices and Working Advisors to Deadlines

Advisors should be accountable in terms of their pricing. As advisors we attempt to work towards a client's pricing preference and often find that a fixed fee approach provides the certainty they seek. We need to be very careful around issues that are in or out of scope of the engagement, but otherwise there is a mutual understanding. Sometimes we get so engaged in getting the work done that we forget to stop ourselves and find ourselves out of scope. When this happens it is important to realize that it's not the client's fault and we that we should honor the original fee unless agreement is previously obtained.

From a client's perspective, it is really important to have clarity around cost. Taking a "no surprises" approach is key and both client and advisor play a part in ensuring this occurs. If not, we can inadvertently over commit the client's cash.

Don't Overcommit Your Cash, Slow Down the Deadlines Instead

Remember advisors often lead you, but ultimately you lead your advisors. So working your advisors to deadlines is important. Also remember that sometimes it is more important to get the sequence of important issues correct, rather than have a certain part done by a particular date.

Nearly always a deadline can be shifted (not always though). Although it may be really important to find a way to keep to the original timeline, it is sometimes better (and easier) to shift an activity out a month if cash flow is an issue.

Knowing your financial situation is key here. It is only when we have top of mind awareness around our financial situation that we can manage intentional delays. If we don't know that cash flow is going to be a problem, it's impossible to make decisions to manage to that issue. And before we know it, we have a problem.

No Egos Allowed—Getting Advisors to Work Together

It can be incredibly subtle but valuable when advisors are prepared to work with each other without ego present. There is nothing worse in my opinion than advisors who operate out of low self-esteem or fears such as losing business; the dark side of the ego. It's best when all issues are considered in terms of the client's best interests.

My experience has shown that working as a combined team is significantly better than working in silos. Synergy is formed that is difficult to create when business owners deal with advisors individually or sequentially, especially with issues involving more than one area of expertise. For example, a marketing issue could involve finance advisors that need to address cash flow considerations, as well as HR to address team management.

Get Advisors to Find the Small Cracks, Before They Become Big Canyons

Experts are people who can notice a problem well ahead of the crowd. I have an ability to see cash flow problems a long way ahead of most. But sometimes I might see a cash flow problem only a few weeks out because it is unexpected, or because so much is happening that I haven't kept it top of mind. In other words, sometimes things just slip through the cracks. Experts can discern whether these slips can force cracks into a massive canyon.

Sometimes as business owners we underestimate our own resourcefulness and resilience. Oh and please note, there is a big difference between resources and resourcefulness. If you feel you lack resources in your business, consider that you may have everything you need already. What you actually may lack is the resourcefulness of understanding how to leverage what you already have. Good advisors can help with this.

Future Proof Your Systems

One area that advisors can assist greatly is to help test your disaster recovery procedures. Do this reasonably regularly, especially ones for the absence of key people. Also consider whether your systems are robust enough to withstand strong growth. Strong growth is a good problem, but can also kill a business. Strong growth makes everyone busy and sidetracks them from a future focus.

If we neglect our future business, we remove our ability to improve our now. And the frustrations of our now tend to perpetuate themselves simply because they are not getting addressed. Whatever your current frustrations, improvements are likely possible via a change in your systems, either manually or electronically. Simply improving how you record information can also help manage your future better.

Improving your systems is best done via a combination of advisor and internal support. In our team meetings we have a regular agenda item simply called Opportunities for Improvement. This facilitates small incremental changes. I often check our ideas with our systems advisor who looks after both manual and electronic improvements. The combination of ideas with some added expertise creates efficiencies that would otherwise not be as effective.

Each time we make a change, the intent is to update our operations manual within a week. Sometimes it takes a bit longer. Pretend you are going to franchise your business and this operations manual is the most important thing you need to communicate procedures to the new franchisees. Taking this approach will improve your attitude around consistent improvement.

Jack's Approach to Advisors

Jack recognized that he has some significant knowledge and leadership gaps. This is surprising, especially given how he came into his business. Just because he is good at growing beanstalks doesn't mean he is good at running the business.

Jack is more discerning now than previously in relation to dealing with advisors. He considers the most important areas for his business and decides he needs external assistance in marketing, risk management, systems, HR and CFO expertise. He gets his CFO to work out the cash flows needed for his growth, and puts placeholders into the annual budget for advisory fees.

Jack ensures that all engagements with advisors are based in clear deliverables and managed deadlines. It is helpful for the advisors to deal with each other about Jack's beanstalk business, and he chooses people accustomed to working as part of a wider advisory team.

All of Jack's advisors are business owners too, with senior general and team management experience. They have all experienced the same growth stages that Jack's business is going through. Jack also discusses his leadership gaps with them, especially the HR advisor, but other advisors provide appropriate perspective relevant to their roles and experience.

Jack feels he now has a leadership/management team created from part time, fixed fee experts very accustomed to working together. He has intentionally picked an "A-team", the best people he could find who relate to his size and stage of growth. He doesn't want any B+ team players because achieving the goals is very important to him.

Their focus is toward 90-day goals, adapting the strategy and tactics as circumstances within the business change. They regularly consider the steps and milestones within the critical path because like all businesses, Jack's business requires constant adaptation of the leadership and management issues.

Over time, Jack improves his leadership, knowledge, systems, and results as he learns how to engage with the various people he has brought on board. Importantly, his own staff are brought onto the management team as his business grows. As time progresses, Jack becomes more efficient at leading both his advisors and staff.

Summary of the Chapter

- Consider the cost versus benefit and risks around the return of using an advisor.
- Know if we pay peanuts we get monkeys—but having the right advisors is gold.
- Pick advisors that know how to be a hot knife through butter with their advice.
- Know your own strengths and work to them.
- Make any advisor a revenue center, ensuring they make or save you more money than they cost.
- Consider the regularity of their quotes, fixed prices and working to deadlines.
- Don't overcommit your cash: slow down the deadlines instead.

- No egos allowed—get your advisors to work together.
- It is better to lead not manage, delegate not abdicate.
- Get advisors to find the small cracks before they become big canyons.
- Future proof your systems so you prevent getting stuck in the now.

Chapter Fourteen

Building a Great Team in Your Business

Important Things to Not Forget

I have learned many things about team building. When I refer to the word team, I do not mean only our staff. I include anyone in a position of influence, including advisors, suppliers, affiliates, and customers.

This concept of team applies outside business too; in family, sports, cultural and social contexts.

Why Not Improve By Yourself?

"If you want to go quickly go alone, if you want to go far, go together." I first heard this African saying when Al Gore quoted it at a TED seminar. Creating a great team is fundamentally the most important thing we can do to create influence and long-term freedom. A loyal, well functioning team creates the leverage needed for time and money freedom for everyone involved.

Why is Having a Team-Based Focus Important?

The answer to this question may be obvious or not, depending on your vantage point. A team concept is simply not that relevant to some because they believe that operating in silos works just as well. In addition, some tend to be emotionally disconnected from the concept of working towards a shared vision. In my experience far better results are achieved when all team members are across issues, and their motivations are aligned.

Your job as a leader is to influence so that the vision becomes relevant for all. Sometimes the relevance of team is missing because of differences in individual abilities, or a lack of individual motivation aligned with your vision. There needs to be a "what's in it for me" context to generate a well functioning team over the long term. Focus on this at a practical, real and specific manner.

When we are all in the same boat, rowing in the same direction, heading for the same target and at the same speed, the concept of a combined team focus becomes relevant incredibly quickly.

Remind People of the Relevance to Them

I have learned to not underestimate how frequently people need to be reminded of the relevance of everyone aiming for the same target with a mutual focus. It can be very easy to forget what we are all playing for. This is especially so if team members are not genuinely aligned with the vision, or do not trust it. Part of our duty to influence includes developing a genuine platform of trust.

We need to remember that team members only tolerate words without results for so long. As leaders in our business, we tend to hold onto the vision longer than most. Others need to see results regularly to trust the vision.

Team members can be fickle, especially if they view progress through the lens of judgment. Sometimes this occurs because people do not realize what it actually takes to achieve the results needed. Or sometimes it's simply because they are operating from a place of blame, excuse and denial, forgetting to take ownership, accountability or responsibility for the part they play in the team. We have all done this before, and I imagine we will all do it again. Dissention within the ranks occurs at the most interesting of stages for the most random reasons. Often it's because of a misalignment of values at the source. Open communication can resolve this. Closed communication (or no communication) will not; it is the enemy of team. Every team member is responsible for ensuring communication is 1) open, 2) empowered 3) sourced in sound values and 4) with the right person.

Creating Freedom For All Within Your Team

We should always consider issues relevant for your team's freedom, not just your own. Why would we do something for ourselves that will not also benefit those traveling the path with us? We wouldn't, if we genuinely wish to obtain the influence we seek. Instead we would want all team members to benefit at least as much as us.

As much as possible, apply their values to situations, as well as your own. Understand that all perspectives are valid and try to not mentally crucify anyone who is operating from a slightly different set of values, unless those values are inappropriate. Decisions will still get made; just factor in the perspectives of other team members.

Often we can learn from the experience of others, both good and bad. Below are some of the more subtle aspects I have learned about practical leadership over the years.

1. Ask, Ask, Ask

We tend to forget things if we are running fast with lots on our "to do" lists. This might include what everyone else has to do, their work priorities, and deadlines. I will typically remember 3 of 5 important things each staff member is doing, if that.

Often I have prevented myself feeling like a fool because I checked a staff member's workload before allocating more work. They explain their important priorities before I discuss or request an amendment to a deadline. We assess priorities and amend deadlines for the next week, few days, and month. This helps prevent me requesting too much and staff members feeling loaded up or pressured.

This level of enquiry helps me slow down, the staff member to feel acknowledged, and most importantly, the priorities to be adjusted to constantly changing circumstances. Asking another's opinion if a perspective might have been missed enables decisions and advice to have more depth.

Others often approach the situation from a very different angle to myself. This results in a more effective synergy than addressing an issue in isolation. I bring value that they would not have considered, and they bring value that I would not have considered. Everybody wins.

2. Collaboration is Key

People I know in associated businesses are clever, as are my staff and my clients. In light of this, it would be dumb for me not to collaborate with them. The key to empowered collaboration is to do so without ego.

In my experience, collaboration only encounters problems when one or more parties operate from a disempowered state, such as a place of fear, wanting to impose control, or seeking validation. Employing compassion and an ability to communicate in a tag team approach will help in these circumstances.

That said, if people refuse to collaborate, either from a place of dissention or incompetence, we need to move them away from collaboration altogether, or change their role.

3. Be the Bigger Person

Stop to assess. Sometimes we focus so much on our goals, keeping to plan, or what we are trying to achieve, that we forget to assess what is really going on. If the perception of your team is something completely different to your own, it could be for many reasons. But whatever they are, their perception is their reality. And if things are important to them, I try to make them important to me too. Sometimes though I simply need to be the person making sound decisions for the benefit of the business overall, despite their view.

When a differing perception presents itself that is challenging from a team management perspective in some way, I still do my best to stop. I believe we need to go back to *who am I being* to have created this situation. My intent is clean, so how come people have misunderstood? I don't over analyze it, but I consciously allow space for their perspective.

I also know that for my own behavioral style, it is very important to consider all factors so that I benefit from receiving others' opinions. Are they always right? No. Neither am I. I remind myself that very little matters unless I want to be significant and dramatic. Things tend to worsen when I try to make the situation about someone else's shortcomings. I try to presume the other person has a very good point and I have an opportunity to learn from them. Of course this is more difficult with issues that are hidden by my own blind spots. I trust that someone else will assist in illuminating them. If an issue is important enough, they do. And then we both learn as long as they are prepared to approach things similarly.

4. Remembering to Praise and Guide

Part of "going far together" is the concept of appropriate motivation and support. Most people want to feel motivated and not taken for granted. Feeling appreciated is important and so is feedback that reinforces the parts that are being done well. It doesn't matter whether we personally feel it is necessary to provide positive feedback—what needs to be considered are the team members' needs, and whether they respond well to positive reinforcement. Adapting leadership to a person is as important as adapting leadership to a situation. Offer praise consistently.

When a staff member needs to be corrected, the sandwich approach of commend, recommend, commend nurtures rather than condemns. An instruction to correct or guide is "sandwiched" between two compliments. For some people a more succinct "recommend, commend" works better (i.e. miss out the first commend). What works best depends on the individual's behavioral style. Some people don't trust commending comments because they think they are falsehoods, or simply a precursor to prepare you for a recommend comment. With these people, giving the recommend comment straight off the bat is received as more genuine. They then receive the commending comment that follows as more genuine too.

5. Acknowledge You Mess Up Too

Being able to be the bigger person is a reflection of how much self-worth we have and allows for more balanced conversation. Acknowledging when I have made a mistake as quickly and simply as possible is the quickest pathway to harmony. I don't need to be gushy with an apology, but simply genuinely apologize if needed and/or acknowledge that I could have done something better.

Making mistakes is human. But we can still stay centered and light-hearted about them. Just own them and say sorry when relevant. If you resist apologizing when appropriate, people sense it and sometimes make it mean something unfavorable. I would ask why I am resisting apologizing—that in itself will likely provide some insight that until then may have been hiding.

There is a strength in the ability to simply and genuinely apologize that will not go unnoticed. The opposite is also true.

6. Awards For Being a Doofus

Keep mistakes light-hearted. In our office we have a wooden spoon award for when we do silly things, as well as for when we make big errors (very seldom, thankfully). It is basically a light-hearted acknowledgement of being human and our capacity to make mistakes. Being reminded of mistakes via an overly negative reprimand doesn't create team. It kills it. Of course consequences to shortcomings are needed and consistently applied, but it's important to keep management of the mistake itself well balanced. One major point about this is that we still set high standards and expect to meet them, while trying to avoid mistakes.

An interesting thing happened in our office when we removed the negative significance of mistakes. Our mistakes created opportunities for laughter and team building across the whole business. The energy in our office shifted because of one simple change in focus. But it can also change back if people get too serious or dramatic.

In our office anyone who receives the wooden spoon award provides chocolate to everyone until the next person receives it. And as the boss, I tend to get it often. Staff sometimes give it to me in anticipation of events that haven't even happened yet. Sometimes when I return from a business trip it is on my desk to welcome me home because they know something will have happened; they just don't know what yet. Or I might provide chocolate before I leave, for exactly the same reason. Staff have also been known to good-naturedly query whether the amount I have left them will be enough. Keeping everything light hearted is the key.

7. Daily Huddles

You would be forgiven for realizing that despite considering myself highly competent, I can also at times be reasonably learning impaired (I say this from a light-hearted perspective). When people I respect make suggestions, I often act on them immediately. But sometimes I resist their suggestions for no conscious reason, or simply because I don't yet see the value in them. I dismiss the suggestion before even trying it. This is unusual for me but it still sometimes happens.

One such suggestion was to hold a daily huddle. Four people suggested this to me over a period of two years, people I highly respect and trust. Despite intellectually seeing the value in it, it still took four suggestions before I finally actually *did* it. I was stuck over the apparent opportunity cost.

A daily huddle is where my team meets in full for 15 minutes (we need to manage it not extending too far beyond this) to discuss what we are achieving today and achieved yesterday, as well as share conversations, events and information important for others to know. These meetings have allowed me to transition further out of some aspects of the business, as well as create more knowledge across the team. I wouldn't have believed the change possible from putting this meeting in place unless I had witnessed it for myself. We can review the position of the entire business in 15 minutes. We are currently at the stage where others run the meetings and I only occasionally attend to check in or address something specific. And if anything is challenging, I attend more frequently to provide regular guidance. Sometimes this includes nurturing the team dynamics.

8. Celebrate

Sometimes we get really busy, don't we? It can be a dangerous place when our business becomes all work and no play. To keep our positive team culture it is important to have celebrations. Even if we as business owners don't feel the need, our team might.

Celebrations can happen in a myriad of ways. We have had competitions where we give a prize to anyone who has achieved a challenge. These prizes are not just for ourselves but also for others and include vouchers, $100 notes, the rest of the day off work, money to take a staff member out for lunch, a late start the following day, or dinner for the winner and their partner.

In one December competition the prize was a holiday basket sent anonymously to a person of your choice. One of the most rewarding things I have ever done was buying gifts for these baskets and then delivering them, along with a note saying "someone thinks you are special and wants to thank you for the kind things you do." It was only a small thing, but the joy I saw these recipients feel when receiving their gifts was heartwarming. As we all probably know, to give is to receive; we share in the joy giving creates for another person.

Also remember to celebrate as a team through team building events such as movie nights, go-karting, staff drinks, and such like. Even as small business owners, it is important to do this with our teams so we don't start feeling taken for granted or that work is becoming a grind. Big companies do team building often; smaller companies should remember that even when we get really busy, we should do the same.

9. Teams Win and Teams Fail—Lose as a Team

Making a team goal mean that we win and lose as a team is critical for the overall success of our business. Team effectiveness can create fabulous results for a business. And the opposite is true when your team is feeling disenfranchised. The way we lead is crucial in times of success, and also in times of failure. If a team member makes a mistake, I subscribe to the view that the team has made the mistake together.

Ultimately the mistake rests with me, regardless of who made it. If our processes, training and supervision were not good enough, then as the business owner, it is my cross to bear. But we still bear it together. Our business has strength that way. When mistakes are made we ensure there is appropriate retraining, feedback and correction with the actual team member concerned.

"Putting my money where my mouth is" can be really important when mistakes are made. If we need to put things right, sometimes it costs me financially. All of this requires me to be honorable and courageous and apply our business values consistently. It is about having open, transparent communication with clients and team members alike when challenges present themselves. If we can talk about an issue, we can resolve an issue. Making assumptions around issues of trust and motivations can be very damaging to client or staff relationships and costly to the business.

When addressing issues of failure with a team it is vital to avoid blame, excuses and denial, instead staying in a place of ownership, accountability and responsibility. All team members need to apply this approach. I might be the only one who apologizes for an error. Instead of being upset if the team member doesn't follow my lead and apologize as well, I do my best to stay in a place of zero and focus on what I can do better. But of course I am human too and sometimes want to throw my toys out of the cot. In those circumstances, I simply try to get back to being grounded as fast as I can.

As the owner of the business, if anyone needs to take a fall with a client, it should be me. Any mistakes made by my team (which are seldom) can always be traced back to less than adequate instructions, training, or procedures. I take responsibility for all of these, even if I have delegated them to others. I believe this creates loyalty within the ranks and buys respect from our client base. Remembering these two points makes for a long-term thriving business.

10. Allowing Your Team to Compensate For Your Weaknesses

Acknowledging our weaknesses is powerful. I remind my team that part of their role is to tell me my weaknesses, and vice versa. This is a great way for us to learn from each other. Some of the people I hire are intentionally quite different to me, not only because their roles differ (and therefore their skill sets), but because I want to create a balance of different behavioral styles.

We try to openly acknowledge shortcomings without being significant or serious about it. And I might add, try our best to improve on our own weaknesses. We also acknowledge that we balance out each other's weaknesses with our respective strengths, so that a strength of one of my team balances a weakness in me, and vice versa. Sometimes this works less well than desired, but the intent remains.

11. Team Players, Not Silo Workers

Synergy is created when team members are able to share information and are encouraged to find solutions together, especially when advisors are included.

It is best when advisors have permission to share with other team members for an overall better result, both in terms of cost and outcome.

In my business I have people in place whom I trust and only check in with on particularly critical issues. The rest of the time they deal with each other. Having competent people allows me to release control.

One critical aspect of being a team player, is for team members to understand the importance placed on team goals versus individual goals. Business owner need to decide which deserves higher focus in their business. I place more weight on team goals, while still employing guidelines for individual goals. Both can be managed and rewarded as appropriate for high or low performers.

Interactions between team members can become strained if there are members who insist on having a strong focus on one over the other. The ideal situation is to achieve both team and individual goals, and for all team members to trust and support the dynamics needed within the business for this to successfully happen. Team members need to employ sound values and respond in an empowered manner in order for issues between each other not to arise. Strong and fair leadership is needed in circumstances where they do not.

12. Create the Vacuum For Your Team to Step Into and Release Control

When appropriate, remove yourself from a situation. This creates a vacuum and the team can be given the freedom to fill it themselves, encouraging freedom to succeed and freedom to fail. By appropriately removing myself, it prevents me getting in the way of progress. This can stir some control freak tendencies. People seldom believe me until they actually start trying to delegate areas that until now have been their own baby. The more precious we are about a topic, the more our control freak natures will surface. From a risk management perspective, it is best to cherry pick issues to delegate, starting from the least risk/easiest gain/simplest solution and continuing to pick the next in the list using the same criteria. Examine your own need for control when you find this difficult. Sometimes this control is valid; sometimes it is not. It can occur not only in you but also elsewhere in your team, so watch out for this.

It is surprising to see what issues people want to control. I suggest you closely challenge whether the need for control is valid. Is the need based in disempowered issues? A good way of learning to release control is getting too busy to maintain everything yourself.

Taking a "least risk of the wheels falling off" approach allows us to get used to releasing control at an appropriate pace. Often at the core of a control freak are concerns about standards, competence and trust…basically fear. If we have confidence in who we delegate to, and they adhere to our standards, then we will learn to trust. It can take a while for some of us to do so.

In my experience, these situations are more about me than the person I am delegating to. I'd like to suggest you viewing this in a similar way. For example, perhaps your expectations or training methods are not clear enough, causing confusion. Or you may not create enough clarity as to purpose, expected outcomes and deadlines. If issues arise because they are incompetent, deal with that as a separate issue.

13. Allowing the Cream to Rise to the Top

Frustration is often experienced when feeling a need for control. Control and frustration usually prevent people from empowering their team. Control comes in two types: good and not so good. Good control is about ensuring the business brand is maintained via sound, well laid out systems and processes, and adhering to them. We manage, or control, via the systems and the issues. Not so good control is when we try to prevent failure by containing people's actions so much that there is very little room for freedom. Or we manage failure in a way that disempowers others, rather than motivating them.

Acknowledge that failure is not a bad word. I am referring to failures that steer us, not failures that sink the ship. Remove your frustration. People will observe this and more cream will rise to the top. The concept of failure can be viewed in a very empowering context if we allow ourselves to do so. Are we failing fast enough? This is only a problem when we don't learn from our failure for next time.

Where possible, lead from a place of patience and tolerance. Remember this is all about who you are being, not what your team members are doing. Use a bigger mirror if need be. And once that is done, forgive them their failings and train them better, so the cream still rises to the top.

14. Your Team is Always Watching— and Looking For Someone to Follow

Welcome to the world of things not always being fair. As a leader in business, your team (including those outside of your staff) will be watching you at a level that is commensurate with the extent to which you are trying to change, grow, and lead. Some of them, more often than not, will see you through compassionate eyes. Others might use a lens of judgment, staying happy as long as things go their way, but quick to judge if they do not.

At times, their own ability to deliver or engage may not seem to factor into their perception or opinion of you. I am blessed to be surrounded by people who are usually able to tell me when I have made a mistake and normally do so compassionately. If not, we need to have a conversation at a different level.

Be conscious to the dynamic that people will always be seeking you to lead and also assessing whether they want to follow you. Placing you into this position of leadership may occur, despite it not being an official position of authority. Or perhaps they mentally appoint you as a leader, but you have no idea that they have done so. Sometimes people may see you as a leader even after you have ceased to be in a leadership level appointment. I have many examples in my life of others thinking of me as a leader without me realizing it. Some are funny, others not.

One funny example hits home for me that we are always being watched. One early evening I was out for a run. I live in a relatively safe country where murder or abduction is unusual, so although it is not that clever to run at dusk, it isn't necessarily a death wish either. So there I was out running. Well, to call it a run is very kind; I think it was more a geriatric shuffle. After a few circuits around the block, I became aware of someone behind me. We were the only two people within sight. I sensed the person was walking and that their speed was increasing. I felt that their walking was faster than my run speed, which made me feel a little silly and inadequate.

I wanted to be a safer distance away from this person, so I sped up a little. This decision was partly fuelled from wanting to be safe, and partly to prove I could run faster. I noticed that as I sped up, so did they. This occurred several times until I could tell they were also running. In the midst of this gradual speeding up, I turned my head briefly to get a good look at them. By now it was quite dark and the person was still far behind me.

I sensed they were female, but wasn't sure. After a few more times around the block, I decided to head back home and a voice called out, "excuse me, excuse me!" It was female and sounded friendly, so I chose to stop. I wasn't fearful, but my senses were still on standby, seeking anything unsafe.

A woman jogged over to me, panting heavily. Remembering that I saw my speed as a geriatric shuffle (and most people would think this a kind conclusion), the woman said she wanted to thank me and found me a really good pace maker! She thought I looked like a seasoned runner and really enjoyed trying to keep up with me. She asked if I ran around this block regularly, because she would love to run with me. She thought I looked really athletic which I found really funny.

I laughed on the inside. She was seeing me as a leader, yet I had no idea. I had a different view of my running ability. She viewed me as more experienced and someone she could learn from, while I was preoccupied with feelings of inadequacy.

She was using me as a pacemaker at the same time that I was embarrassed I might be overtaken by a walker! In those few blocks I had made my speed a negative issue for myself and had created a sense of failure. One of my board members, Todd, would be smiling as he reads this. I often joke about his international skill level in marathons, versus my feeble attempts to shuffle around the block.

The point of this story is that leadership relates to individual situations and perceptions, as well as skill levels of those following. It had never occurred to me that my geriatric shuffle could create a leadership situation. Recalling this conversation put a smile on my dial for over a week. Actually it still does, years later.

People can see leadership everywhere. Leaders are like eagles: we find them one at a time and when we do, people want to follow. Leaders need to be worthy of being followed. For their part, followers need to have a desire to go to the same place as their leader, so they are aligned with their vision.

15. Sometimes Relevance is Missing and We Need to Ask Why

As a leader in business I have learned that some things that I regard as highly pertinent and relevant do not even nudge the outer edges of my team's radar (remembering my wide definition of team). I need to recognize this and ask why. If being part of a team were relevant to my team members, logic would follow that they would more often act as a team.

So, either my influence is lacking, or there really is a lack of relevance for them. Either way, the issue is partly sourced in my ability to influence and my ability to learn why their relevance is missing. Remember too that under the Guardians of Leadership Model, influence is a by-product of the cornerstone pillars of resilience, honor/courage, compassion and loyalty. So somewhere in these four pillars may be the root cause of the issue.

I don't give this too much airtime, but when contemplating relevance for others, I first ask myself, what have I done to reduce the perception of these cornerstone pillars in my team members? If I see any connections, I address them with my team and see if their perceptions alter. Especially important to consider is whether I have done anything to reduce their loyalty, and to check for myself if there is anything I can see from the perspective of reduced honor/courage, compassion and resilience that may be an undercurrent in the situation. They may not even be conscious of this undercurrent.

If I cannot see any connection between my application of these cornerstone pillars and my ability to influence, I would ask a general question of any relevant team member; to what extent do they feel my leadership has reduced in relation to these four cornerstone principles? It may only be when you ask the question that they realize the answer. I mean it when I say the issue may be operating at an unconscious level. The issue may be held deeply and difficult to uncover. It is clearly a choice whether you go to that space with your team members, or instead talk around the issue. It takes some skill and ability to approach the topic from a tag team approach, as discussed in chapter five. If the lack of relevance is because the team member is genuinely disengaged, or being disempowered, there needs to be serious consideration as to whether their place in the boat is unhelpful.

These points all have the same core focus; how do we get everyone into the same boat, to achieve the same vision, rowing in the same direction, and at the same speed? If we can work that out as a team, we will arrive at the correct destination, on time and within budget. If not, we won't. If the boat doesn't achieve these things, then all team members, including you, may be swimming to shore alone to find a different boat to help row. All team members need to have enough resilience to identify with this point without finding the concept threatening. Otherwise they will eventually need another boat anyway.

16. All Team Members Need to Seek Opportunities to Lead, as Part of Following the Vision

Whether we are a team member or team leader, we can all demonstrate leadership. The team works infinitely better when everyone considers themselves a leader, regardless of their role. Not surprisingly, team members often don't view themselves as leaders. But if everyone seeks ways to actively lead within the context of their individual roles, overall results will benefit greatly.

Sometimes recognizing ourselves as leaders within the overall vision is not conscious. It can be similar to situations when we fail to recognize our ability to serve one another in our day-to-day tasks, or assist with hosting others at events. Varying contexts of leadership can be found in almost any situation when we look for them. Not seeking ways to lead indicates a disconnection from the overall vision, and an absence of definite purpose in a team leader or member. Or simply indicating a team member has adopted a disempowered approach.

In any given circumstance we need to decide whether we want to be a leader or a follower. Based on my experience I believe there is a strong correlation between:

1. all team members wanting to lead
2. an alignment of the main leader with the four cornerstone pillars

But the team members have to want to engage. They tend to want to lead more within their role when they and their leaders increase their resilience, honor/courage, compassion, and as a result loyalty. The opposite is also very true.

The values of leaders and team members also need to be consistently aligned. Cracks in the application of one's values will impact a team member's desire to lead. Applying the highest level of integrity in:

1. what one does,
2. what one condones in oneself, as well as other team members and
3. what one refuses to ignore to ensure the business values are upheld, will impact the financial results massively. The above can also be very revealing for highlighting the individual values in play.

When a team member chooses to do nothing in a situation that goes against the business values, it highlights either their integrity or lack thereof. What we don't condemn we condone. Take care to realize that inaction can define and incriminate as much as actions. Whatever the circumstances facing your business, talk about them with team members concerned if they are contrary to your values.

Finding another boat, sometimes

Depending on the extent to which team members feel their values are misaligned, especially in regard to the cornerstone pillars, a team member sometimes needs to acknowledge they are in the wrong boat and change vessels.

Sometimes the team leader needs to change the vision and direction of the boat. Life changes so very quickly for all of us, so it can be a very delicate balance between genuine acceptance of a vision, versus paying lip service to the boat one is currently rowing in. It is a most difficult thing to realize as a motivated leader that team members are not in the same boat, despite best efforts to support, train and inspire to that end.

Sometimes as team leaders we need to free up another's future and allow them to recognize they might be best to move on. This can be of benefit for all concerned if they are not well enough aligned with the vision, or they operate from a disempowered place. Any significant vision needs the whole team to get them there. So if they are not on the team, it can benefit everyone if they leave the boat.

If we are not all in the same boat, rowing in the same direction, at the same speed, we need to not leave some too far behind, before forging ahead.

Unless of course it is better for all concerned that they are left behind. If a team member wants to stay in the boat, but doesn't know how to apply a new vision, supporting them in areas in which they want help can be very rewarding for all concerned. It is not until this occurs that our financial results become the best they can be.

JACK AND JILL'S TEAM

Jack's personnel have changed periodically. Jill is now an integral part of the management team. They are recently married and she has an active role in both this business as well as focusing on the development of some of their other business ventures.

Part of Jill's main focus has been trying to harness the golden egg laying genetics of their goose, with not much luck to date. They are both very interested in creating an income stream that is not reliant on their own personal efforts. They hope to benefit in perpetuity from doing the work once. Keenly aware that few achieve this type of income generation, they are focused and inspired, investing a lot of their time and effort into it. It will be some years before we learn how they got on.

Together they manage their team and performance of the business. They continue to utilize their A-Team of management advisors as relevant, meeting with them at least every 90 days to discuss strategy and practical implementation. Their A-Team members focus is to support Jack and Jill to become like hero CEOs. Both knowledge and leadership skills are passed across from the experts.

Their staff are more competent and engaged than previously. Despite this, the team still needs good leadership, management and focus to avoid difficulties. Most of the team players are in the boat, but occasionally they need to realign to have the right people on board. They consider this with the assistance of their A-team members.

Summary of the chapter

- If you want to go quickly go alone, if you want to go far go together. Creating a team is necessary if we want our business to go far.
- Ask, ask, ask your team their priorities, so you can be reminded before you load them up with yet another deadline. Include their opinion into your decision-making.
- Collaboration is key to continual development and creates a synergy from wider expertise being involved in problem solving.
- Be the bigger person. Stop to recognize that your perception may be very different to others and that theirs is also highly valid.
- Acknowledge you mess up too and recognize what you need to apologize for.
- Make mistakes light-hearted within your office and have a reward system but try to not make mistakes again.
- Have daily huddles to keep in touch so everyone knows what's going on and you can manage the whole business quickly.
- Remember to celebrate success.
- Teams win and teams fail—lose as a team. The whole team gets the team across the line. Your team needs to know you have their back and if anyone is going to fall on their sword in front of a client it will be you.
- Allowing your team to compensate for your weaknesses allows you to openly have some. Transparency around this creates better overall results.
- Team players, not silo workers, are needed if you want to go far. People who are not accustomed to teams might need to be taught how to do this and why it's valuable.
- Create the vacuum for your team to step into. Remove yourself from the situation so they can have freedom to shine and freedom to fail.
- The cream will rise to the top if you let it. Remove frustration.
- People are always watching. Be the leader you would want them to follow and understand that perspectives will often differ. Worry less about the perspectives of the disempowered, but still manage them well.
- Sometimes relevance is missing for our team members so ask why.

- Within the contexts of our own role, we all need to seek opportunities to lead, serve, host. Maintain integrity at the highest level and take care to not be guilty by association through your inaction. What we don't condemn, we condone.
- Sometimes a team member needs to find another boat, or else realign with the vision.

Chapter Fifteen

How to Delegate

Make Your Business Better Instead of Worse When You Release Control

We've referred to some delegation and control concepts and now we will get more specific. The key question is, why should we release control?

Unless we do, the business cannot grow. Neither can we. Both are needed if we are to achieve the freedom we seek. We need freedom to achieve the things we want, either for our chosen causes, or our own version of wealth. To get that, we need to release control. This sounds easy, doesn't it? Yes and no. This chapter details strategies I use that have allowed me to release control—all learned over the years the hard way by making mistakes.

Eating the Elephant One Bite at a Time

I believe the reason business owners are challenged by releasing control is largely because we don't even realize the areas where we could release more of it. This often involves issues others believe should be delegated. As business owners, we are often Kings or Queens of justification and think something a valid reason, even when really it is not. Sometimes maintaining control can put a significant handbrake on a business, so we do need to consider letting go quite carefully.

Regardless of the significance of an issue, releasing control should normally happen gradually, over time. This allows for a reasonable handover and for unpredicted issues to arise and be resolved. No matter how good our planning, we cannot foresee every challenge.

Where is the fear and control playing out in your business; is it in you, or is it in your staff? Sometimes control issues are found within the team. Delegate as appropriate and when one of the team has resistance about receiving more responsibility, recognize this and manage both your expectations. Sometimes the resistance is valid, sometimes not.

Taking a Leap of Faith—Who is More Scared?

Let's face it; releasing control can be scary, for both you and your team, but it doesn't need to be. Look through all areas of your business and continue to manage the areas that concern you the most. Reduce inherent risks with good training, good operational procedures, good systems and a thorough review process. Have the right people in the right seats.

Personally I think that if we are feeling anxious about something, it can be helpful for all concerned if we admit it. Doing this humanizes us. We need to recognize we are sensing resistance and find a way to release control safely anyway, maintaining good systems and standards so we continue to ensure that safety.

Know Thyself: How to Surrender and Get Out of Our Own Way

When we experience fear/apprehension, it can be because we just don't have the right people in the right seats. Or it can be because of something within us. Sometimes we need to learn to surrender to our apprehension and allow the situation to just 'be.'

This surrender number can sometimes take years to truly achieve. From my own experience, some things are easy to surrender to, others are not. Surrender to one new thing regularly that scares you (or you simply sense resistance about) and just try that. Be committed to finding a way to teach someone else this one task, why you do it and what is most important about it to remember. Pick small things to begin with.

Choose to surrender to your apprehension, or choose not to; just make the choice conscious. Sometimes our fear is based in an absence of capable resource to delegate to, so we "do it ourselves." One thing I will say to that conclusion is this: remember the Guardians of Leadership Model. If we have enough influence in our world, we can always find a way to be resourceful, meaning delegation doesn't need to be scary. We just need to employ more influence to gain the right resource needed.

If we are focusing on being resourceful, we will always find enough resources. We can make massive progress in our resources when we surrender to whatever emotional blockage about fear or control is getting in our way. Then the energy improves and assistance arrives as if by magic.

Releasing Fear, Building Trust

We need to learn to trust things will be okay. Trust yourself, or trust spirit, or trust your advisors; just trust whatever is valid for you! Whatever you belief in, trust this will keep you safe. We all need safety—and we all need to trust in order to feel this. Trust allows us to release the apprehension. Releasing your fear can only occur if we learn to trust; there is no middle ground.

In case it is not already obvious (it may well not be yet, depending how connected you are internally), releasing fear is needed so our financial beliefs improve and our money style gets closer to Sorted. My observations of clients and team members over the past 25 years strongly suggest that people who operate out of a basis of fear seldom achieve their version of wealth. They sometimes achieve money, but not the wealth they seek. Remember the wider definition.

So if we want to achieve our version of wealth, we need to learn to trust. This concept applies regardless of your role within an organization, business owners and employees alike. It also strongly applies within your family. We therefore need to explore further any underlying issues creating distrust in ourselves, or others. To not do so will hold us back, sometimes permanently. We are the only thing stopping ourselves surrendering to this.

Document Processes

Let's not forget that at a practical level, we also need sound process in the delegation and implementation of any new task. This allows us to surrender the task to others. Sound, documented process helps us release control, and others can learn/apply the process effectively. Whenever you delegate a task for the first time, briefly document the following for the person learning it—the task's purpose, important values/perspectives involved, the process itself, common mistakes to avoid, and time allocation suggested. Include a checklist for them to review prior to finishing the task. Although brief, the documentation should be done from the perspective that if someone was not told anything, they could understand the written instructions alone. Remember to include the obvious points as well as the subtle.

Understand the learning style of your protégé and work to their strengths—kinesthetic, visual or auditory. Adapt your teaching method appropriately. And write everything significant down about what is being taught so next time around you can teach it even faster to the next person.

This above all, to thine own self be true. Remember your values, always.

As I mentioned earlier, my Dad used to quote this most famous Hamlet speech often.

"This above all: to thine own self be true, and it must follow, as the night the day, thou canst not then be false to any man."

It's easier said than done, huh? Don't believe that any of us are perfect; we're not. But consider this: what exactly is your molecular structure when the chips are down? Individual character is revealed very clearly when we are grumpy, stressed, tired, resentful, or broke.

Anyone can be honorable when things are easy or everyone agrees with conclusions reached. How honorable are we with our financial and other commitments though when things get tough? How quickly do we run away, or else judge? How likely are we to have real conversations with those involved, because we believe it is important to discuss the issue? How easily do we simply act without talking and not worrying about another's perspective? Where is our loyalty placed and how accurate are our memories? How empowered are our perspectives rather than being fear or control based? How easily do we want to discuss things at this level? Many knee jerk reactions are misplaced feelings of control, based in fear.

Everybody judges. It's even easier for someone to do when we stick our head above the crowd. Somebody will often try to chop it off if they not feeling empowered. But it is how we react when someone else acts that matters most. I suggest we simply stay true to ourselves at all times and try to reduce or remove being false to others concerning finances or other issues. All we have is our own integrity.

The Link Between Delegating and the Ability to Honor Financial Commitments

If someone does not perform as well as perhaps you would have, then delegation can negatively impact our profit. This in turn can impact our ability to honor financial commitments (and therefore our ability to be true to everyone). So if delegation does not work well, it becomes more difficult to stay true financially to others.

It is also more difficult to stay true financially to those to whom you delegated. One key question is who's responsibility it is to wear any financial consequences arising from delegation not working well. Is it purely your responsibility, is it the team's responsibility, or is it one individual's responsibility? Who pays the price of poor performance? I think it depends.

Each person makes different decisions in relation to varying circumstances, and we are all impacted by the consequences. Personally I am a fan of pushing any consequences to the area where the performance or behavior was lacking. But there needs to be a balanced view employed as to the cause of the poor performance—sometimes it occurs from poor training.

We need to make a decision as to what is more important: 1) sticking to our goals and doing our best to communicate fully about issues and consequences, so we stay true to ourselves and others, or 2) worrying about what others think when they try to chop us down for something we did wrong, in circumstances where we did our best to communicate well. As much as possible we need to make our decisions from a balanced and empowered state.

It is important to consider all vantage points for delegation issues which impact financial commitments and results. This is because an error in judgment re: the appropriateness of delegating can result in an inability to pay your debts (if the error is significant enough).

Inaccurate Assumptions Underpinning Judgment Around Finances

In my 25 years experience as a qualified accountant, I can tell you that little of what others believe or presume about someone's financial circumstances is accurate. Others do not know your financial situation. Often nobody outside your innermost circle does. On my reckoning, the impressions assumed by people are only loosely accurate about half of the time.

We can often have circumstances that others know little about—family members we support, debt that needs servicing, health issues, costly and acrimonious matrimonial issues, business interests gone bad, mental health issues impacting….you name it. And it is often the case that few other people know these type of issues are relevant.

Others from the outside looking in however, can make assumptions about someone's circumstances and also base their financial actions or judgment towards people on these. And often they do this without having the common courtesy to discuss an issue with them before jumping to conclusions. This is human nature at its finest, isn't it. Not.

So if someone is criticizing you for being false and you are not, don't wear it. Leave it out of your wardrobe. But do talk about it. Whenever something arises, communicate to those relevant, so you are given the opportunity to discuss the issues.

Staying Honorable

Remember to forgive yourself when you completely and utterly forget things that are important to others financially. For example, we might genuinely forget to pay someone money that is owed which for them is a big deal. Part of being true to ourselves is accepting our mistakes and re-tacking once realizing our error. Remember to apologize for the part you could have done better. Personally I think it is never too late to do so.

Staying honorable is a big aspect of growing your business and becomes even more important when delegating. Have you considered that we become a guardian of leadership each time we delegate? We need to guide and protect so the leadership or delegation request we pass on to others is kept safe. So we need to ensure our staff or others being given any instructions can see that we are doing our best to guide them well. And that guidance will continue as necessary.

They also need to do their part and perform the assigned task competently, as well as need less guidance over time as they become practiced. But the fact remains that most poor performance issues are firmly sourced in how competently we are leading. Doing so from a place of honor permeates your entire organization. We can well remember this when we are next disgruntled with the performance of an employee. If they are in the wrong role, that is our fault for keeping them there. If they are in the right role, train them better.

Staying true to your values while delegating, is an example of an issue in the Honor/Courage Pillar in Chapter 11's Guardians of Leadership Model. Having the real conversations, being genuine with your actions even if the outcomes are challenging, and being vulnerable takes courage.

An absence of courage to talk or act appropriately with the correct and relevant person, (rather than gossiping with others), can be a reason many fail, or self-sabotage. This is especially true for topics involving money or topics about performance, subsequently resulting in money issues. Embrace any opportunity to discuss the issues without reacting emotionally, or running away from the topic or relevant person. Avoid discussing the issue with the wrong person. Doing that lacks integrity.

Checking In On Your Team

Our discussion so far relates mainly to our work team (which remember is not restricted to just staff). Other teams, like family, friends, and sports teams are also relevant. We have to remember to check in with them if we have a need, putting aside any idea that they should be checking in with us since we are the ones with an unfilled need. The person with the need should be a demand to get it resolved, actively engaging in a manner that achieves resolution from a common ground.

One of the most difficult things I have found that prevents me being really good at checking in with my own team members, is that I can easily forget some of the specifics around things like agreed timing, deadlines, status etc. Thankfully others remember some aspects very clearly. Busyness can create a few communication problems if I am not careful. To ensure communication is effective, I document things well, acknowledge how busy we all have become (not just me), and have staff I can inherently trust. I do my best to check in with them regarding their opinions, progress etc.

If I trust my staff, I know they will tell me the truth about anything. Trustworthy staff will tell me the good, the bad and the ugly in an unbiased manner, without mischief. If I do not trust them, or doubt their ability to communicate openly and truthfully, I shouldn't have them as staff. I don't need to over complicate it.

Keeping Your Frustration in Check & Examining Your Own Insecurities

I need to own that I have had periods in my business where I have experienced frustration for an extended period of time. And at these times, everything was about a lack of resource and a lack of the right people for the roles we needed. What I also needed to acknowledge for myself was the lack of leadership and ability to inspire at levels we most needed. And to simply focus on making that better over time with the help of others.

I also needed to examine closely my own insecurities. Sometimes I needed a massive mirror for this one—there were days it needed to be so big I wasn't sure it would fit through the door. This was because I had trouble seeing them. But I can laugh at myself for this. I don't need to make moments where I messed up significant. It is part of what makes us all special. I just try to not let it impact how or when I delegate. We need to lighten the hell up, and laugh, a lot. It is amazing how little frustration there is when people are laughing whole-heartedly, like nobody is looking.

Having the Right Team

I love my team. It makes me smile that some people may not even realize that I think they are on it! Sometimes people in my wider team might forget I include them in my version of team. Regardless, it is a privilege to work with them and I am proud of their efforts to do their best.

We all have different skills. At times I have needed to look very closely at our strengths and weaknesses, and decide whether we need other team members to take us down the path we are heading. On occasion we need to change our team members (again in a wide context).

Everybody in the team needs to decide whether they are in the boat with both feet, even if they are only occasionally needed to help row. Team members that do not align with the vision should get out of the boat altogether. Sometimes the team is committed, but the crewmembers are on the wrong seats. Change that when needed and don't prolong it. When we have the right people on the right seats, there is more plain sailing towards our goals.

Crossing the Street—Together or Alone?
Managing Tasks So Cracks Don't Appear

We get to choose as leaders whether we lead or manage, or worse, neither. Ownership, accountability, and responsibility are three words that can improve almost any situation in the context of leadership. It is far more important to focus on being a good leader because then all team members can focus on their respective aspects of management.

A good question to ask is how do you behave when nobody's looking? This is important *because you will know*. Being truthful about who we really are allows us to feel authentic as sound leaders. The person in the mirror is the most important of gauge this. When we lead, we lead via example and inspiration. When we manage, we expect others to do as we say, instead of as we do. I don't know anyone who doesn't do a bit of "management" in this context at times. And some of the time it is valid.

We also need to learn from our mistakes. A big part of this is to change our procedures whenever we learn something isn't working. One example might be when we have a customer complaint that could have been prevented via different processes—change the process so it doesn't happen again. Good training and communication are crucial when delegating so customers are delighted regardless of who assists them. I think of the following analogy when training…and sometimes it even works (I mean that light-heartedly).

If I am teaching a child to cross the street, I have a choice as to how to do this. I can either:

- Hold the child's hand and cross with them because the task is new or scary, or
- Stand on the sidewalk, suggesting where and when to cross—they may know what to do, but need help with sequence or timing, or
- Stand on the sidewalk and watch in case they need help, looking out for any danger—guiding from a distance and letting them know I am available for questions, or
- Tell them to go cross the street, sometimes getting them to tell me when they have done it if it's important for me to know—they basically have it covered at this point and can discern when to involve me.

Taking a staggered approach depends on the competency of the person at hand for that given situation. Consider both the competency of the person and also look at the situation itself. If need be, I go through all the stages with someone until they learn, even though I may think it would be easier for me to just say "go cross the street."

Whatever You Do Duplicates—Bad Stuff Duplicates 10 Times More Than the Good Stuff

A mentor of mine taught me this principle about 20 years ago. I hated accepting it at the time and I am yet to fall in love with it. Why can't people just copy our good habits and overlook our bad ones? I get that it isn't "fair," but human nature is that we tend to seek out areas in our leaders that lack integrity.

You may feel uncomfortable acknowledging this one for yourself, but this is what I used to subconsciously do as a staff member. I don't think I am alone, except perhaps in relation to my ability to admit it. Any perceived shortcoming in the boss can become a valid excuse for our own shortcomings.

Sorry, no. At some point, we serve ourselves much better when we can apply our standards all of the time, regardless of the circumstances surrounding us. To do this we need a conscious awareness of what these are, compassion without judgment for others, and integrity in ourselves. Otherwise we will sell ourselves short. Sometimes our standards differ to those of others. In these situations the best approach is to discuss it with them without judgment—and part ways if you cannot align well enough.

As a boss, we need to remember that despite my comments above, our bad stuff will still be copied more often than our good stuff, so take care with what you don't do. I ask myself a simple question whenever I want my team to do something: am I doing that same thing well enough? Often there are good reasons for me to not do what I am asking my team to do. In those circumstances, I had better hope my team agrees, otherwise they might use this as an excuse for their own behavior or results. Communication assists with ensuring everyone understands why there are valid inconsistencies.

Choosing Whether to Interfere With a Butterfly's Wings— Do We Want Them to Never Fly?

Sometimes we stay too close when we delegate, feeling a need to maintain control. Our staff sometimes prefer this if it make things easier for them. This dynamic can be very subtle. Believe me this is definitely one of those, "we are here to learn what we are here to teach" issues.

I was a playcenter mom for 8 years, part of the team responsible for the early childhood education of up to 25 children each session. It taught me a lot along the way, and is one of the proudest and most fun things I have done. It amuses me that lots of what I learned there I can also apply to my business. Dealing with a 3-year-old tantrum requires similar techniques to dealing with a disempowered adult. It fascinates me that sometimes a 3-year-old seems to return to an empowered state quicker!

One of these playcenter learnings involved butterflies about to emerge from their cocoons. There would be 25 under-5-year-olds hovering with bated breath for each butterfly to emerge. Once this happened the butterfly would wave its wings for an extended time to let them dry.

Every child wanted to touch the butterfly's wings as they were flapping. But if they did, there was a very real chance that the wings would be damaged or torn, and the butterfly would never fly. They didn't know this and only the bigger, more experienced children understood when told. Most of the children simply knew what they wanted to do. They had their own perspective of importance about the situation, and their individual relevance within it.

To allow a good chance of success, the children needed to leave the butterflies alone with their process. They found this difficult to understand; they only wanted to "help." If they had interfered, the butterfly may have had its path and abilities irreversibly altered, causing it to fail, despite the good intentions of those watching over them.

Sometimes delegating to our staff is exactly the same. We need to allow them to grow, firstly going into a cocoon, and then re-emerging different. And it is at this time of emergence that we need to take most care. We need to allow them to transition, and sometimes fail. We need to protect all of this from the customers of course, but still allow the failure internally. Of course review processes for both staff transitions and failure should also be in place.

It takes something to allow others in your team to risk failure; it risks brand integrity and could compromise the success of the business. But business is full of varying risks and we need to manage the ones we can. Delegating allows both the team member and business to grow, so we can eventually move into other things as desired.

Also get others to help train your team, and to train you. Allow your staff to do things their way, and don't worry too much if that way differs to your own (as long as your values are being applied consistently and legal risks managed). Remember, the concept of failure is not to be avoided, but to be embraced. It is through failure that we learn and also build resilience.

Like most things, there is wisdom found in the discernment of whether to risk team members learning through the chance of failure (or temporary defeat). Some things are too important not to step in. Discernment is fundamental and we need to choose wisely. If something has the potential to create a significant issue, I step in and assist in managing that issue. This requires that I know enough to discern both need and timing. Sometimes I get this right and sometimes I do not. The main point is to improve the balance and ability to discern well over time.

JACK AND JILL'S AREAS OF CONTROL

Our fairytale couple has some interesting control issues. They have recently read this chapter and have some insight, albeit with vulnerability, illuminating a few of their blind spots.

Jack is often viewed by others as having a highly reckless and cavalier nature, appearing foot loose and fancy free. And yet he swoops down on the smallest detail when it is not done to his satisfaction by others. He withdraws into himself and carries a grudge that he finds difficult to shake. He sometimes creates unrest and undermines confidence in others because of his inability to release control.

Guiding and correcting is a valid need; that is not in question. It is the way in which he leads that Jack could do with some insight around. Jack realizes his whole organization could benefit greatly from documenting processes (currently none are documented) and managing training back to the process each time this "need to correct" occurs. The consistency of working to documented process is Jack's personal conduit for being able to release control. Doing this will be a turning point in his leadership. Taking care to not turn into the red tape brigade, Jack starts gradually implementing change in the way things are done in his business. Human error is greatly reduced over time and Jack's sense of comfort in delegating improves.

Jill on the other hand has very different control issues that impact her ability to delegate well. People don't like her approach with them; she is perceived as lacking compassion and seems very direct, judgmental and bossy. Her mood changes at a moment's notice and she is prone to either anger or sulking. When she is delegating, she prefers to do things herself because she feels nobody else is as good as her. (I think we all know quite a number of people that sometimes fit this bill.)

We all have moments of being something less than that which is to be desired. Drawing on our acceptance of humanness from within the compassion pillar can help Jill's team with their ability to float on through the conversations when dealing with her. They forgive her for her insecurities, but also try to discuss a suggested improved approach with her.

Jill's control issues impact not only her delegation method, but the way in which the team feels when they receive instructions, carry out their duties and maintain a sense of engagement within the business.

Her need for control comes from her childhood. From a very dysfunctional childhood background, she often still experiences a shakiness sourced in the way she was parented. This instability comes from fear that erupts from the depths within. This fear represents itself in low self-worth, a need for control and desperate need to erect a façade. Most around her can see this, despite it seldom being named. Her team generally have compassion for her background, but also wish she could operate from her wound less often.

Jill could benefit from some healing in relation to her past. I may sound a little cheesy, but Jill needs to learn to genuinely love and accept herself more. She will then be better able to operate from a place of authenticity, and her disempowered responses (which impact her delegation methods) may improve. Considering these issues takes courage for Jill to address. Gradually over time, an improvement in her inner feelings correlates with an improvement in her ability to lead her team.

Summary of the Chapter

- When it comes to releasing control, eat the elephant one bite at a time, making small changes incrementally.
- Acknowledge that you are taking a leap of faith and that this is okay.

- "This above all, to thine own self be true." Always remember our values including integrity.
- Master how to keep your frustration in check and at the same time, check in on your own insecurities.
- Manage tasks so cracks don't appear, by crossing the street together when needed.
- Whatever you do, duplicates: bad stuff duplicates 10 times stronger than the good stuff.
- Choose which areas of your business are okay to allow your team to learn through the risk of failure (or temporary defeat) so you can leave the butterfly's wings alone.

Chapter Sixteen

Managing that Oh So Lovely Symptom of Poor Cash Flow

I often refer to my belief that our treasure ships come in over calm seas. Here we will explain how to build cash and discuss things which may prevent the seas of your cash flow being calm.

Cash flow is an output. So we need to examine the inputs needed to improve this output. Some of the generic cash flow inputs include most key performance indicators such customer numbers, average value sales values, average purchase times per month or annum, customer churn rates, productivity percentages, conversion rates, gross margins, stock turn levels, debtors days, to name some of them.

Cash flow or Profit?

One really obvious aspect about poor cash flow is that sometimes it simply reflects a business that is not profitable. We fundamentally need to offer something in our business that people want enough to cover costs. If we aren't achieving this, poor cash flow is very tricky to resolve.

So if you are struggling with cash flow, your first point of reflection is to ask whether you have what is needed for a profitable business. If so, is it just temporarily cash strapped? Or is there a fundamental issue creating poor cash flow at a systemic level? Let's assume that your business offerings have enough demand to make adequate profit (most months at least). If they don't, managing cash flow is a futile topic and you should discuss creating enough profit with your Chief Financial Officer (CFO) without delay.

Why is Positive Cash Flow so important?

Ask anyone who has experienced both positive and negative cash flow this question. Get them to list how negative cash flow impacts them, and compare this situation with times when cash is easy. Negative cash flow can be stressful, impacting performance, happiness, relationships and business growth. Extremely negative cash flow can put someone's house on the line, attack their sense of security, and affect their health.

Equally important is the ability to act like a squirrel and 'save nuts for winter,' accumulating enough cash for later. In most cases, this means having a beginning goal of one month's operating expenses always available. Over time and depending on the size and type of business, this is often best built to three months expenses. With some seasonally dependent and specific business types, having even more stockpiled is better still.

Poor cash flow is only ever a symptom of how the business is going— an output or indicator that something else is not working well enough. Profit is another output that has a high correlation with cash. Profit should occur every month unless it is seasonally dependent. So you need to make generating enough profit a mental and actual necessity. This is because you won't have sustainable cash, unless you first have adequate profit. Many business owners take a significantly high level of risk by working on making *future months* become profitable, instead of focusing on making *this month* profitable.

As the saying goes, cash is king. This is because it affords you the ability to do what you want. People with cash can make choices that others cannot.

It doesn't matter which one of these reasons resonates for you for improving your cash flow—you only need one reason to want to change. But let's keep it simple: how would you feel if cash was more readily available to you right now? Consider your wider version of wealth. If you know you would feel better with different or better cash flow, act on that feeling to generate motivation, and apply the following suggestions.

How to Build Cash

Working to your money style is important when approaching the best way to generate cash. One of the most common things I have come across over the past 25+ years is people getting stuck in the 'how to make this better.' These are often the same people who also feel constrained by negative cash flow. They feel like they have little choice in how they pay their commitments and/or themselves when there is simply not enough money. They forget (or simply don't know) that *any* improvement is a valid improvement. Small improvements to actions and attitudes can be the start of big shifts in the energy around their money.

The general steps to building cash are listed below. Some of these center around improving your cash flow and others around ensuring it becomes no worse. I realize that some of these may almost seem insulting, as they are so obvious—I list them mainly for those of you that realize these things, but aren't actually *doing* them.

- First and foremost, ensure your business makes a profit every month, unless to not do so is a temporary part of your business plan. If your business isn't making a profit, get some help with changing that quickly. Seriously. Consider all avenues for ensuring income is higher than expenses.
- If you are not in business, ensure your household has more income than expenses each month. Both these first two points come back to living within your means.
- Know how your actual position is tracking against the planned (budget) position.
- Understand how much additional capital is needed in situations where profit is absent or you are in strong growth phase—assess the risks of this situation and make decisions around the future viability of your business. Train wrecks are sometimes waiting to happen so

get some outside perspective on this. Strong growth can be equally as risky as low profit.

- When your business is making a profit, pay yourself first and make this an achievable amount. Gradually increase your own pay to ensure you get to market salary levels as soon as possible. If your business is not making a profit, find a way to get paid somewhere outside of your business. This helps ensure the net equity position of your business gets no worse and you have enough cash for your household expenses.
- Know the dollar figure you need for biweekly or monthly expenses.
- Have a business and personal budget and stick to it.
- Once you have built up at least a fortnight's expenses in savings, start to put easy, small amounts aside into a savings account every time you are paid anything.
- Live within 90% of your personal income (know whether you are or not) —find a way to achieve this. Contrary to popular opinion, it isn't impossible in the vast majority of circumstances.
- Apply the other 10% of your income to a combination of debt reduction and/or an increase to savings—say 5% to each but this depends on individual circumstances.
- Increase the amounts you save, gradually over time. Small steps can be important to achieve consistent sustainability.
- It's hugely important to work on the above gradually, rather than trying to transition all at once—always remind yourself that the habits of savings and philanthropy are more important than the amounts.

Your Core Beliefs Underpinning Your Finances

The above are all important to operate under for improving cash flow. But more important is whether there are financial issues occurring because of attitudes you have about yourself, money and your business.

Your financial situation is a direct reflection of your wider world. If there are areas of your life that remain unresolved from your past, not in sync, or out of integrity with your values, your cash position will be a mirror of those areas that need work.

Reasons for Business Failure

Clearly it is important that the business "plans the work and works the plan." Not doing this is a major reason businesses fail. There are many other reasons for business failure including sometimes people just don't want what you've got—i.e. it is just not a financially viable concept.

Four other common reasons for business failure include:

1. Lack of capital
2. Lack of skills
3. Lack of understanding of applicable tax laws
4. Death or disability of key personnel

All of these reasons can be well managed. So too, can a lack of profitability, as long as the business concept itself is sound and the public are receptive to it. Request your CFO covers these topics with you as they may not suggest it themselves. In relation to the "Lack of skills," remember to assess the team you need for improving this. Any legal issues need legal input, any marketing issues marketing input, etc. Get the correct expertise for the type of commercial issue in question.

Financial Questions to ask yourself

If these types of commercial gaps are properly addressed and your business is still not progressing how you want, answer the financial belief questions below for yourself. Perhaps you have lots of money, but you do not yet have the time freedom you seek. Make sure you are truly honest and open with yourself when considering these questions.

In cases where the answers are not what you would want for yourself, go back to considering the root cause and some of your financial inhibitors. The business itself may be fine; it may be you as the owner (or else your team members) that still has issues to be resolved. It is also often the case that the business itself is not at fault, but rather the key personnel running it in relation to their own money style and financial inhibitors.

If you have a business partner other than your life partner, the questions about fears etc. should be considered for every key person. Taking due care about these discussions via a professionally facilitated session is recommended because these areas can become quite personal for people and may be best done one on one.

The first question to ask is how much money would make you feel significantly more in control of your finances. For the purposes of this example, let's say it is $100k. Then ask the following questions applying a similar example, mentally inserting your individual correct number instead of the $100k:

- If I transferred that $100k amount into your bank account, what would you want to do with it?
- How much of it would be to pay off debt? How much would be for savings?
- How much would you leave in the bank account?
- How much additional money would feel like too much for you personally to cope with?
- What fears, if any, do you have around money?
- What goals, if any, do you have around money?
- On a scale of 1–10, how much certainty do you want around money issues?
- What relationships do you currently have with people about money issues—how often do you change advisors? i.e. banks, accountants, financial planners, insurance agents. Why do they change? Is there a common theme as to why?
- Have you ever had investors in your business? Do you still, and if so, how long for? How often have these people changed? Why? Is there a common theme as to why?
- On a scale of 1–10, how do you rank your competency around money issues?
- On a scale of 1–10, how do you rank your self-discipline around money issues?
- Are you getting the most return on your investments? How do you stay informed about that?
- Do you save regularly? For what purpose? How much of your income in percentage terms?

- On a scale of 1–10 to what extent do you buy things because you deserve to have them?
- How often would you buy something you don't really need, but just want for the fun of it?
- How often do you buy something that results in you being stretched financially?
- Do you feel you really struggle with your finances? How long has this been the case?
- What do you believe is getting in the way of your finances being better? What could you do differently to change this?
- Is your perspective on money different to that of your partner's? If so, how specifically?

What to do with the answers to the above questions

The purpose of the above is to get you to have a closer look at your money style and to acknowledge for yourself the way your money style may be playing out in your business. Where are your fears? Where are your actions? What emotional needs do you have? Are they trust/giving based, or control /fear based? Your answers will reaffirm which money style you are.

Remember that regardless the extent to which our awareness becomes heightened, we still need good balance between financial beliefs and financial actions. Know that to not create balance will be your nemesis. Decisions will always need to be sensible, just not fear based. Sound controls and processes will always be needed, just not ones sourced from an unhealthy need to enforce control onto others.

A heightened awareness of all of the above will influence the actions you take with your cash transactions on a day-to-day and month-to-month basis. It is through improvements in your awareness that your cash flow will be impacted the most. Especially so with improvements over time in your awareness around the way financial energy flows when your beliefs are in the highest levels.

The Impact of Your Team on the Financial Results

As a small/medium business owner, your business is a reflection of you and other people within it. Help your staff understand the role they are playing in the overall ability to generate results. Are any of them operating out of fear or unhealthy levels of control? This will need to be addressed if so.

Get your team to read this book to align with what needs to improve. They should each have a working copy, to do their own highlighting and make notes. This is a study book, not a novel. Treat it as such. If achieving your financial freedom and wealth is important for all of you, they would be serious about wanting to learn and adapt as well.

Your Vision and Goals

Revisit your business vision and goals developed from chapter twelve and the critical path created for them. Do any of these steps, or the sequence of them, need revision due to increased awareness of your money style and the impact of this on your business? Do any of the five financial action steps need their own step in your critical path?

If it is not already there, also include in your critical path steps to take for your team to increase their understanding around their money style, behavioral preferences and biases. Help them understand how they are operating and provide perspective on how this impacts overall results.

All of us have differing issues to address. Most people can identify with one main money style; some of us identify with two. It is relevant for you and your team to broadly understand the money style of all team members because the team's combined financial beliefs and actions will impact the results of your business. This happens at a very practical and also energetic level. The energetic level can have the stronger influence on the business's ability to grow and prosper.

If a staff member is operating out of fear, it will impact the energy needed for the business to be abundant. Sometimes the general energy in a business is incredibly positive. Remove or reduce the aspects that are not. Take care in removing attitudes that differ to yours simply because you do not agree with them. Sometimes these disagreements have the effect of keeping your business safe or sustainable over the long term. There is learning from every perspective.

Key to self-awareness is the ability for team members to discuss their own beliefs and feelings. Sometimes acknowledging one is fearful about financial circumstances can have a positive effect. This is because it can allow others to recognize that others are viewing their actions as highly risky. This perspective is helpful in that it can temper actions and ensure risks are well managed. Sometimes fear is not fear at all. Sometimes it is simply well placed caution, after taking into account all of the commercial risks at hand.

I believe it is never a bad thing to 'call it' when someone believes the risks are getting too high for the long-term safety of the business. As a result people are able to disagree and to reach a well-managed middle ground with lower levels of risk. What is of more concern is when people see the risks but the culture does not allow freedom of speech, either formally or insidiously due to the way people react when issues are raised.

The most reckless reaction a business owner can have is to assume a financial concern raised by others is simply based in an inappropriate level of fear, instead of genuinely considering it as potentially valid. To consider concerns from a perspective of reducing risk is a far better approach because it ensures balance. It isn't always possible or valid to raise concerns (if they are baseless) but it is still valid to at least consider and communicate any concerns raised from the perspective of wanting to minimize risks.

What's Next

When working within the strengths of your money style it can take at least a year of improved focus to achieve the right balance for your business and personal financial goals. Once you have mastered the various strengths of your money style and compensated for the weaknesses, it is much easier to draw on the attributes needed for any financial situation at hand.

Take care not to return to unhelpful habits. I have done that many times and now recognize the tell tale signs I personally need to look out for under my individual money style. This is very valuable awareness. Most of my insights are based in a need for self-discipline, prefaced in self-awareness of the issue itself. For example, I can tell that I am stating to shift back to the survival quadrant if I take more cash from the business without it also having first created enough profit to cover this.

Ensuring we apply the seven steps to wealth creation for ourselves personally, as well as our business, provides the insight needed to discern the next steps needed at any point in time.

Increasing the flow

Once this improved awareness is present for all concerned in your business or home, increasing *the flow* of money is the next step to address.

Firstly blockages need to be removed from your internal belief system. Just as it is difficult for water to flow if there are rocks wedged in a pipe, the flow of money is halted by unhelpful beliefs. Remember that some of your beliefs control whether you feel the five financial actions are a necessity or simply a "nice to have." They are in fact a necessity if you want long term-sustained wealth.

Some think removing blockages in your beliefs or applying the five financial actions is difficult. I believe it is a choice, quite simply based on your motivation to seek healing, awareness and focus. Over time you can learn to genuinely love yourself and others, forgive yourself and others, and embrace your shortcomings. As this occurs, your self-esteem and self-worth will start allowing beliefs around giving to yourself and others unconditionally. This is a turning point.

Allow it to happen and allow time for changes to take effect. This may not happen overnight. You are reprogramming years of conditioning, so give yourself some compassion that your mind might need a little bit more time to achieve permanent results for change.

Once your blockages are removed, you can create an obstacle free channel through which money flows to you. There is an ability to call in money whenever it is necessary to receive. Our mental expectations around money create our reality, as long as we are in balance. This concept of financial flow is linked in to the Financial Laws of the Universe explained in chapter seven. This concept requires that we are in a place of inner calm and we can be with any financial circumstances without fear, trusting that all is as it is meant to be.

Next we focus on widening the width of the channel in which wealth flows, followed by increasing the speed that it flows down that channel. Note

I said wealth, not money. Increasing the speed is achieved from stronger beliefs and actions.

Five Financial Actions and Gauging Success

Remember the five financial actions needed. The most critical one is learning to live within our means, and being able to do so at a very modest level. Once this is learned, no matter what happens in the future, we can always revert to the lessons learned from a more modest financial stage of our life.

Sometimes we can make living within our means difficult for ourselves, because we allow financial pressure to spend unnecessarily to be placed upon us by others. In any given moment, we choose whether we want to be personally defined by the financial state we have chosen to move to, or achieved thus far.

We have a choice to change how we live at any stage, so that we become financially more sensible in alignment with our current situation. This can be a difficult pill to swallow if it means we need to down size any aspect of our financial life because our situation has worsened compared with previously.

Consider whether you wish to adopt a different focus than monetary results for your sense of success. Personally I don't think it is overly useful to be defined by our monetary achievements, or lack thereof. There are more important things in life. Don't get me wrong—enjoyment of genuine financial success is warranted and in my opinion a helpful thing. It's just that it is not the same as using financial success as a basis for assessing one's overall achievements. So choosing to adapt our spending to live within our means does not need to be viewed as a negative in terms of our success. On the contrary; living within your means is a big point in your favor.

Humility and Shifting Our Spending When Needed

Regardless of how we gauge our success, it is useful for us to learn to be humble when the situation warrants it. Humility can be especially critical in circumstances where finances have become tighter than normal. Being able to shift yourself up and down the spending ladder is important so you can adapt your budget as needed, being mindful to only commit to manageable levels of debt.

As your money increases with your age, the level of appropriate debt to equity will most likely change, but not always. Increase your savings/investments accordingly if you can. Get advice on the specifics for your own situation from a really good financial planner.

Specific Steps to Improve Cash Flow

Other things to do to achieve better cash flow include the following:

- Chapter nine's seven steps to personal wealth creation can be applied to your business as well as personal life. Applying the steps creates sound working capital situations, as well as empowers financial energy underlying your business results.
- Know what's coming up with your cash projections. Get your CFO to assist with this knowledge. In order to prevent poor cash flow, managing any down side risk is just as important as managing strong growth.
- Trust others with your finances, but don't be stupid about it. Still know your financial situation yourself. The best way to not abdicate this situation is to delegate the financial processing and work, while still staying close to the financial information.
- Follow your financial policies—they need to override your financial 'currency'. Remember financial currencies include the following examples.
  a. security or certainty,
  b. a sense of belonging or connection,
  c. self-actualization, being significant, or to want to grow
  d. or to want to give,
  Take care to not sell yourself short in terms of the actual cash portion of your value exchange.
- Take care to not give beyond your means (in time or money), or at the other end of the scale, require too much certainty. This is relevant if either of these examples come at the expense of the amount of cash you receive.
- Put into your calendar money tasks you need to remember and also a reminder about respectful actions to focus on—things that you do

to respect the source that provides for you. Do one small thing every day to demonstrate respect.

- Consistency is key—remember the obvious points like being commercial and consistent with your debtors to ensure you get paid on time, or have the ability to charge interest if you don't.
- Remember other basics such as sound terms of trade, good credit risk assessment, customer acceptance criteria (for new or ongoing work), and capacity planning.

Give an amount you can afford a bit more regularly. Periodically increase the amount and frequency while still keeping it at an easy level. This will help to loosen the financial flow around you.

JACK AND JILL'S BUSINESSES

Let's look again at Jack and Jill's situation and how they have applied these learnings. They have shifted gears. It's a few years since we last engaged with them. They have been running their beanstalk centre and beanstalk climbing competitions successfully and have two small children, Thomas and Sarah, are aged 7 and 5.

For the first few years their businesses were thriving. But they struck harder times when the worldwide economy took a major dip, coupled with Jill no longer working full time. She cares for the children after school, but Jack wishes he and Jill could both work part time and that he could help more with the childcare too. Unfortunately the businesses need his particular skill sets full time.

Together Jack and Jill have done a really good job of building a competent team around them. Jill stills holds a management role in the business, albeit part time. Cash flow is currently their biggest challenge.

They endured a few very challenging years after they both had an accident. Luckily, their team and insurances were both strong enough for their businesses to survive. Jack suffered minor head injuries when he fell down a hill that had him off work for six months, but he was able to eventually fully recover.

At this juncture, Jack and Jill sit down and analyze the application of all points they have each noted so far. They realize they are very good at many of the issues suggested but a few points need attention. Their habit of savings is not yet strong enough, so they agree to improve this. They also need to apply closer attention to their team management. They fully accept the need for these issues and have done so for many years.

One of the biggest points to resonate for them is that although they understand the logic of some of the points, they aren't actually doing all of them. So they commit to each other to address these things in their business and to actually make real changes to their actions. From the business perspective, they implemented these improvements into 90-day plan process and their situation improves gradually over time as a result.

Unfortunately, they forget to apply the same discipline to their personal life. As we learned in chapter 9, it was to be another 8 years before they realize this point for the improvements needed personally.

Learn from the mistakes of Jack and Jill. An imbalance between suggestions applied in personal versus business contexts often occurs. Sometimes people are consistent with these things personally, but allow their business to be neglected. Or vice versa. It can be quite difficult to ring fence business and personal worlds from each other because the results of one impacts the other. Jack and Jill were very stuck in the 'busyness' of their businesses. It was no wonder it was easy for them to miss the simplicity of consistently applying the suggested steps to both their business and personal worlds. Luckily they will learn this in good time.

Summary

- Poor cash flow is only ever a symptom of something else that is going wrong—focus on the cause to fixed this more easily and permanently.
- Ask yourself the key finance questions so you understand the root causes of your money style dynamics. This directly impact your results, because they are a reflection of you and your team.
- Your money style will impact the best approach to building cash reserves —we need to work to our strengths and adapt our approach depending on what we each find easy.
- Follow the five simple financial action steps for both your business and personal life. Remember that the only reason most people don't have a good financial situation is because they don't DO the steps suggested.
- Learn from the experience of Jack and Jill. Apply their suggestions to both your personal and business worlds consistently.

Chapter Seventeen

How to Get the Best Out of an Internal Chief Financial Officer (CFO)

Why Does the CFO Sit at Your Right Hand?

Jack and Jill

One of the team members Jack utilized was a talented Chief Financial Officer (CFO), a trusted advisor Jack had worked with for many years. It had become increasingly apparent how important it was for Jack and Jill to use their CFO well to maintain a healthy business. They applied this sentiment to their other advisors too.

Together with the rest of their management team Jack, Jill and their CFO helped navigate the path to grow their businesses. Assistance from their CFO was invaluable throughout their journey, especially when Jack and Jill had an accident that left Jack out of the business for months due to the fall that injured his head.

Whether stress on the business comes from an accident, an illness, severe financial difficulty or external circumstances, Jack and Jill now know that they need a team to help them manage significant events. They never thought this type of accident would happen to them, but they now know how commonplace trauma, illness and disability are for people before they retire. Luckily they were well insured, but they still needed help from others as events arose. Despite still having money coming in, it would have been too difficult to manage the business if they had not had their management team of advisors. Along the way Jack and Jill applied the points suggested below with great success. There were many occasions where having experts with an integral understanding of their business was crucial.

Why have a Chief Financial Officer (CFO)?

Given that we know cash is king, it's no surprise that one of the most important roles in a business is having an accomplished Chief Financial Officer (CFO). Some also affectionately know the CFO as the Cash Flow Officer. The CFO traditionally sits at the right hand of the business President/CEO. But why is that?

Using a nautical analogy, the front of the ship always hits rough seas first. The ship needs to be steered with skill to avoid disaster. Given we know our treasure ships come in over calm seas, it can be beneficial to have more than one mind helping to steer.

The President/CEO stays at the front of the ship, directing it into calmer waters. Because everything you do in your business has an impact on numbers, (either through your action or inaction), it is the core role of the CFO to stand alongside the President/CEO and help gently guide it to calmer and profit rich waters from a place of high competence.

What the CFO actually does for you is key. So too, is how often you ask them for assistance. If they don't know what's going on, they can't help you.

How We Lead Our Advisors and How Changing this Impacts Our Results

We get the best results from our advisors when we lead them well, not when they lead us. That said, the reverse situation of your advisor doing the leading is still preferable to nobody doing it at all. As the business owner, you should make the decisions. This is true despite the advisor being significantly more qualified in the matter in hand, or the solution suggested being clearly the best option.

In order to provide context for the topic of effectively "leading" our advisors, we need first consider our leadership style so we can communicate effectively with them for most value and least cost. Some advisors need to be led differently, for the same reasons we need to lead staff in varying ways—to accommodate their individual personalities and communication styles. The strengths and weaknesses each advisor brings also need to be factored in so you ensure balance in skills across your team.

Management of your advisors involves being clear about expected fees, specific deliverables, deadlines and performance management. It is similar to managing other personnel. These issues all require you to have an appropriate leadership style for the relevant relationship. There is a subtle difference: you are still the client. It depends on the dynamics of each relationship as to what works best for you.

Looking For Places of Low Accountability

Low accountability can occur with your staff, and also with your external advisors. With advisors, it usually relates to how they view your business, or what they view as a higher priority compared to you. It can be helpful to ask why if their accountability seems low.

Your strategic and commercially focused CFO can explain the relevance of these three issues:

- How accountability levels provide a direct link to the results achieved and why most accountability is sourced in everyone "being your brand" throughout the entire business.

- Why the combination of your behavioral culture, values and standards specifically impacts the dollar results achieved from your team productivity.
- Why the underlying behavioral styles of both you and your team directly impact:
  ◊ leadership preferences
  ◊ leadership capacity
  ◊ inputs willingly offered from all stakeholders in the business

The above three points often uncover root causes that might be preventing your desired results. Aligning accountability with our behavioral and leadership styles shows us the most important aspects to monitor in a business.

When we find the places of low accountability, we will also find the places we most need to lead in. Knowing how to lead in these areas often comes from improvements in "being our brand." This presumes that as business owners we know the essence of our brand, as do our staff and wider team.

The "Wider" Team and Your Leadership of it

Advisors can only jump on deck when we let them. You are still their leader and they simply assist in applying the navigation systems with appropriate levels of advice. As small business owners, we often need to significantly improve the way we develop and nurture a good team. This tends to be because most small business owners are competent at their particular craft, but less aware of general management and leadership principles. Remember that my definition of the word team is wide and involves:

- ALL stakeholders together (i.e. directors, management, employees, and external advisors).
- ALL consistently "rowing together" in the same direction and at the same speed.
- ALL focused on the same main purpose.
- ALL "knowing" they are ALL still consistently rowing together as one cohesive unit.

- ALL under the direct, consistent inspiration and guidance of ALL of the directors/leaders.

When the above team based approach occurs, the improved financial results can be phenomenal. Unfortunately I don't see it happen that often, and the absence of a true team based approach is one of the main reasons a business stays in "survival" mode.

Choosing Whether to Jump in the Boat

Some advisors and employees are spectators, instead of jumping in the boat as fully participating crew members. Resistance usually occurs when there are differing core values, or people don't connect with the vision (especially if it hasn't been clearly articulated). So the first thing to do when a team member is not in the boat, (or no longer in the boat) is to reinforce your business vision and core values.

Ask them how they see themselves fitting in with these and offer whether you share their view. Sometimes they just need reinforcement that they actually have a place in the boat long term. Our silence can be very misleading in the minds of others, if we forget to explain how we see everyone fitting into the plan. This is especially true when the business undergoes significant change.

Occasionally there are differences in the capacity or motivation levels of the differing owners themselves; this can have a high impact on other team members. If the working owners are supposed to be in the boat, then they need to be in the boat, just like other team members. If even one working owner is not motivated, it will impact the overall results because it affects the others' motivation. This should be addressed by either 1) improving the working owner's commitment so a drop in another's motivation is prevented or 2) managing the impact after the fact (once we realize it is happening).

The working owners also need to have enough capacity and competence to occupy their seat in the boat for other crew members to stay consistently motivated. Otherwise other crew members are at risk of building negative views. While this is not an empowered situation, it is unfortunately for some their nature. Usually these issues are known throughout the organization (despite seldom being voiced) simply because inconsistent performance is apparent to all. Working owners should either decide to be in the boat whole-heartedly, or get out of it altogether to benefit the overall business.

Aligning With Your Leadership Style

We need to consider the extent to which our leadership style helps or hinders the team. If your leadership style has elements that are unpalatable for others, this will be evident in a lack of commitment and low engagement further down the track.

You may not be concerned with the impact you have on others, but I guarantee you others will be. Sometimes our leadership style is a perfect fit for the rest of the team; sometimes it is damaging to the success of the business. Now is a good time to state we all mess up in our ability to lead (catastrophically at times) despite having good intentions—we all "push buttons" along the way.

A mismatch in leadership style can be sourced in different levels of priority placed upon the four cornerstone pillars (resilience, honor/courage, compassion, loyalty). Differing leadership preferences can highlight a misalignment of core values. Financial topics tend to misalign the most. Tolerance levels can be surprisingly low if our actions do not line up with our words.

Sometimes the first time we learn there is a mismatch in leadership style preferences is when a team member puts a boundary in place that you hadn't realized was important for them. This might come from anywhere within your wider team. Often it occurs with financial matters, but other areas such as being treated with respect can highlight differences in leadership preferences.

With issues that are highly important, sometimes the boundary put in place is them walking out the door. They could be voting with their feet, or they might walk because you want them to. Key to ensuring we don't lose team members unnecessarily is everyone adopting the four cornerstone pillars. Remember that loyalty is the key pillar to nurture and this happens by guaranteeing the other three.

We need to choose whether to align our leadership style with the needs of our team, or instead get a new team. You may have this choice made for you. Sometimes we simply need to recognize that our team members do not want to be in the boat. It is not always about a mismatch of core values. It's just that most other issues such as low motivation are initially created from some mismatch of core values. When there is a strong enough difference, it tends to be best from all perspectives that the team member gets out of the boat.

Depending on the extent of their involvement, a good CFO is able to either be your eyes and ears in relation to the above topics, or else a sounding board for you to discuss them from the outside looking in.

Why We Need Our Advisors to Operate as Part of the Team

According to Abraham Maslow, a sense of belonging is a core human need. Whether we personally identify with this or not, know that most people do. The concept of team is integral to growing a business as it enhances a sense of belonging. Any business involves humans—even if your business is a one-man band, you still have external advisors.

Some advisors want to feel part of your team, and others don't. The stronger their connection with your business, the more likely they will want to feel part of it. Sometimes this results in increased engagement and commitment, as well as wanting to offer better targeted assistance.

This does not suggest any professional boundaries are crossed. It does suggest however, that the stronger the concept of team within a business, the stronger the business. So actively include your advisors. They do not need to become your friends, but they do need to be viewed as team members, and see themselves this way.

The business will benefit from taking a team based approach, even if some members want it more strongly than others. If their connection to the business reduces, their sense of engagement and commitment tends to as well. Be aware that a team approach is foreign to some though, especially some advisors. This is usually linked to concerns about losing their individuality, autonomy or professionalism. A team approach means every person receives more assistance than they would if going it alone, while pursuing the main purpose. Achieving together makes it easier. So as the leader in your business, promoting a strong team based on the four cornerstone pillars is wise.

A competent CFO is just one team member who can bring value to your team. Remember to include other advisors too. Depending on need and relevance these often include marketing, legal, insurance, systems, HR, and branding people. But don't make your team too big too soon. Add appropriate team members as relevant.

What should your CFO do for you?

In circumstances where the CFO is at the President/CEO's right hand, they should do the following:

- Make profit every month a standard necessity of the business. Have a "not for sale" attitude about this, (unless the business is in a phase that has allowed for alternative results).
- Assist with (or at least be across) all significant decision-making and assess the impact on the numbers.
- Assist with the strategy and structure of the business, making the words/ideas work from a numbers perspective.
- Ensure that financial failures are "failures that steer" and not "failures that sink."
- Plan your cash flow well enough so red flags are both clearly communicated and well managed.
- Plan and manage your tax requirements.
- Provide commercial perspective and call on other expertise in legal and HR areas when that is not available in house.
- Assist with pricing and margins management.
- Assist with actually creating more revenue for the business.
- Utilize their connections for the benefit of the business.
- Brainstorm ideas for new income streams, product lines, restructuring.
- Ensure the business is compliant with all relevant legislation. If not in anyone else's brief, they should also raise commercial issues outside of the pure CFO areas to ensure somebody qualified is addressing them. (e.g. issues such as health and safety, and employment/HR issues).

- Hold a monthly review meeting to discuss results.
- Manage relationships with creditors, tax authorities, and bank managers.
- Provide assurances to your Board from a place of expertise.
- Always operate in your best interests, especially when that requires difficult conversations.
- Assist with the development of your own leadership and knowledge.
- Make sure you do not trade recklessly or cause the company to become insolvent.
- Create cash flow models to tie in with your business plan.
- Help you manage costs and increase profit.
- Help create and manage both growth and succession plans.
- Sometimes be the "bad cop" for you in negotiations.

In circumstances where the CFO is not an integral part of the management team, (but you prefer them to be more of an ad hoc advisor), they should:

- Discuss trading results with you regularly—quarterly is a good benchmark, but monthly is needed if you are in "rescue" or "high growth" mode.
- Brainstorm goals for the upcoming 12–24 months.
- Manage your tax planning circumstances.
- Have competencies for the skills required to become an integral management team member, so they can grow with you, should you wish.
- Alert you to any commercial issues identified.
- Utilize their connections on your behalf, to create more income generating opportunities.
- Create cash flow models to tie in with your business plan.

How should you manage your relationship with your CFO?

There is a reality that as the CEO, you are the decision maker. Some points to note however:

- You should have a CFO input that is commensurate with the size and growth stage of your business.
- Seek appropriate assistance in areas that you do not excel in yourself, at least so that company legislation responsibilities are covered off. And also so your business thrives.
- Your CFO should have wide ranging commercial experience that they draw on when assisting with decisions. You should recognize both their strengths and limitations and discuss issues openly with them.
- Have very good knowledge of your own strengths and weaknesses—whenever you delve into an area of your management or the business that you are weak in, get your CFO's perspective—this may be from either a commercial or numbers perspective.
- Trust your own instincts in areas where you thrive, but still ask for perspective in areas that have a significant impact on the numbers, or on your tax responsibilities.
- When one has the wisdom to ask for advice, it is wise to also apply it.
- Ask relevant questions of your CFO. For example, direct marketing questions to a marketing person rather than your CFO, but if required ask the CFO to build models, break even points or to assist the marketing person with pricing impacts.
- Determine whether you can get the skill set you need internally, but if not, treat the outsourced resource as if they are internal to your business.
- Be fully transparent and vulnerable.
- Remember to own the management of the relationship. So should your CFO, but as the business owner you need to decide when it is important to engage.

As business owners we sometimes forget (or not realize):

- Who is responsible for a decision—who should lead/decide versus who should "recommend."
- How to create and apply strategy.

- When and what is most important to communicate, to whom.
- When it is best to ask for assistance from experts, and when we should rely on our own instincts.
- How to lead external advisors, or even to realize that we should.

The easiest way to answer almost all of these is to ask, "whose business is it?" Business owners need to take the ownership, accountability and responsibility on all of the above. It is also critically important for advisors not to "assume the position" simply because nobody else has, or at least not for long.

Business owners often don't know *how* to do something and that's why we need assistance. We still need to stay responsible though for leadership. The gap in the "how" is always possible with communication when we seek advice and choose which options to implement.

Our advisors need to be led by the directors/leaders, in order for them to serve us best. Ask your advisors how you can best lead them, acknowledging that they also need to lead us from time to time. But not for very long.

Advisors are better placed to recommend or guide—not lead or direct at a decision making level. This distinction is really important. And who leads who changes over time as our knowledge, confidence and understanding increase.

How I suggest we should "lead" our advisors

Your advisors form part of your wider team, even if everyone does not realize it. Many management concepts focus on leading your employees, but few focus on leading your advisors. At the end of the day, the President/CEO needs to lead everyone, advisors included. Here are some tips:

- ALL business owners should assume the essence of leadership within their role—sure, get guidance on how from your advisors.
- Share your lifelong goals and business strategy with them.
- Introduce them to your other advisors—for example your CFO should meet your lawyer, banker, financial planner, insurance broker, marketer, HR personnel, and systems advisors, as well as have a working relationship with all the business owners.

- Ensure they understand your appetite for risk, and which risk types are/are not palatable for you.
- Take responsibility for ensuring open communication.
- Teach them how you prefer they disagree with you, such as whether it is okay to disagree in front of employees and stakeholders, or whether dissension needs to be voiced privately. Help them understand your appetite for differing opinions.
- Help them understand what "pushes your buttons." If it is important, talk to them whenever this occurs—they are unlikely to know otherwise. But if it's not important, get over it.
- Advise them when strategic direction has significantly altered.
- Call meetings for regular updates, driven by you.
- Request specific advice on anything in their specialist area that has strategic importance or could impact your ability to be compliant with law.
- Agree the areas you want them to report to you about, and areas you report to them.
- Remember that you know your business better than any advisor. Trust your instincts, especially around timing. The "why" questions are the most important to ask continually, but second most are the "when." If you have any nagging doubts about timing, trust and explore these fully before proceeding with any advice. It's your business, so your decision whether to proceed or not. Learn discernment around instincts that are sound versus instincts based in fear.
- If your advisors are offering what they perceive to be critical advice, listen with an open mind. Discern carefully before choosing to ignore it.
- Creating an empowered team takes time but it's never too late to start—you always get better results than if you do nothing.

It's also important to recognize we all have varying leadership styles. I believe it's important for advisors to:

- recognize when a situation requires leadership.
- allow the client to lead if they want to.
- lead us (for a short time) if the client does not, until such time as they have enough "tools in their tool box" to make an empowered choice—then create the space for them to choose who should lead.
- understand the demarcations between "recommendations" (the advisor) and "responsibility for decisions" (the business owner).
- always act in what we believe are the client's best interests, even if they do not see this themselves at the time.

What if you think you cannot afford a CFO?

If you think you can't afford a CFO, talk to the person you want to utilize anyway. Their first job can be to work out how you could afford them. Part of their role is to increase revenue (but more importantly, profit and cash.) So make their first assignment working out how their fees can be covered, so they can then assist you improve the sustainability of your business.

If they can't do that, I wouldn't hire them.

When is the best time to raise issues with your CFO?

No surprises here: the answer is at the start. They should be an integral part of the decision-making and planning, not the ones to clean up the mess. Remember "Think It, Plan it, Skill it, Drive it." Your CFO input should be requested at either the "Think it" or "Plan it" steps.

Avoid taking an approach that is simply "Think it, Drive it." Allow your CFO to fill in the "Plan It," and "Skill It" steps for you if need be so the full process is followed. Your CFO should assist you in achieving your critical path developed in Chapter 12. This assumes they are a commercially focused CFO (rather than simply a bean counter). Have discernment as to which CFO you hire.

JACK AND JILL'S CRITICAL PATH

It is now some years on. Every 90 days, Jack, Jill and their management team (including their CFO) continue to review and adapt their critical path to navigate through the various business building stages. Between the experts involved, all business risks are addressed and they have achieved goals detailed.

They weathered the storms thrown at them better than other businesses as they developed a sound combination of improved leadership and knowledge. Keeping their leadership and knowledge levels well placed, they have stayed progressively longer in the "mission accomplished" quadrant for their business, and it has worked its way up the seven steps of wealth creation.

Initially they found it difficult to get past step 5 of the 7 steps to wealth creation. But once they fully studied this book and understood its subtleties, they realized that they needed to apply the wealth creation principles to both their business and personal lives. They also realized that their personal beliefs and actions directly impacted the results in their businesses. At a personal financial level they became much better at staying in the sorted quadrant.

Although they cannot fully explain why or how, they also now know the Universal Laws impacting their financial results are sourced mainly in their ability to be still, treating their financial beliefs and actions in unison as if they are one. Key to their success has been the alignment of their financial issues with each other.

They have achieved a sorted financial situation and are now consistently giving back to society through many of their chosen causes. This was a main objective of their personal version of wealth. Their focus is now turning to assist their own children to achieve their business goals, as well as helping them personally. Jack and Jill are focused on creating a legacy for Thomas and Sarah—not so much specifically for their material achievements, but more from the perspective of passing on the information held within these pages. They want them to thrive.

They believe that by doing so, they will be creating a legacy to help them grow and achieve whatever they want. They are doing their best to assist them understand what they have first learned for themselves.

Jack and Jill sought out a good CFO to help them understand the financial intelligence needed to apply the subtleties of this book. Many are focused purely on financial actions, so it took a bit of effort to find one who also understood the impact of financial beliefs. This however was less important than their own learnings. The most important people to understand all of this were in fact themselves. The addition of a CFO helped quicken their awareness.

Summary

- Your CFO should sit at your right hand, helping you steer yourself through challenging seas into calm waters from a place of high competence.
- Leading your advisors is critical. They provide advice, you make the decisions.
- Have advisors who want to be in the boat and align with your leadership style.
- Get your CFO involved early in the process of significant issues, and assuming they are commercially focused and skilled, get them to help you achieve your critical path.
- Like Jack and Jill, review your critical path every 90 days and remember to involve your CFO and other management team members as part of this strategic and tactical process. Decide what or whom you want to help create a legacy.

Chapter Eighteen

WE ARE HERE TO LEARN, WHAT WE ARE HERE TO TEACH

The Love to Grow Story

The first time Jack grew a beanstalk, it needed to be chopped down. This was because Jack didn't manage the risks (the giant) very well. Applying the metaphor of that story to business, the beanstalk was the business itself, or at the very least, all of the systems that form it.

As we all know, many businesses suffer the same fate as Jack's beanstalk and need to be chopped down due to unmanageable risks. But hopefully we can avoid a similar fate by learning from the experiences of others. I am lucky in that I have not been forced to close any businesses to date, but I have had to deal with some highly significant challenges in my business career. I am not alone in that. Staying ahead of the challenge curve has been a real feat at times, both for my business and some of my clients.

Originally a Survival Mode money style, (I now stay in the Sorted quadrant with self-discipline and continuing personal growth), I have needed more focus to stay Sorted than those blessed with a natural affinity to be there. If you are like me, it is comforting to know that few are Sorted by nature; most need to work on something about themselves to both get and stay there.

Where we all differ is the degree to which we manage our vulnerabilities while shifting to the sorted quadrant. Shifting can take some time even when we are conscious to it. Our ability to both 1) be with our vulnerabilities and 2) manage our vulnerabilities impacts our progress. This is one reason a lot of this book focuses strongly on our belief system, whether applied to our business or ourselves.

Even when we are more sorted financially, most of us still need an ongoing conscious focus on change and improvement. This prevents us shifting back insidiously to where we started. Like you, I am only part way through my own business journey (and hope this will always be the case.)

Now it's time for me to share some of my personal background so you can understand from where I have come. I tell you these things as a reminder that such circumstances are commonplace. Sharing helps generate connection with others experiencing similar things to ourselves. And knowing a bit about another's past allows us to communicate at a similar level of understanding, strength and empathy. You may feel a sense of resonance with my story, or you may not. Either is fine.

Lessons For A Good Work Ethic

Our experiences as children and young adults shape our futures, including our work ethic. Mine created a good work ethic for me, and it has held me in good stead. With a few more years under my belt, I have also sought balance in my life. A good work ethic is why I now have choices around balance, instead of having my hand forced into either working hours or doing things I don't want.

Our parents often pass down our work ethic, and we each get taught different things, don't we? Below is a list of some lessons I learned from my Mom and Dad. I believe they were significant in creating both 1) my wider perspectives and 2) specific results in my life:

- To go the extra mile, to always do more than I was paid to do.

- To seek out ways to serve, no matter who the person or situation was.
- To seek out ways to host another, even if I wasn't the host.
- To seek out ways to welcome others, to put people at ease, and to lead.
- To consciously use my initiative and to ask questions, so assumptions were not misunderstood.
- Above all, to have integrity and honor in business dealings. To recognize this takes courage.
- To honor decisions and perspectives that were made in the past, as well as those made in the present.
- To have compassion for both the perspectives and situations of others.
- To apologize for my part in a miscommunication or unhelpful situation.
- To love the good and forgive the rest.

What specific childhood experiences contributed to my good work ethic? One example is if I ever wanted something that was more than a necessity, I needed to find my own way to pay for it. This was either with cash, or when younger, by spending time on a task/chore as a means of exchange. Consequently I was totally financially self-sufficient when I left home at 17. In my era, this was not unusual.

These lessons were my personal recipe to guarantee a good work ethic and as a result I have many blessings. You may have other ingredients that achieved the same thing. If not, borrow mine. I believe it is through the combination of 1) this good work ethic and 2) sound values, that have created longevity in my business relationships. I am blessed by the people surrounding me. There is a synchronicity in play that is fuelled in part by these lessons.

Another blessing was to have had the situation where there was a *need* for a good work ethic to be instilled in me, rather than simply a *want*. I didn't have any choice about needing to generate funds; I simply did what was needed. By having no choice, I learned things easier. No matter what our personal background, our parents have an ability to create a *need* in this regard, if they choose to. Affluent parents can still teach the same principles. I feel I was blessed by being taught such things.

Through school I had various part time jobs. When I was 19, I switched to part time study and full time work with an international accounting firm. To become a Chartered Accountant (the equivalent of a Certified Public Accountant), New Zealand college graduates need wide practical experience for a minimum of three years. This is coupled with additional exams to ensure technical and ethical requirements are well addressed. One year I upped the ante, working and studying full time. It was really important that I stayed highly focused.

It was this focus that taught me a lot about setting and achieving goals. As a young adult, most of these centered on getting enough assignments done so I could reward myself by socializing. I wouldn't socialize unless I had first achieved what I had set out to do. I still defer a reward until the result is achieved. I am an advocate of this approach; it's about being true to your own subconscious.

Mentors

It was a privilege to work for the partners of that accounting firm. As individuals they were very different, and I learned from each of them. I will be forever grateful for what they taught me. Outside of a sports coach, these partners were the first non-family adults I trusted. They were genuinely predictable and consistent in their behavior towards me, something that surprised me. I don't believe they realized it at the time, but their support towards me was significant. It provided an element of stability in areas where I hadn't experienced much before. We often have someone like this in our lives. They seldom know the impact they are having on us, but allow us to grow, and at our own pace.

I have had many mentors over the years who helped me grow. They include my Mom and Dad who had massive strengths, despite their very human weaknesses, my siblings who helped to look after me and with whom I have an incredible bond, my very special and awesome husband Craig, and various business and personal development mentors who have taught me many things by simply being around. I have been blessed to have them in my world and I believe it was by no accident that we found each other.

Learning from Customers

We learn from everyone we engage with. My clients have been wonderful in this regard. Some have been massively successful in their own right, and many have been fabulous characters. At times some clients have been rat bags, but they have been wonderful rat bags.

Some just seemed determined to persist in their survival mode activities to run their business. And it has been challenging to help some of them create a shift in their results. I am proud to say though that I have genuinely done my best to be supportive and compassionate toward everyone's situation, within the resources available at any given time.

Learning from our Team

For the most part, my own Love to Grow team now run my accountancy practice, so I can focus on teaching my leadership and financial information. They have also taught me a lot. For all of these people and many more, I am eternally grateful. I wasn't always the best student, so appreciate their tolerance. I'm sure we can all think of moments where we have not learned as quickly or effectively as we might have liked. I believe it is important to simply try better next time. It is our progress and ability to adapt that is relevant. Like any business, Love to Grow has happened because of the people in it.

Remembering to Learn From Our Children:
Out of the Mouths of Babes

My children have taught me with some of their amazingly apt and timely comments about business. They are very quick witted and funny with their observations. Some of my business observations have originated from unrelated conversations with them and their very simple questioning of me. This questioning requires one to examine things at a much simpler, but often ironically, deeper level. Children can also sometimes tell us what everyone else is thinking, because they are brave enough to do so.

Learning from Subtlety in My Messages

Remember that according to Charles Darwin, it is not the strongest of the species that survive, or the cleverest. It is those most adaptive to change. When we make incremental changes, (rather than always intending changes for tomorrow), we learn better and quicker through our actual experience.

People often intellectually understand the logic of my suggestions. But it is when they actually do them that they say things to me like, "It's quite weird, since I've started to save, my business is also getting more income than before." Or "I'm not even missing the money I'm saving, it's as if I never needed it." Or "Since I've started knowing my financial situation better, I've started to win more work." There is an energy that creates what seems to be financial magic, and that energy is based in all the factors discussed for living within the Sorted quadrant.

Sometimes you need to subtly adapt your actions. Even then you might sometimes still fall down. So stand up and brush yourself off. Remember these lovely Chinese proverbs: 1) to know and not yet to do, is not yet to know, and 2) fall down seven times, stand up eight.

My Personal Story

We all have a personal story and that story is important to each of us. Regardless of what it is, we all have learning, healing, growing, compassion, honor and resilience to learn. I am no exception, and I'm sure you aren't either.

For my part, I was the youngest child in a family of four. My Dad was a World War II veteran who, in my opinion, suffered from undiagnosed post-traumatic stress disorder. My Mom was a nurse who had significant health issues throughout my childhood. My two older siblings left home when I was six, and my last when I was ten.

Before my siblings left home, I effectively had five parents to care for me (in varying capacities), so most of the time I was well protected from any challenges. Home life was unpredictable, including alcoholic related violence, packaged within a layer of genuine compassion and unconditional love. This was confusing and scary through a child's eye, and dysfunctional through an adult's.

Parts of it still confuse me as to how it all "worked out." My family are highly functioning, caring adults, albeit with some underlying dysfunction that we light-heartedly acknowledge and, for the most part, have healed. Significant events in our lives had themes of life threatening illness and situations, some affecting my own ability to feel safe. These events were reasonably chunky and regular. I felt abandoned, fear, anger, shame and guilt. I'm happy to say the vast majority of these past-related issues have been healed with help from skilled professionals. It is a lovely thing when we are ready to be who we really are.

My past, for the most part, is in my past. But the richness of resilience and deeper understanding remains in my wider tapestry. I am blessed to have all of the threads woven into it. I cherish the contrast between my younger and current worlds, and I also cherish many of the empowered and healthy moments my past has brought into my present. I feel so very blessed to have a strong sense of what is truly important in life.

It took me considerable time to allow myself the freedom to grow, and more importantly, to fail. And to have shortcomings that I allow others to see and help me with. Like all of us, I have had some growth and development cycles, some having occurred alongside significant life events. Sometimes we need healing, sometimes we just need a better attitude. Sometimes we need unconditional love for others and ourselves. Sometimes we need to allow ourselves a sense of worthiness strong enough to become successful. But most of the time we just need to "be where we are" and choose to change. Or not. It is all about the choices we make as wisdom unfolds.

Whatever your story, know that the root causes of any challenges you have faced are unlikely to have been your fault. It is also quite unlikely to be the fault of the person who created your challenges. They are all instead likely to be sourced in someone's personal background.

Applying some awareness and compassion goes a long way towards explaining why someone thinks or acts in a particular way. We can benefit by focusing less on what "happened" and instead consider our own reactions and feelings. Sometimes our responses need a different way of thinking, and sometimes we need a different amount or type of healing. What is our responsibility however, is whether or not we want to change our situation. We can choose to thrive, heal our past and move forward. To love ourselves, so that we can grow.

Whatever our story, it is a story. It may be massively challenging or it may be massively enriching. It is probably both. Either way we choose whether to allow it to impact us now. My background still impacts me some of the time. Not very often, but when it does, it fascinates me as to what bits still do. I can truck along for ages, feeling really empowered and not engaging at any specific level with hurts of my inner childhood self. Then something I hadn't seen coming really affects me. Sometimes I even realize it. I'm only partly joking when I say that—at times I have no clue that I have been impacted by my past. Either way I do my best to just "be" with whatever arises.

There are often times where I need to buy a really big mirror in terms of my own awareness of all things business, money, relationships and purpose. Some days in order to show me things about myself, this mirror could benefit from having a flashing light and loud alarm, plus a snooze button that keeps bringing it back. This is normally because I haven't realized something about myself that is incredibly obvious to others. I tell you this because we are all just learning, no matter how good we might be at a particular area. It can be helpful to remember this about everyone we deal with.

My Work Lessons

What follows is a summary of what I have learned in my career. These lessons were sourced in many places, including the accounting firm, my corporate career and my own Love to Grow business. Some things I learned to do often, others I learned to never do again.

One thing you may note below is that I have used the word try in " try to do" and "try to never do." I am aware that it may sound like an excuse to some of you. I am also aware that I am human and have erred at times with nearly every example listed. It is through this element of failure that I have learned. It has never been intentional, yet I have erred nonetheless. And I have forgiven myself my humanness; I recommend you do the same. Reset the bar and do your best to consistently exceed it.

- I always try to do these things at work and in my wider relationships:
- Be real—with yourself and others.
- Have a vision and purpose. Remind people of it! Don't just pay lip service to it.
- Create and refer to a code of conduct when needed to provide consistency and a strong base.
- Consistently base decisions in well-defined values.
- Be consistent and fair when managing the team.
- If someone has to take a fall, I normally take it.
- Check what else team members have on before "loading them up" with work.
- Ask my team's opinion on lots of things.
- Have highly transparent conversations: we refer to these as "calling the pink elephant." When something is there for one of us, but we are hesitant to discuss it, we label it a pink elephant so we can talk about it.
- Know and love my culture.
- Promote integrity at a core level.

Things I try to never do:

- Forget to apologize.
- Take people for granted.
- Be unfair or inconsistent.
- Blame a staff member for something that is my fault.
- Get them to "cross the street" without me the first time.
- Put others too far outside their comfort zone.
- Think I no longer need to grow/learn—instead I stay focused on wanting to learn.

Through the process of applying this book in the coming months and years, I would love for you to genuinely learn and deeply understand:

- the impact your behavior has on your finances.
- the difference between "reckless" and "respectful" financial actions.
- the difference between fear and control based beliefs to giving and trust based beliefs.
- the way to have real time application of sound leadership.
- how and when to get advisors involved in your business.
- the critical path factors needed for growing your business.
- how to be where you are, so you don't miss your life.
- a conscious awareness of want you want to learn and what you want to teach for the benefit of others.
- how to achieve your legacy.
- what to teach your future generations.

JACK & JILL

Both Jack and Jill read their own copy of this book so they would be in a similar headspace to each other. Each of them gleaned different insights and highlighted things to review later. They both feel they want to read the book again in about 3 months. In a month's time, they want to review their progress with the five financial action steps. In the meantime, like you they have other action points to address, including assisting with the legacy they wish to create with Thomas and Sarah.

Jack and Jill are now well advanced in achieving their desired version of wealth. The causes they want to support are all benefitting. Their life will not be all plain sailing, but their treasure ships are now on calm seas. And they have an implicit awareness that any rough weather can be managed well.

They understand the wisdom of a lighthouse. They can see now that it is less effective to be busy-busy, running around in their world, looking for boats to save. It is more effective to simply stand there, shining.

Summary of the chapter

- Create a work ethic that holds you in good stead.
- Learn from your mentors, customers, team and children.
- We all have a personal story and we all can benefit from healing, shifts in attitude, and anything else that empowers us to move to a place of making a choice.
- Learn to have a healthy relationship with the word failure.
- Learn how to generate support from your team and others.

Besides learning the impact of your past on your present and the impact of this on your finances, I have explained the richness that can be created from combining consistent and fair values, with solid business building practices. Financial improvement is almost a by-product when this is done well.

Are any of us perfect? Of course not, far from it. But we do try to love. To grow. And in my humble opinion, everything else tends to fall into place when this happens. Business and financial growth is a great by-product when you adopt sound practices and values.

Be still. Love yourself. Love others. And you will grow.

CPSIA information can be obtained at www.ICGtesting.com
Printed in the USA
LVOW07s0018021113

359627LV00001B/1/P